THE ENERGY-SAVING HOUSE DESIGN HANDBOOK

Your Super Guide to Earth Sheltering, Solar Heating, and Thermal Construction

Frederick Uhlen Hop

PRENTICE HALL, Englewood Cliffs, New Jersey 07632

Library of Congress Cataloging-in-Publication Data

HOP, FREDERICK UHLEN.
  The energy-saving house design handbook.

  Includes index.
  1. Earth sheltered houses—United States.
2. Architecture and energy conservation—United States.
I. Title.
NA7531.H66 1989   728   88-28953
ISBN 0-13-277427-5

Editorial/production supervision
and interior design: *Carol L. Atkins*
Cover design: *Wanda Lubelska Design*
Manufacturing buyer: *Robert Anderson*

The publisher offers discounts on this book when ordered
in bulk quantities. For more information, write:

  Special Sales/College Marketing
  Prentice Hall
  College Technical and Reference Division
  Englewood Cliffs, NJ 07632

Printed in the United States of America
10 9 8 7 6 5 4 3 2 1

ISBN 0-13-277427-5

Prentice-Hall International (UK) Limited, *London*
Prentice-Hall of Australia Pty. Limited, *Sydney*
Prentice-Hall Canada Inc., *Toronto*
Prentice-Hall Hispanoamericana, S.A., *Mexico*
Prentice-Hall of India Private Limited, *New Delhi*
Prentice-Hall of Japan, Inc., *Tokyo*
Simon & Schuster Asia Pte. Ltd., *Singapore*
Editora Prentice-Hall do Brasil, Ltda., *Rio de Janeiro*

Contents

PREFACE   vii

PART 1
CONSERVATION PRINCIPLES

1 **PRACTICAL PRINCIPLES**   3

Energy-Saving Systems *4*

2 **HEAT TRANSFER**   4

Conduction *5*
Infiltration *6*
Insulating Glass *7*

3 **COMPARTMENTED ENTRY**   9

4 **TEMPERATURE RETENTION**   11

Free Heat Source *11*
Heat and Cooling Retention *12*
Insulating the Foundation Exposure *12*

PART 2
EARTH SHELTERING

5 ADVANTAGES OF EARTH SHELTERING   19

6 SITE FACTORS   23

Topography *23*
Orientation *26*

7 GENERAL CONSIDERATIONS   30

Mechanical Heat *30*
Mechanical Cooling *31*
Ventilation *32*

8 STRUCTURAL CHARACTERISTICS   34

Suitable Soil for Earth Sheltering *34*
Thermal Insulation *38*
Waterproofing *39*
Encroachment Situations *43*
Aesthetics *44*
Positive Design *45*
Facade Styles *46*
Floor Plan Principles *48*
Light and Ventilation *49*
Effects of Solar Heating on Floor Planning *50*

9 OWNER-BUILT MODIFICATIONS   51

Partial-Bermed House *52*

10 FULL-BERMED WOOD EARTH HOUSE   56

Unique-type Nails *65*
Subfloor Drainage *67*
Buttressing Long Walls *69*
Confidence in Treated Lumber *71*
Conclusions for the Conservation Builder *72*

PART 3
USE OF SOLAR ENERGY

11 SOLAR COLLECTORS   77

Active Solar Systems *78*
Passive Solar Systems *79*
Greenhouse Collectors *83*
Tilted or Vertical Glass *84*

12 SOLAR STORAGE   88

Heat Storage Bin *89*
Masonry Storage Wall *90*
Trombe Wall *92*
Heat Storage Media *93*
Central Heat Backup *94*

13 DOMESTIC HOT WATER CONSERVATION   94

Conventional Economy Measures *95*

14 SOLAR-ASSISTED WATER HEATING   100

Flat Plate Water Heaters *100*
Mounting the Flat Plate Collector *103*
Breadbox Collector *109*
Vertical Integral Solar Water Heater *114*
Efficiency Concept *117*

PART 4
SUPER ENERGY-SAVING HOUSE DESIGN

15 THE DOUBLE-WALL FRAME   121

Double-Wall Section View *121*
Material Savings *130*
Double-Wall Framing Procedure *132*
Salvaging Studs *144*
Other Double-Wall Designs *147*
Double-Wall Coordinates *148*

16 **FLOOR INSULATION**   150

Double-Wall Insulation *155*

17 **THERMAL ROOF DESIGNS**   156

Thermal Truss *157*
Extended Span Truss *159*
Web Location on Extended Trusses *162*
Ventilation of Thermal Structures *163*
Roof Ventilators *166*

18 **COST EFFECTIVENESS OF THERMAL CONSTRUCTION**   171

Inspection by the Buyer *173*

19 **ENERGY-SAVING HEATING SYSTEMS**   175

Solar Systems *175*
Orienting the Collector *176*
Collector Angle *177*
Sizing an Integral Collector *179*
Constructing an Integral Collector *181*
Details of Construction *181*
Heat Pump *188*
COP *188*
Two Water-to-Air Systems *189*
Water Heating Assistance *190*
Conclusions *190*

GLOSSARY   193

INDEX   213

Preface

There is much interest among certain professional and amateur builders in the quest for comfortable and attractive housing that is economical in the realm of interior climate control.

There are a number of motivations for this interest. Professional builders and realtors recognize the advertising and sales potential of catchwords such as "thermal." Home owners, especially permanent-consumer residents, are vitally interested in the size of the monthly utility bill and the long-range cost comparison of one system to another. Fixed-income retirees are crucially interested. There is also an enthusiastic category of folks who delight in the quest for innovative, cost-saving utility systems, especially those systems that harvest nature's freely-given elements. Each part of this book contains something of value for those who have an interest in utility cost conservation without loss of comfort.

Part 1 presents the principles that are basic to understanding how warmth and coolness are generated (collected) and how they are adapted for use. Materials and types of construction that are susceptible to temperature loss are cited. Effective construction methods and designs that produce superior heat and cool retention are illustrated and explained.

Part 2 explores the advantages of modern earth sheltered housing. Many suggestions and solutions for overcoming early incompatability factors are given. These suggestions will create a sense of the modern-day potential for this form of construction.

An innovative system of combining earth sheltering, solar heating, and superinsulating, suitable for pro or do-it-yourselfer, is explained in detail in this chapter.

Part 3 takes the reader into the realm of cost-free solar energy. Active water heating systems are explained and illustrated. An emphasis is placed on economical, passive space heating systems that will cause life-long utility cost containment. Sun angle, glass angle, eave overhang, ventilation, materials, heat storage, the trombe wall, circulation, distribution, summer and winter modes, and much more, are to be found in this practical section.

Part 4 describes how to hold and disperse the energy gains from the earth and the sun. Sheltering, eliminating infiltration, using economical construction designed for optimum insulation space—all are topics laid out in understandable terms.

The superb, double-walled conception of framing and coordinated thermal truss designs also are featured. Illustrations are thorough and complete enough for emulation by those who have yet to experience this exciting way to build.

The objectives of this book are to provide the knowledge to:

- Construct a comfortable, thermal-conserving dwelling
- Sustain a reasonable initial cost factor
- Make use of nature's thermal gifts
- Feature long-range utility economy

Good luck and have pride in your project.

Frederick Uhlen Hop

Part 1

Conservation Principles

1 PRACTICAL PRINCIPLES

Many features that produce fuel savings in a home have been known for a long time. Early settlers to the great plains areas of the midwest built sod homes because of the shortage of trees and lumber. Although the sod home was not prestigious, it was quite efficient in a thermal sense. The temperature below the frost line is approximately 52°F. This reservoir of constant warmth needed only a small supplement of added heat from a fire to provide a livable temperature in the cold winter months. In the heat of summer the cooler earth temperature provided a tempered comfort zone.

When cheap fuels were abundant, homes were most often built with little or no thought of insulation. Indeed, insulation in most of its present forms was unheard of as recently as 50 years ago. However, some recognition of insulating principles could be seen on a seasonal basis. Farmers would stack bales of hay or straw around the high foundations of the farmhouse to ward off the penetrating cold. Detachable wooden framed screens were taken down and replaced by storm windows when winter approached.

Some insulating products came on the scene quite accidentally. At Iowa State University in the mid-1930s, experiments were conducted to see what salable product could be made from a surplus of cornstalks. Such experimenting led to the making of fiberboard. Beaverboard was an early name given to a product which became popular for use on ceilings. As time passed, many names and insular uses evolved. Some of the names are Celotex (a brand name), fiberboard, building board, brownboard, and blackboard. For a period of years, blackboard was the standard sheathing material. It gained a reputation for causing a house to be snug and cozy—not at all the drafty character terms used for the old wood-board-sheathed houses. More recently, sheet forms of Styrofoam are proving to be more heat conserving per inch of thickness than is fiberboard. As fuel costs soared in the late 1970s, a great amount of attention and concern was focused on and will continue to be directed toward energy-saving systems and materials.

ENERGY-SAVING SYSTEMS

There are three basic types of houses that will accomplish the energy conservation principle at construction costs comparable to conventional designs.

- Earth-sheltered house (and berm modifications)
- Solar-heated and -cooled house
- Superinsulated house

There are some good books available about earth-sheltered and solar-type construction. The following parts will be devoted to principles of basic construction and to innovative and practical, above and below ground, superinsulated house designs. Construction methods and details are presented that are practical for the novice, the professional, and the tract builder.

2 HEAT TRANSFER

It is not the purpose of this book to make a heating or cooling engineer of the reader. The focus is not on complicated formulas and computations. That is left to the theorists and universities.

They have given us the fruits of advanced technology in the form of readily available resource materials. The emphasis that follows is placed on how to use currently available materials to the best long-range advantage of both the builder and the consumer.

The Btu rating (British thermal unit) is the term used, for purposes of this book, to denote heat transfer (energy loss) through a material or combination of materials. Each type of material is given an R rating, which indicates *resistance* to the passage of heat. A low R number means that passage is more rapid. More heat is lost from a room because it passes through a wall more quickly. A high R number indicates a better insulating value. R values are established for materials per inch of thickness. On the wrapper the R number refers to the full thickness of the material. Roll-batt fiberglass insulation of 3 ½″ thickness is usually labeled R-11.

The superinsulation principle is simple. The higher the total R number from the addition of all the materials in the wall, the greater will be the potential resistance to the loss of heat or coolness.

CONDUCTION

In house construction there is a factor called *conduction* that can lead the builder and consumer astray. When heat is applied to an inside surface of an exterior wall, it passes through dense materials, such as studs and plates, to the cold side and is lost there. A false sense of comfort results when an owner rationalizes that a wall has an adequate quantity of insulation in the stud and ceiling joist cavities. The system is fundamentally flawed because the whole framework structure is a conductive envelope—each member a potential bridge—which bleeds off precious heat. Add to this the quantity of glass in windows (especially windows with aluminum frames) and doors, and it becomes quite clear where the weaknesses of conventional construction exist and consequently where the greatest potential for improvement is concentrated. An objective to keep in mind is to follow or improvise practices that will balance component retention factors throughout a structure. To do otherwise is like insulating a wall while omitting the insulation from every fourth or fifth stud cavity. This ludicrous example is comparable to the common practice of insulating all wall cavities adequately and then using the lowest R-rated doors and windows available because they are a "good deal" or money is getting tighter. Neither rationale builds responsibly towards the future. A little further along it will be shown how the loss by conduction can be effectively eliminated or greatly reduced when contemplated on a five- to ten-year consumption plan.

INFILTRATION

In addition to heat transfer through materials, there is another significant source of heat loss, called infiltration. A poorly constructed house can lose as much heat as if it perpetually had a window open. Infiltration means cracks that permit heat to escape or cold wind to blow in. A house that seems drafty when no circulating fans are operating is probably suffering from excessive infiltration. An investment of a few dollars in caulking can make a tremendous difference in such a place. For new construction, however, there are better ways to prevent infiltration than the patch and putty, after-the-fact technique.

Key infiltration zones are well known. Poorly sealed doors that enter directly into a living area are first-rate culprits. Windows run a close second. Electric boxes that are not carefully surrounded with insulation allow cold air into a house. Fireplace chimneys draw a lot of warm air out on calm days and allow drafts to blow in on windy days when dampers fit loosely and there are no glass doors to seal the opening at the hearth. Brickwork that connects outdoors to indoors may have a poorly sealed junction with the wooden framework that adjoins it. The list goes on and on.

The type of window used has a major effect on conservation. It is not at all uncommon for a single window of poor insulating character to lose more heat than all the rest of the wall. Buying cheap windows is one of the poorest economy measures a consumer can take.

There are three types and qualities of glazing. The poorest and least costly is the single-glass pane in a metal frame (steel or aluminum). The insulating R factor is so low as to offer little more than a windshield. Next comes double glazing. There are several designs falling under this term (some of them masquerade as "thermo" or thermal windows). Originally "double glaze" indicated one framed sash with a second lightly framed insert which could be removed for washing. A more advanced form has two panes of glass set in mastic in a U channel. The thermal conserving feature of the latter is a little superior to that of simple double glass. The design is supposed to produce an air-sealed dead air space. Most doublepane windows accomplish this objective. A common complaint after a few years of exposure, however, is that leaks develop, followed by fogging and condensation buildup between the panes. Reputable manufacturers will make adjustments in most cases. Triple glazing is another way of adding an additional dead air space.

INSULATING GLASS

The most effective heat-conserving type of window is the hermetically sealed insulating glass best known by the name *Thermopane*. Similar to the way that a vacuum bottle contains heat in a confined liquid, a Thermopane window does the best job of containing the heated air in the house. Over a period of years, Thermopane will be the best choice, even though the initial cost may be considerably more.

The economist on the job should consider all factors both initially and in the long run. For example, inexpensive aluminum-framed windows do not have integral casements (the surrounding interior jambs), whereas most wood-framed sashes are complete with jambs. Windows such as those produced by Pella and Anderson may be had with all weather-affected parts encased in vinyl plastic. The initial cost of the unit may be as much as twice that of the other type. This is a deceptive comparison. The aluminum-framed window will require additional skilled labor and expensive finish lumber for the jambs and sill. Each piece is custom fitted to the individual opening. Although the glass may be on a par, the fact remains that the aluminum material conducts at a rate about 19 times that of wood.

Doors present a similar comparison, but the materials situation is reversed in the case of panel doors, Fig. 1-1. An exterior

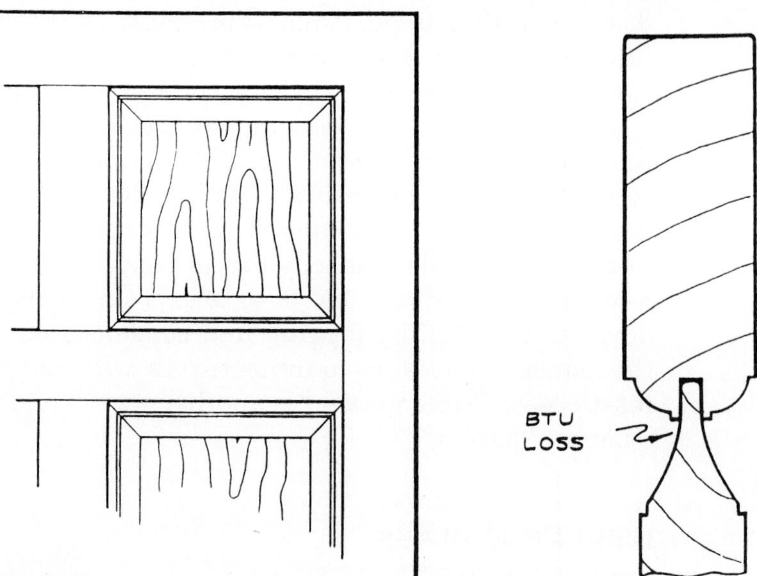

Figure 1-1 Solid doors with molded panels provide severely limited resistance to heat loss.

wood panel door usually contains contoured panels with edges that are very thin. The coved edges that form the tongue in the groove may be as thin as ¼″. One-quarter inch of wood between the heated side of a room and the outdoor winter elements could scarcely be considered adequate. Tightly sealed storm doors are required to salvage a modicum of economy.

Insulated doors, Fig. 1-2, are available in many styles and materials. They all have a common feature. The core of the door is filled with a rigid form of insulation. Less costly models are covered with prime painted steel. Some doors give the impression of carved and molded panels with overlays that do not detract from a full-thickness insulated core throughout. Others have shallow impressed panels which do not offer as much insulating quality but which nonetheless surpass wood doors by a considerable margin. More expensive doors are available with real wood overlays or vinyl pressure-molded wood imitations. As with windows, it can be a false economy to install a seemingly economical unit.

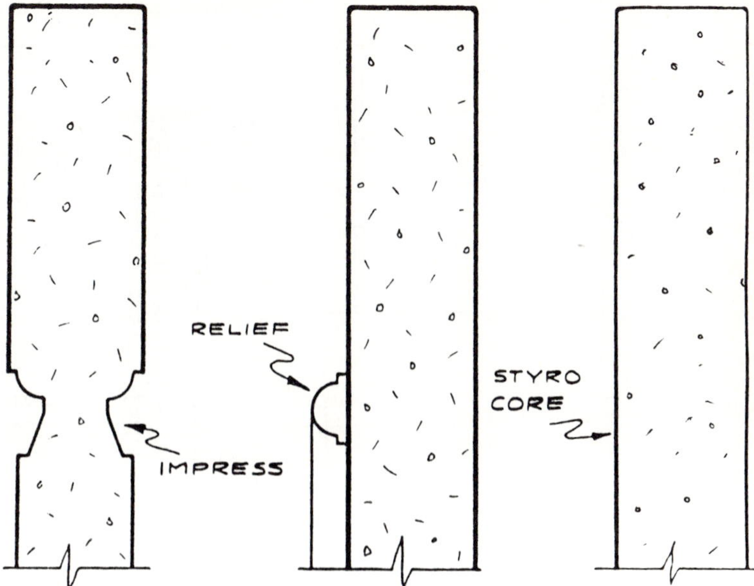

Figure 1-2 Insulated steel doors with impressed or reversed relief panels offer reasonable thermal characteristics when combined with storm doors.

3 COMPARTMENTED ENTRY

The compartmented entry principle has gained in interest as a result of the energy-saving concern. Designers of earth-sheltered and solar-heated homes stress the importance of a closable foyer (Fig. 1-3). A compartmented entrance is an anteroom. One can enter from the outdoors, close the exterior door against the drafts, and then proceed through another doorway into the living area. Frequently, it is possible to add this feature to an existing floor plan simply by adding a door in an existing archway. The compartment admits only a limited amount of cold or hot air upon entry or exit when the interior door is in the closed position. A sizable amount of energy can be preserved by having a compartmented entry design at all exterior entrances.

The principle does not necessarily preclude that an anteroom

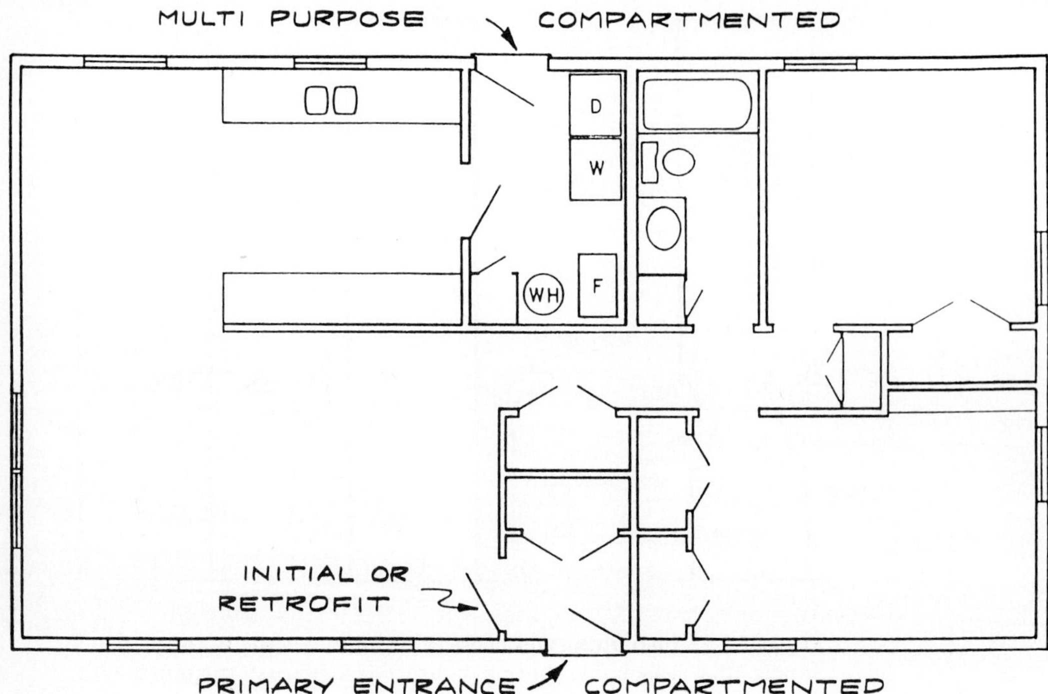

Figure 1-3 Compartmented entries perform the conservation objective and other useful roles.

is required for that sole purpose. A secondary entrance can frequently be adapted to the compartmental type by incorporating it with an existing small room. A utility room or a laundry room that lends itself to a logical traffic flow may serve well as a compartment entrance. Care should be taken in the design, however, not to route the traffic pattern directly through a work space (a common fault on many floor plans).

A modified compartment exists where the service entrance is inside an attached garage. The principle works only moderately well with this design. To work at all, the garage door must be shut. Even then the efficiency is minimal, as the garage area is usually too large and too cold.

The floor plans of many existing homes lend themselves to minor remodeling which will make a compartmented entrance possible. An arch between an entranceway can be framed into a doorway. An entrance alcove can be separated with a retrofit partition, including a door.

It may be noted that most commercial buildings make use of compartmented entrances. The reduction in heat loss by this design is well known. The design is universally practiced by commercial architects. Compartmental entries are basic to the overall conservation principle.

4 TEMPERATURE RETENTION

FREE HEAT SOURCE

Certain elements of free heat and cooling are available in most regions and climates of the earth. Throughout history human beings have cycled to and away from the sources. Now, through necessity, it appears that in the United States, the pendulum is swinging back toward the use of our free sources of energy. What are these gifts of nature?

They come in several forms. It is only a task of finding a feasible way to harness each source that remains to be perfected. The sources are the *sun,* the *wind,* the *water* in the earth, and the *earth* itself. Solar energy is readily tapped with a variety of collector types. Wind is put to work with windmills and generators. Both of these sources are free for the taking, but they suffer from a common feature: unreliability. Unless the sun shines or the wind blows, the energy gain may degenerate to nothing. By contrast, the earth, and the water in it, are more consistent sources of a known quality and quantity of heat and cooling potential.

There are devotees of these four sources who will expound at length on the advantages of one or another. There are a growing number of people who are taking advantage of feasible combinations of the four sources. As the technology improves, the use of the various combinations will be more attractive to contractors and individual builders alike.

HEAT AND COOLING RETENTION

Whether the structure is an earth-sheltered home, a solar-collector design, a conventional structure with a heat pump that draws water from a well, or some other type, one feature is supremely important. Once the heat has been gained, it must be efficiently retained. The methods of retention are well within the reach of the conscientious builder.

INSULATING THE FOUNDATION EXPOSURE

The above-ground portion of the exterior face of a foundation wall is called the *exposure area.* Most building codes mandate a minimum exposure of 8″. Frequently the actual exposure is much greater, especially in heavy snow country, where home owners may be concerned about potential water damage to wood that is exposed to melting snow. It is quite common to see whole neighborhoods of houses sitting atop two or three courses of exposed concrete foundation blocks. Where there is a basement with approximately one-fourth of the wall exposed above ground, an extreme heat loss factor exists unless insulating measures are taken. Even a minimum 8″ exposure will comprise a notable conductive escape zone all around the house. When one stops to consider that the two sides of a concrete block comprise scarcely a 3″ thickness of porous concrete, a mental picture is drawn. The cavities add no thermal barrier as they are not airtight. The webs in the block provide conductive bridges.

Solid concrete (poured) walls, though containing more mass, are also radical conductors. The installation of sheet Styrofoam, applied to one or both surfaces will do much to eliminate the window of vulnerability that a basement wall represents. Such techniques successfully complete the overall envelope concept of house insulation.

A well-coordinated system is to run the wall sheathing (Styrofoam) continuously down the frame wall, over the exposed foundation, and down to or below the frost line. This effectively blocks the thermal bridge (the sill and floor header). Another layer is then installed full height on the interior face of the basement wall.

Protecting the Styrofoam surface along the exposure area is mandatory (Fig. 1-4). Styrofoam sheets are so vulnerable to damage that a shield is a must. The Styrofoam must be installed before backfilling, as it should extend at least to the frost line. For basements that are intended to be used as full-time living space, a full wall covering of Styrofoam will add to comfort and to the economy of maintenance.

The shield is provided over the exposed part of the Styrofoam and extended down below grade line a few inches. Many material choices are available: copper, aluminum, galvanized iron, treated plywood, vinyl, and other materials in sheet form. The shield is

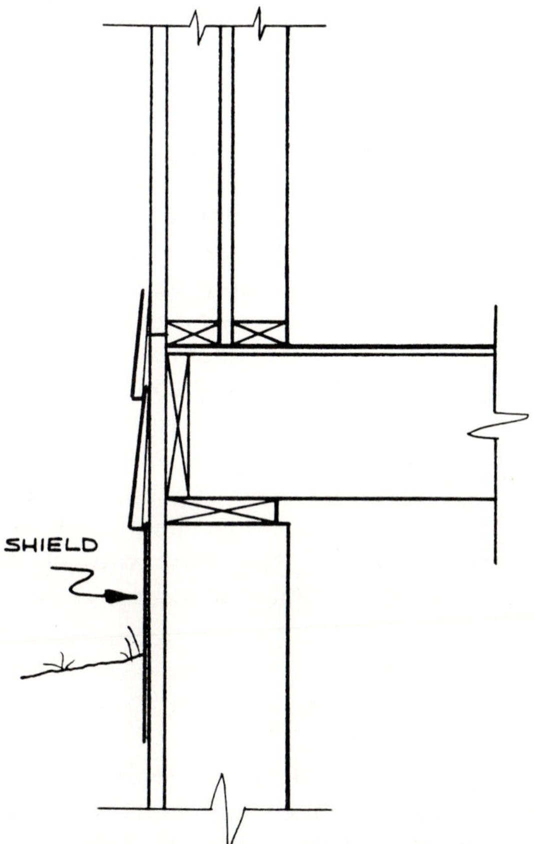

Figure 1-4 A shield of wood or metal is mandatory to protect a Styrofoam-insulated exposure zone above the grade.

tucked up under the siding in rain-shedding formation. It should be secured in a manner that is permanent. Though the shield is trapped at the top and pressed against the Styrofoam by dirt at the bottom, it still may benefit from adhesives or fasteners, particularly at the top.

Styrofoam may be fastened with adhesive to the masonry. A grid pattern is better than spotted pads. Some parge sealers will perform double duty as moisture sealers for the wall and adhesive backing for the Styrofoam. Obviously the Styrofoam must be placed on the wall while the asphalt sealer is wet and sticky. Spray-on sealers will not hold Styrofoam in place.

The 6″-studded exterior frame wall is a mild approach to greater thermal retention in above-ground walls. This 5 ½″ cavity wall is a step up from the 3 ½″ cavity of the traditional 2 × 4 stud wall. Obviously it gains cavity capacity for insulation by a little over 50%. In Btu resistance, this is an advance from R-11 to R-19 with fiberglass batts. This is a significant improvement. Teamed with a proportionate advance in ceiling insulation, such as R-19 to R-38, the home owner, new builder, or retrofitter will realize a substantial saving. There will be a cost-effective payback in a few years that will completely offset the additional initial material cost. From that day forward the difference in utility cost will be pure savings—the harvest from good planning and execution.

Superinsulation is a term that was coined to describe high-level R-rated house designs. An 8″ double-walled house was classed as superinsulated when it was first conceived. In reality, it is now cost effective in all regions that require either house heating or cooling or both. Times change and with them, life styles. Full house air conditioning is now commonplace throughout the heat belts. This means that superinsulation is feasible wherever climate control is practiced. This way of life gives impetus to the double-walled concept of building as described in Part 4.

REVIEW TOPICS

1. What is the approximate average temperature below the frost line? How does the frost line vary from the south to the north in the United States?

2. What are the three basic house categories that accomplish the energy conservation principle? Describe how each of these types accomplishes the conservation principle.

3. Tell what the abbreviation "Btu" stands for and how it applies to the discussion of heat and cool conservation.

4. What does the letter "R" mean? Give the most common ratings for fiberglass insulation of 4", 6", and 12" (nominal thickness).

5. What does the word "conduction" mean to the conservation-conscious builder? Explain how it applies to the design of exterior walls.

6. What is "infiltration"? Describe several places where it is most commonly found in a poorly constructed house.

7. Discuss the pros and cons of using single-glazed metal windows, as compared with double or triple glass, or Thermopane-glazed wood windows.

8. Explain why the Styrofoam-cored door with external relief designs is so superior to a concave relieved wood door.

9. Explain what a compartmented entrance is and how it functions to conserve heat in a house.

10. List and discuss the three most practical forms of conservation construction available to the modern builder (*reference:* Parts 2, 3, and 4).

Part 2

Earth Sheltering

5 ADVANTAGES OF EARTH SHELTERING

There are a number of compelling gains to be made by using the earth in its natural state to shelter a dwelling. Mankind has used the warmth and the coolness of the earth for many thousands of years as a means toward human comfort. Only recently has enough technical data become available to eliminate some of the problems encountered in producing a wholly suitable habitat of this type. Even so, the construction of an earth-sheltered dwelling that meets the basic demands continues to be thought of as one which requires the services of a contractor, due largely to visions of prefabricated concrete components and massive hoisting equipment. These limitations often discourage the home owner-builder and the do-it-yourself family team. The facts to be learned in this part can be assembled in combinations of systems that will make it possible for the previously mentioned builders to take on an earth-sheltered project with confidence. In fact, some of the designs shown and described can be constructed by only one person.

Seasonal lag creates an advantage well worth taking into account. In any given area, the earth cycles between a warming season and a cooling off season. It takes about three to six months to reach the extremes before the cycle starts its return swing. The earth is always behind the atmospheric seasonal cycle. As winter runs out, the warming winds of spring begin to thaw out the ground close to the surface. Eventually the atmospheric temperature penetrates deeper into the ground until the frost line is reached. Then, as summer wanes into fall, the temperature above ground begins its annual descent and the earth begins to cool again. This means that the earth, from the frost line up, contains coolness (albeit in diminishing measure) throughout the summer and sustains stored warmth into the winter months. In an earth dwelling, these lagging temperature characteristics are used to counteract and reduce artificial heating and cooling needs.

Constant temperature is found below the frost line. This is to say that the earth varies little below the frost line, year round, at any particular locale. In most of the United States this temperature is about $\pm 52°$. This constant earth temperature greatly reduces the temperature differential in a dwelling that is completely below the earth. It also helps save fuel for those dwellings which are partially earth sheltered and adequately insulated above the frost line level.

Temperature differential is large in the northern states. This translates to large differentials during an extended part of the winter. For example, the temperature is $-15°$ on a certain January morning in South Dakota. Desired room temperature is $72°$. To meet the need, it will require an $87°$ rise in the temperature. In the same location, in an earth-sheltered home, it will take only about $20°$ of heating to reach the same level of comfort. For air conditioning, no artificial auxiliary is needed. During summer months, when the outdoor temperature is above $72°$, circulation of just enough outside air to raise the temperature will produce the desired level of comfort. By using the fan on the conventional heating system in the manual mode, a good circulation can be had while fresh air is introduced from intakes that draw from the outside atmosphere. Lacking an outside duct, the same effect can be produced by simply opening entry door(s) or windows on an exposed side.

Solar coordinates constitute logical and superior ways of reducing the fossil fuel cost to practically nothing. There are a number of systems for collecting and storing solar heat that can be coordinated with the exposed wall of an earth shelter when it is properly faced to the south. Incumbent with the technique is the responsibility for effectively warding off the undesirable heat of the solar rays that will bombard the shelter during the summer months.

Unwanted solar heat can be dealt with in several ways. All should be practiced where possible. Hardwood trees, properly situated, will provide shade in the summer and will shed their leaves to permit winter sun rays to penetrate to the collectors during the winter. The exposed front-wall windows may comprise the extent of collector devices. In this circumstance, trees should be adequate in shade capacity and location to shade all of the exposed south facing wall. Even the retaining walls of an earth berm that adjoins the dwelling wall will benefit from the shade.

An adequate roof overhang is necessary to shade the front collector wall. Trees are great, but the dependability factor is subject to breakdown. Sometimes nature takes its toll without our permission. High winds may destroy large limbs or even whole trees. Drought may kill a tree and its effectiveness is lost overnight. It takes too long to replant and wait for adequate growth. A structural overhang, on the other hand, can be designed to shade the collector surfaces during the summer and expose them in the winter because the angles of the sun rays are much higher in the summer.

Venting the collector in the hot months is the third measure that should be planned in advance. Collectors that are made with absorber plates and designed heat-transfer corridors must have provision for automatic or mechanical venting. To leave such a collector unvented in the summer sun is to court disaster from spontaneous combustion. A minimal problem will be the rapid depreciation of materials from overexposure and excess heat. Where the collection system consists of Thermopane windows, no escape system is available. In this situation shade is mandatory and must be created by external blinds if it is not provided throughout by an adequate overhang.

Quietness is a fringe benefit of the earth-sheltered dwelling. The earth and frequently the ultimate shape of the contours act as deadeners and deflectors of sounds that might otherwise be considered objectionable.

Storm protection is another feature that appeals, particularly in cyclone- and hurricane-prone regions. The usual one-side-only exposed type of earth-sheltered structure is well protected on the other three sides.

Low maintenance is a most attractive feature of the earth-sheltered home for those who prefer other activities to those of caring for the exterior of a house. Typical house maintenance will be required only on the structure's exposed wall. The rest of it is equivalent to yard maintenance.

Life cycle cost effectiveness is a term which draws a comparison between the proportion of the initial cost with the useful life of a specific property and that of a similarly used property. In this category the earth-sheltered dwelling comes out far ahead of other more conventional housing. There simply is little to depreciate from either nature or time. Of the structure itself, there is little to wear out (assuming proper construction). There will always be the short-lived appliances and mechanical-moving accouterments to replace, but the basic structure is about as impervious to the ravages of time as any form of habitat that man has designed.

Payback is a term we frequently hear as an item to consider when choosing how much insulation to use or whether to install Thermopane windows or single glass at half the price. To the discredit of some builders, it is unfortunate that the decision is solely made on profit motives to the detriment of the owner-consumer. Put simply, the owner gets an inferior house product while the contractor attempts to improve his or her company's financial position. It is also a sorry state when a prospective house purchaser will buy a minimum quality house for a few hundred or thousand dollars less when a close study will reveal that four or five years down the road the higher-cost house will have reached the payback point on some construction features. From that point on, the owner could have deposited the savings in the family account instead of continuing to spend on utility cost. The extreme, but possible, example of payback time is the earth-sheltered, solar-heated home that requires no heat and cooling utility cost. In some areas of this land, the savings in fuel could be as much as the monthly mortgage payment. The earth home is literally paying for itself; and after payback is reached, it will be free rent and free heat and cooling from then on.

6 SITE FACTORS

TOPOGRAPHY

Optimum exposure of an earth-sheltered dwelling is south. The greatest potential for heat and light reception is thus realized by situating the structure on a south-facing slope. An earth shelter may be excavated and constructed on a level site but it complicates the design and forces much recontouring of the site. Aesthetically, it does not present as many design alternatives as a south-facing slope (Fig. 2-1).

The soil composition should be of a heavy type. Earth-sheltered homes with earthen-covered roofs will be excavated considerably deeper than conventional surface homes with base-

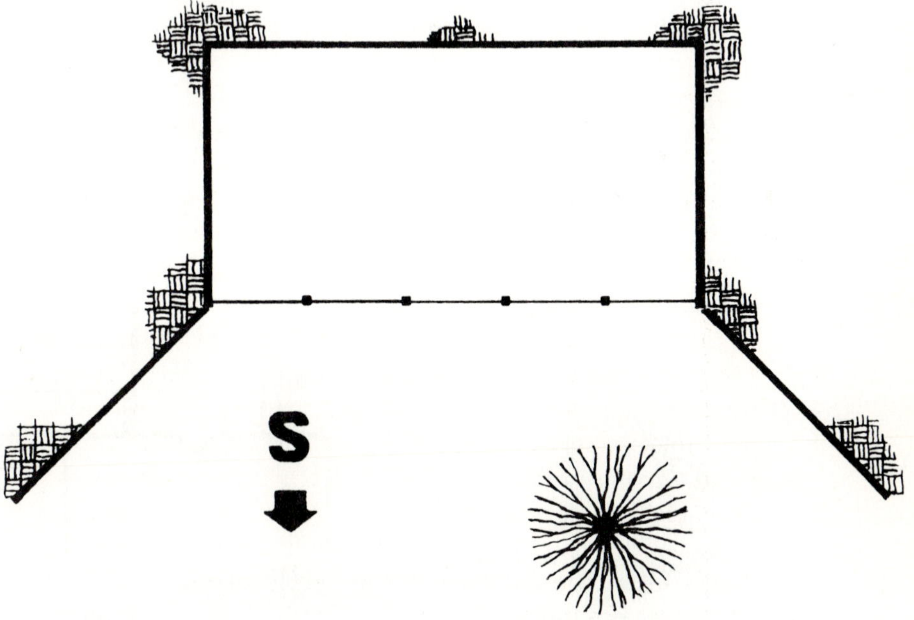

Figure 2-1 The optimum facing direction for an earth-sheltered house is south.

ments. The water table level and the presence of ground water must be known before serious planning proceeds. There must not be water present above the contemplated foundation level. Bore testing is always advised to confirm the suitability of the projected site of an earth dwelling.

Drainage is an important characteristic of an earth home. With proper drains and gravel bedding, an earth home will be as dry and healthy as any other type; it can even be more comfortable. Surface water from rain should be handled so that it runs away from the house vicinity and toward the lower-altitude boundaries of the site. On the high side of the yard (usually north), small drainage contours are strategically placed to guide the water around and away from the back side of the house. To detract from possible erosion, the slope pitch of the grade should not be greater than 4 in 12 (1' of rise for every 3' of run). Directly behind the house, some extra gravel bedding is required beneath the topsoil to carry the water around the perimeter foundation drains (Fig. 2-2). These drains will conduct the water to a spillway or evaporation field that is at a lower level than the footings. The minimum successful slope for drain tiles is ⅛" per foot (Fig. 2-3).

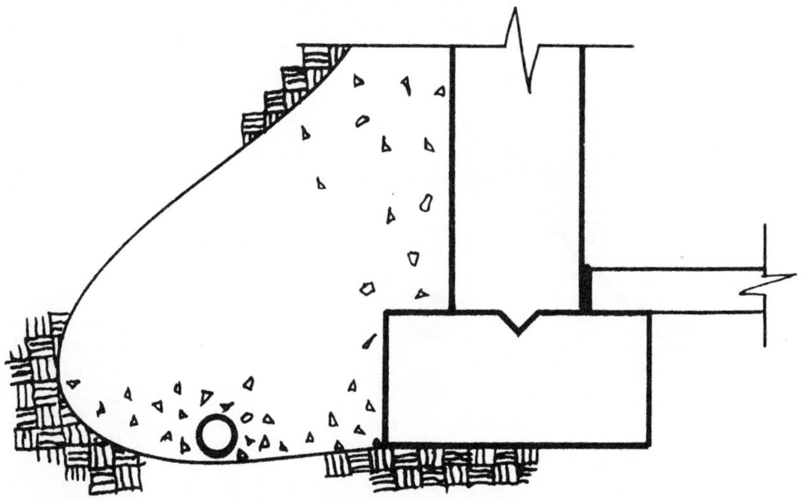

Figure 2-2 Perforated drain pipes laid with the holes facing down in a filter bed of washed-crushed rock will carry unwanted water away from an earth-shelter foundation.

Reflective heat and light will enter the front windows from large expanses of concrete. In winter this reflection will bring in warmth and light (Fig. 2-4). In summer, unless shaded by large trees, shade must be provided by artificial means. Where either

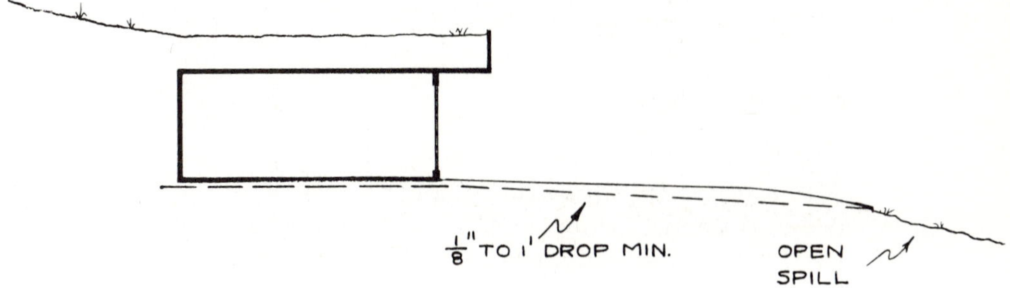

Figure 2-3 The water from the footing drain may be routed to an open spillway at a lower elevation away from the house.

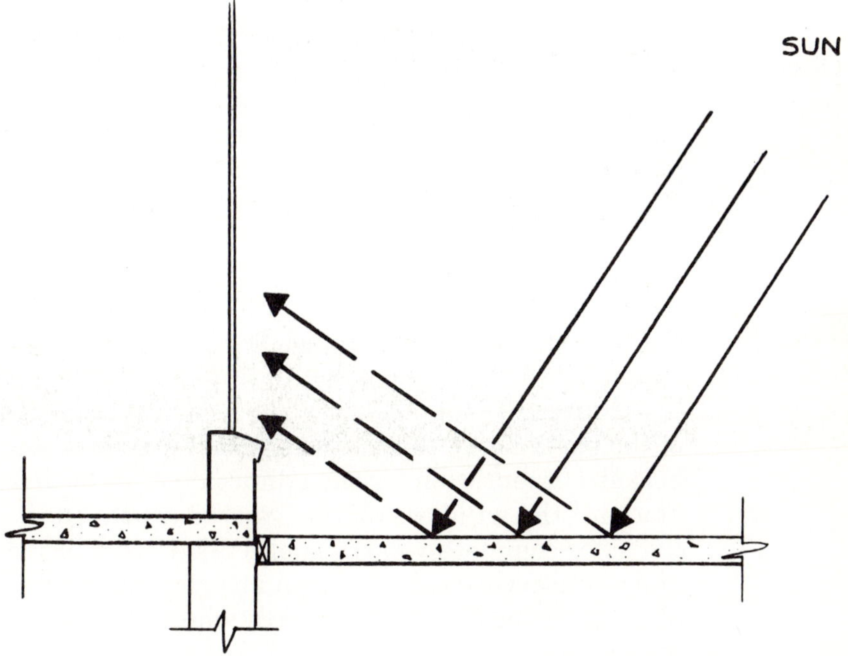

Figure 2-4 Too much unshaded concrete, exposed to summer sunshine, will reflect a lot of unwanted heat into the earth shelter.

exterior blinds or overhangs, or both, are principally relied on for shade, there should be as little flat concrete used for walks and patios as possible. In summer the concrete will reflect great amounts of heat toward the face of the house and provide a serious detriment to the natural earth cooling of the interior. Earth with grass, on the other hand, will be a much cooler surface where overall shade of the area is unavailable.

ORIENTATION

The sun is the focal point and therefore the key to successful orientation of the house. This is especially true when a great dependence is placed on passive solar heat as a staple source for winter comfort. In winter, the hours of beneficial sunlight are much less. The arc of effectiveness is limited to less than one-third of a 24-hour day. The hours of daylight during the crest of the summer are more than double the potential heating hours available in the winter (Fig. 2-5). However, the effect of this disproportion is not as simple as that due to the varying difference in the sun's angle as the calendar progresses. The generally lower arc of the winter sun permits deeper penetration of light and energy into the dwelling. The floor (particularly if it is a masonry type) and the solid objects touched by the sun rays all take on the role of a heat sink (a solar storage system). Thus, the extreme difference in daily sunlit hours between summer and winter seasons, in terms of heating potential, is offset to some degree by the added penetration potential for heat gain. Considering all these factors, solar optimization will be realized when the facade of the hillside house is faced between 10 and 30° east of south (Fig. 2-6).

Sunlight is an element to be considered. An early drawback of the earth home concept was that it was dark and cave-like. The best site orientation for the admission of light and solar gain is to place all the windows on the exposed south side with the remaining sides completely earth sheltered. With a broad front exposure and a conservative depth, such an orientation will provide a light, pleasant atmosphere. All rooms where daylight is desirable are placed on the front. Closets, general storage, and utility areas can be placed on the backside (Fig. 2-7).

Wind direction is another element of house orientation. When the earth house is faced optimally as described in foregoing

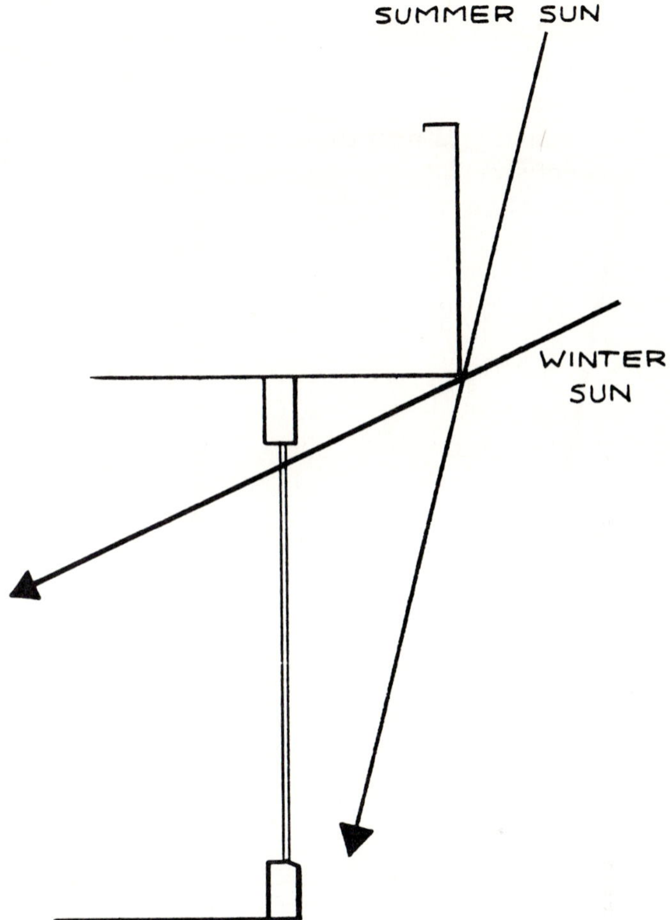

Figure 2-5 In the winter, sunshine penetrates deeply into an earth shelter when the parapet is correctly extended and the solar orientation is right.

paragraphs, it will be on a south slope. The predominant wind directions will be from the northwest in the winter season and from the southeast during the warmer season. This generally holds true, though some features of the immediately surrounding terrain may cause unique wind deflections which alter the mode. The south exposure orientation favors the normal wind direction. The northern winter gales are deflected by the earthen shield on the uphill side. In summer, the cooler breezes are wafted up the slope to the exposed front of the house. With some careful plan-

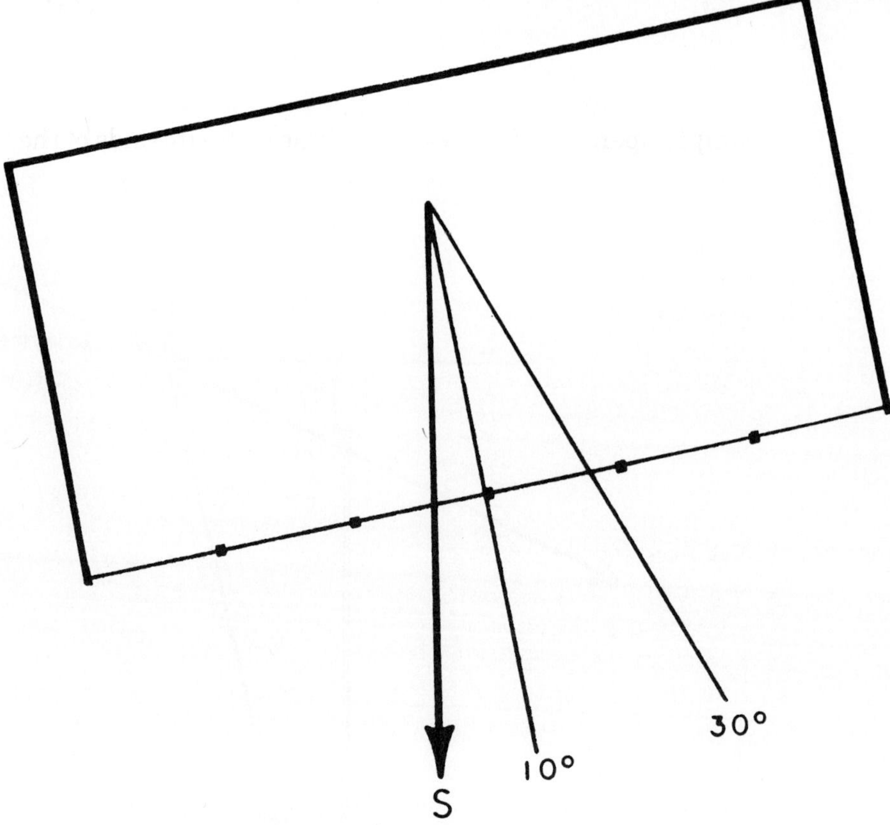

Figure 2-6 An earth house that faces within a range of 10° to 30° east of south will optimize the effects of wind, site characteristics, and solar gain.

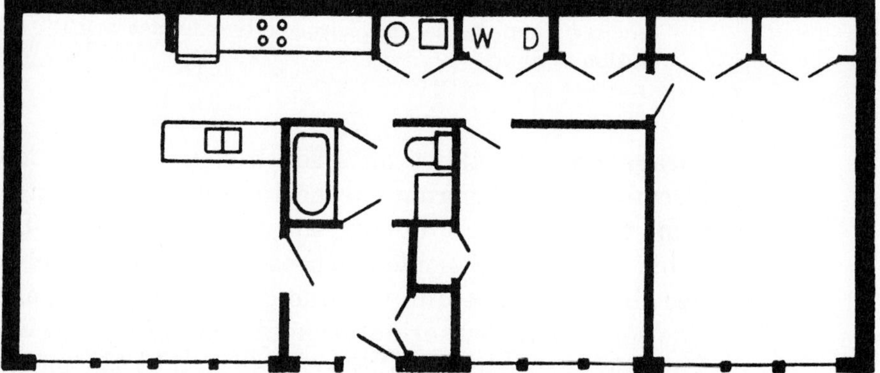

Figure 2-7 All major rooms receive natural sunlight when this basic floor plan is used.

ning, these gentle and refreshing drafts can be taken into the house and used as moving ventilation (Fig. 2-8).

Ventilation can be attained passively in some localities by simply opening windows or doors on opposite ends of the front wall and allowing the length of the house to act as a long duct. In this system it is advantageous to use partitions that go clear to the ceiling or full transoms above regular doors. A conventionally closed area above a standard 6'–8' door will act as a baffle and seriously restrict the outflow of air currents. The open concept of design (as little partitioning as possible) will produce the most potential for good lighting and natural ventilation in an earth-sheltered home. Rapid air exchange and heavy venting needs may be accommodated with power fans and vent exits in the rear of the house. The advantage is that such a mechanical means of moving air is under the control of the occupant at any desired time or for any level of performance. A disadvantage is that mechanical ventilator ducts and hoods are difficult to make attractive where they jut through the earth's surface above. Nevertheless, there will be other vent pipes from plumbing and power lines to contend with and, in some cases, these items can be clustered and camouflaged to minimize the incompatibility with Mother Earth.

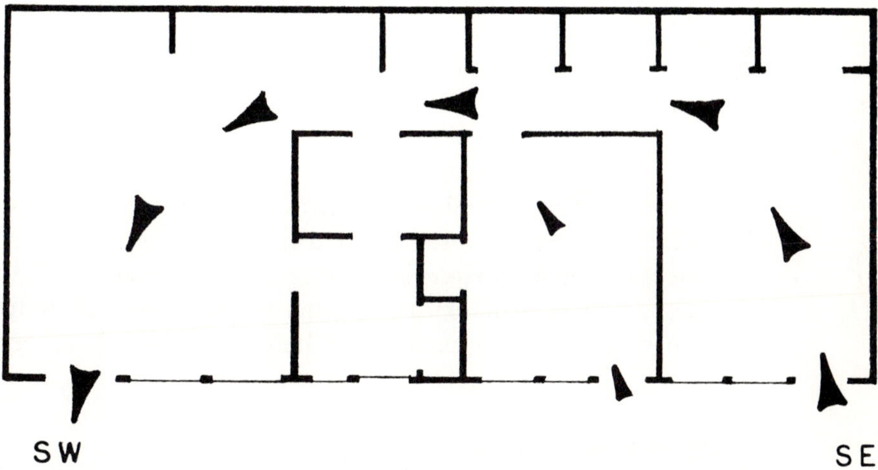

Figure 2-8   Summer breezes from the southeast can be channeled through the bedrooms and corridors to exit at the southwest window. Other rooms can be ventilated by narrowly opening windows. A window fan in the intake window and another fan facing outward in the discharge window will accelerate the movement of air.

The view seen from the exposed windows of an earth home is sometimes one of the outstanding reasons for considering the concept as a whole. A beautiful hillside property is found and from the slope of its possibly limited acres can be seen range after range of mountains and valleys stretching their misty profiles away as far as the eye can see. What a place to own an earth home. Not always so! First we must get out the compass and reconnoiter the facing direction; then we must consider the potential locations that will meet all the criteria established so far. When our homework is done and our criteria confirmed, then the spectacular view is one of the final aesthetic considerations that will affect our construction choice.

7 GENERAL CONSIDERATIONS

The main theme of this book is conservation. Its purpose is to shed some light on methods and means of construction that will net significant savings down the line without initial cost that nullifies the goal. It is believed by many earth home enthusiasts that the solar-heated earth dwelling comes the closest to 100% self-sufficiency of any form of house devised to date. It may well be. Nonetheless, anyone contemplating such a measure of future independence from climate control costs should be aware of what it takes to put the package together.

It is the purpose of this section to give a broad background of information that will acquaint you, the reader and potential builder, with the general but unique character of earth house design and construction. In the next section we shall look at some innovative modifications of the earth house principle that are within the construction capabilities of an amateur or novice.

MECHANICAL HEAT

All of the alternative forms of heat generation that apply to a conventional above-ground house are feasible in the earth house but some have distinct advantages. The use of ductwork, for example, is advantageous because it provides a conduit system for the movement of air by artificial means. The heat exchanger fuel options to accompany a duct distribution system are gas, oil, all electric, and the heat pump. Of these, the most efficient is the heat pump with a buried water coil (a free source of earth-temperature water, such as an artesian well, is the ultimate heat pump system).

MECHANICAL COOLING

The heat pump again reigns supreme as a coordinate system of heat and cooling efficiency. Its mechanism reverses the heat-draw function and draws the coolness from the earth-temperature water. Starting with water in a 50 to 60° temperature range, the differential is much smaller than an air-to-air type of heat pump which has to make up the difference between outdoor air temperature and desired indoor coolness. Should the temperature outdoors be 100° and the thermostat set for 75° indoors, the change required is 25°. With the water-to-air heat pump, there is no differential to make up, as we are starting with a temperature that is lower than that needed. The cooler air is simply introduced until room temperature lowers to the desired level. This takes place with no energy loss (cost outlay) other than the electricity to operate the controls and fans.

COP (coefficient of performance) is a unit symbol for comparing the efficiency ratings of different types of heating and cooling systems according to the energy source. Electrical heating, which stems from resistance (red hot wires), is the most costly. Therefore, this form is given a COP rating of 1. The higher the COP, the more efficient (less costly) the heat source is. The heat pump varies from two-and-a-half to four times greater than the simple electric furnace. It also performs the air conditioning job, thereby eliminating the necessity of another separate utility. The size of a heat pump is so much smaller than either a furnace or an air conditioner that it can easily be camouflaged on the exterior of the sheltered house.

Many earth homes do not have any mechanical cooling facility other than circulation fans and venting systems. Most well-designed earth homes will require no outstanding mechanical means of air conditioning but will function adequately with only the natural cool resources of the earth about them.

Solar heat provides two alternatives for the earth shelter builder. Active heaters will involve separate collectors of commercial or home fabrication. With these collectors comes the necessity for lots of piping, pumps, valves, and discharges. All of these components are relatively expensive. Keep in mind, however, that the true test comes in how much is saved over the long haul. A practical advantage of the collector system is that regulation is somewhat easier. To reduce or increase the temperature, you simply set the thermostat and wait a little while. With passive solar it is more apt to be a case of opening and shutting windows and vents manually (it is entirely possible to construct shades and vents to operate by electrical impulse in as automatic a way as the nonpassive system).

Double-pane glass is recommended for a passive solar window bank. The added retention of the heat after collection hours will more than offset the more difficult penetration task of the sun. Triple pane is not advised as the ratio of retention is then overcome. The penetration resistance is too great, thereby canceling out the retention gain. Keep in mind that the heat waves of the sun penetrate cloud banks and misty skies enough to collect significant heat even though the sun is not visible to the eye.

VENTILATION

Some provision for air movement and exchange in an earth house and a superinsulated house is needed because both of these types are theoretically devoid of infiltration. We should not regard infiltration as a viable system for air exchange for it is this fault in a structure that defeats the principle of conservation and cost economy. Rather, the objective is to make a tight house and provide for proper air control at will. Control of air movement and freshness should be in the hands of the resident, not the weather.

Air exchange is controlled efficiently by fans and ductwork with properly placed intakes and discharges. Most above-ground conventional houses do not have provisions to take in outside air and discharge stale, interior air. This function is provided for by adequate opening of windows and doors. Minimum requirement for code passage is usually 4% of the square-foot floor area of a room for ventilation and 10% for light. These percentages regulate the minimum size of the window area in any given room. A combination skylight and fan duct, placed toward the back of the house will serve a double role as a controllable ventilator and another light source. With thick Styrofoam (2″ or more) sandwiched between 3 mm of plywood paneling for doors, this square in the ceiling can be closed off whenever desired and brought into play when needed (Fig. 2-9).

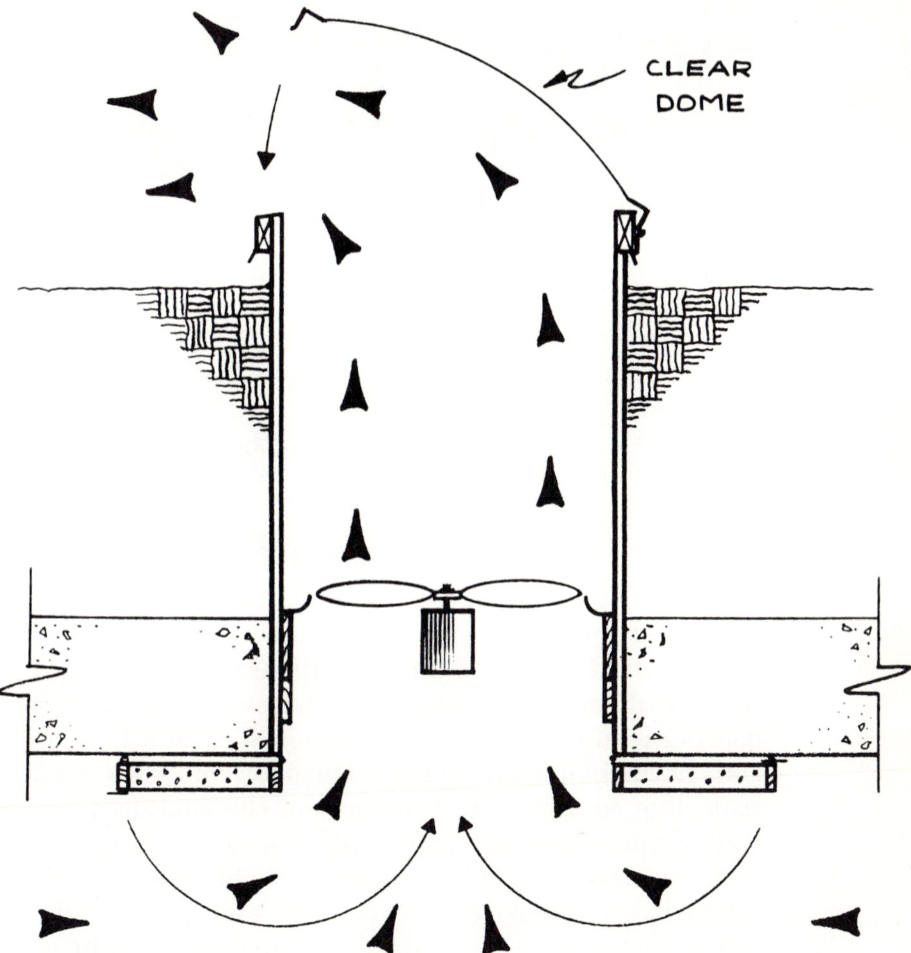

Figure 2-9 A full-house ventilation shaft with insulated closing doors and a clear plexiglass dome will emit light to a rear corridor when the doors are open (spring, summer, and fall mode). On heating days the insulated doors are closed to contain the warmth.

Humidity control is an important feature of the earth-sheltered home. There is usually no need for a humidifier in the wintertime as there often is with a conventional house. In the milder times of the year the humidity is readily controlled by the same methods described for venting and air exchange. The earth house will not exhibit the seasonal extremes of humidity found in other house types.

8 STRUCTURAL CHARACTERISTICS

It is not within the scope of this book to delve deeply into the technical information required to design an adequate earth-sheltered structure to fit a specific piece of ground. That type of project is left to the individual who owns such a piece of property. What follows are general principles to give an impression of the relative complexity of earth-sheltered construction. None of these impressions are intended to frighten off would-be considerers but rather to delineate the areas of construction that require various levels of professional training. In the next section there are examples of alternative designs that are within the scope of do-it-yourselfers and family building teams.

SUITABLE SOIL FOR EARTH SHELTERING

Soil characteristics are more important to the earth shelter builder than to conventional builders in general. A basement house with one story above ground does not pose much of a weight-bearing load on a foundation. When we think that all the materials in the house can be placed on one semi truck load, it does not seem like so much. By comparison, the sheltered roof accrues a load of approximately 100 to 120 pounds for every square foot of roof area and for each foot of depth. A 4-foot-deep (average) earth-covered roof comprises between 400 and 500 pounds per square foot of roof area. This is about 10 times the weight of a composition-shingled wood roof. The prefab concrete joist-and-plank roof system, used on many earth homes, is comparable to those used in large industrial buildings.

There are many other roof shapes such as domes, arches, and

vaults that are designed to handle the earth load. Getting into these types of designs for the roof (and ceiling) will frequently have a drastic effect on the floor plan and the general decor of the entire interior.

One might think that construction on such a seemingly grand scale would be prohibitively expensive. If there are earth shelter builders in your area, the cost could be comparable to a conventional house. These builders will have the equipment, the sources, and the know-how to proceed on a competitive basis. In addition to these advantages, there is the savings realized from the absence of finished materials around at least three sides of the structure.

The earth shelter is much deeper in the earth than a conventional basement that is excavated somewhere between 5 and 8′ deep. The footings for a flat-ceiling earth house of conventional height are often twice that deep. The footings themselves must be proportionately larger to support the much greater load that is placed on them (Fig. 2-10). Framed houses above ground fall within general bearing load capacities which can be obtained from tables. Each earth house is unique in its design and its intended

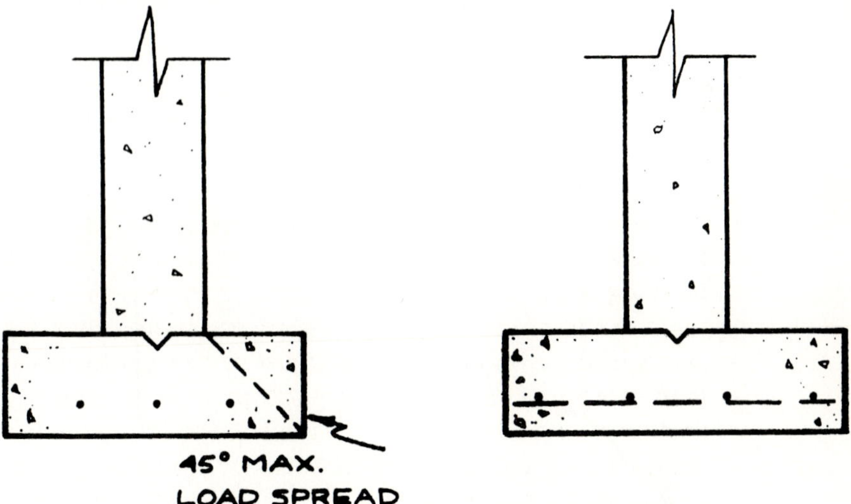

Figure 2-10 A footing for an earth shelter is usually larger than required for an above-ground house. (a) The maximum load spread is 45° from the base of the projection to the face line of the wall. A footing, whose width causes a wider spread than 45° (a smaller angle), should be reinforced crosswise with steel bars in the lower third.

environment. Knowing the specific characteristics of the earth's composition, in advance of the planning and specification writing, is vitally important to the success of each earth shelter structure. Excavation in rock may not be cost feasible. Shifty clay is to be avoided. Sand and gravel will require an enormous excavation and backfill weight will be treacherous.

Walls come next on top of the tailored footings. They will usually be poured concrete with steel reinforcement bars spaced vertically and horizontally throughout. The bars are field welded or tight wired together into an unending grid so that continuous reinforcement is sustained throughout the walls.

Interior partitions that intersect the outer walls can and should be designed to perform a buttress effect (Fig. 2-11). The pressure exerted on the outside of the exterior walls is considerably more than on conventional basement walls. The full height of the earth-retaining wall is laterally pressured. The longer the wall, the more vulnerable it is to inward collapse. This inherent weakness can be strengthened by using the interior partitions as braces, particularly along the back side which usually has the greatest roof weight on it (high side of the watershed).

Concrete interior partitions, in the buttress mode, should be poured simultaneously with the exterior walls. The entire wall

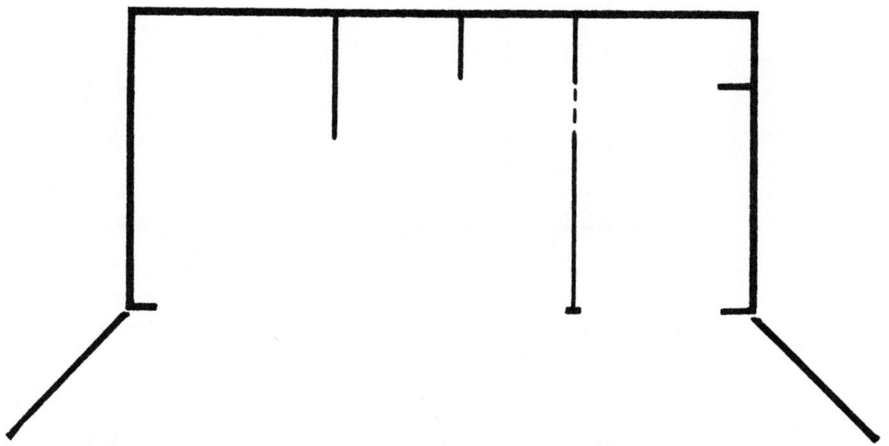

Figure 2-11 Interior partitions that intersect walls can provide a buttressing role to counteract the earth pressures from without.

and partition complex should be reinforced and poured as a integrated unit.

Bearing partitions in the earth shelter are all of those that run perpendicular to the roof joists. Though situated at interim locations of the span, they still may support a portion of the roof deflection (some concrete deck joists are prestressed and, hypothetically, do not bear on an intermediate partition). These partitions, and any other masonry ones, will call for concrete footings—integrally reinforced and poured at one time—to maintain the integrity of the system as a whole. Finally, the floor and roof both act as lateral pressure resistors to the pressures against the outer walls (Fig. 2-12). It is very enticing at this point to complete the drainage and the gravel filling, then to backfill the trench around the wall; so much safer to work, we rationalize, and so much more convenient to reach the deck area. In a few cases where the earth walls are quite vertical and sound and the space is narrow, some contractors might opt to backfill at this stage. The disaster that is courted by giving in to this impulse is not often worth the risk. A collapsed wall is a major financial setback, not to mention the potential for injury to workers on the site. Where the surrounding soil is quite stable, it is sometimes possible to place fill at the two rear corners in order to create a bridge. For greater

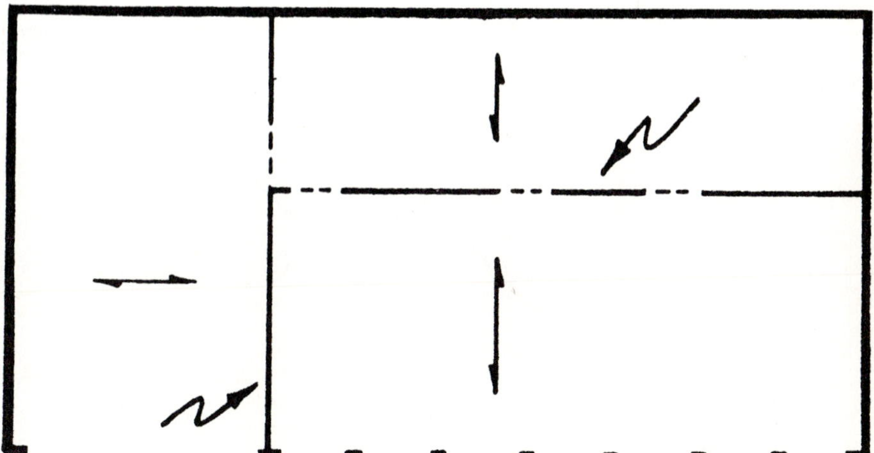

Figure 2-12   Interior partitions and header columns must have adequate footings under them.

safety and support, the floor and the structural roof deck should
be in place before the walls are subjected to the backfill pressure.

THERMAL INSULATION

Thermal breaks were not given much attention in early earth
house construction. Like so many other types of hidden defects,
thermal breaks escaped notice for a long time. *Nosebleeds,* as they
are nicknamed, take place wherever sheltered construction materials are permitted to emerge into the atmosphere unbroken by
thermal barriers (TB) (Fig. 2-13). Tests have shown that a signif-

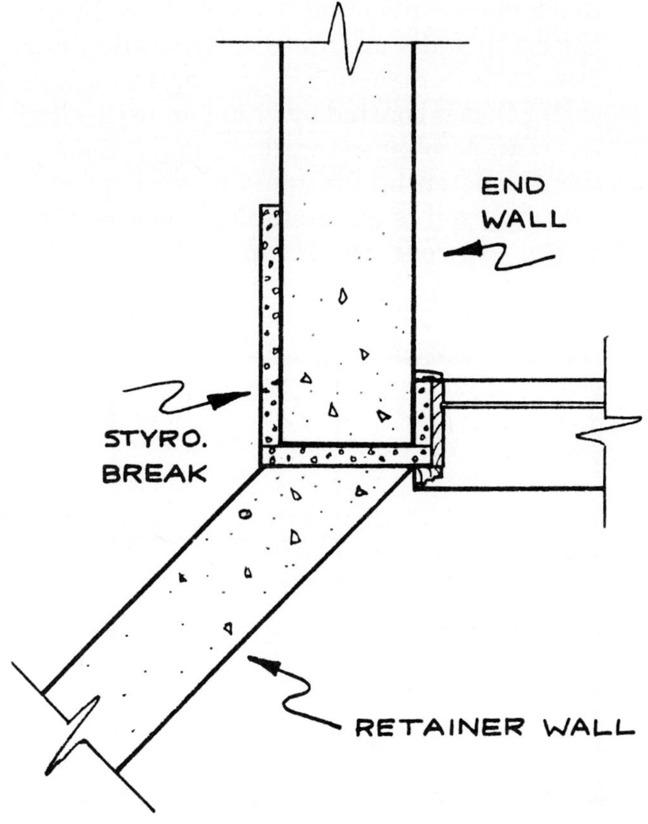

Figure 2-13 Thermal breaks reduce "nosebleed" (the wick effect).
This Styrofoam break effectively isolates the foundation wall from
the exterior retainer wall at each front corner.

icant quantity of bleedout takes place where a sheltered foundation wall is integral with, and an extension of, the external retention wall that holds back the earth from a front patio. At a certain stage of development, the practice was altered to form a break in the wall. The joint was similar to an expansion joint, but the steel reinforcing rods were still continued on through into the retaining wall. This design served to break the concrete connection, but the steel rods continued to act as significant conductors. Rods act as thermal wicks. In winter they conduct the earth's warmth outside and turn the retaining wall into an effective diffuser. In summer the rods become solar conductors in the retainer wall (a collector wall is an effective solar storage sump) and shunt the heat into the rods in the interior walls. In reality they become heating elements in the wall, which heat the coolness we are attempting to harvest from the earth.

Other areas require thermal breaks. A concrete patio or sidewalk that touches the edge of the floor slab will bleed detrimentally in both seasons from the conductive element as well as the solar reflective aspect. Green belts of grass or flowers will form an attractive barrier. Structural overhangs of concrete that are part of the shading requirement are conductors (down the columns) unless some kind of break is provided. Due to their weight-bearing structural function, the design in this area is critical. Any passages, revetment windows, shafts, vents, and skylights should be separated from direct contact with the basic structure to insulate it from nosebleed. Pressure-treated wood is a material that can often be brought to play in acceptable and attractive ways to form a needed thermal barrier. Styrofoam is another excellent insular barrier. It must be kept in mind that Styrofoam is a nonstructural material and that it will not survive wear and tear unless completely covered.

WATERPROOFING

Drainage is fundamental to any waterproofing system if a dry interior is to be realized. Moisture must be taken away from the foundation quickly and not permitted to puddle or stand in low spots. The gravel drainage bed must be of adequate width, depth, and cubic footage. Perforated drain tiles are ideally laid with ⅛″

drop to the foot of run starting down from the middle of the high side of the drain course, the uphill side of the house. This system of tiling in a gravel channel is called a French drain in some regions and the Swedish type in other localities. Regardless of origin, it is the standard procedure in the United States for removing moisture around a foundation (Fig. 2-14).

On a long foundation it is not possible to slant the tile system as much as the formula would prescribe because the end of the tile run would be much too deep. In such a situation the tile is laid with less pitch and the gravel bed is relied upon to eliminate puddling. The bottom of the gravel channel is gently sloped so that water works its way to the discharge point. At no point should the gravel bed be lower than the footing. Such a condition will weaken the foundation bed. The foundation bed is usually strongest and most supportive to the footing when left in its virgin condition rather than dug deep and refilled. Foundation water will attack refill, and erosion often results causing structural failure.

The double row of holes in the tile is placed down so the water will enter but sand and silt will not clog the system. If the tile is laid level, the drainage will take longer because the gravel bed will be saturated before the drain tile begins its fast transit work. With adequately sloped tile, the gravel channels (each side of the house) will start to purge as soon as water backs up far enough to reach the holes in the lowest tile in each of the discharge lines (see Fig. 2-2). At the lowest end of the tile, the gravel bed and the bottom edge of the tile should be on the same level, otherwise the gravel bed becomes a sump and holds unwanted water.

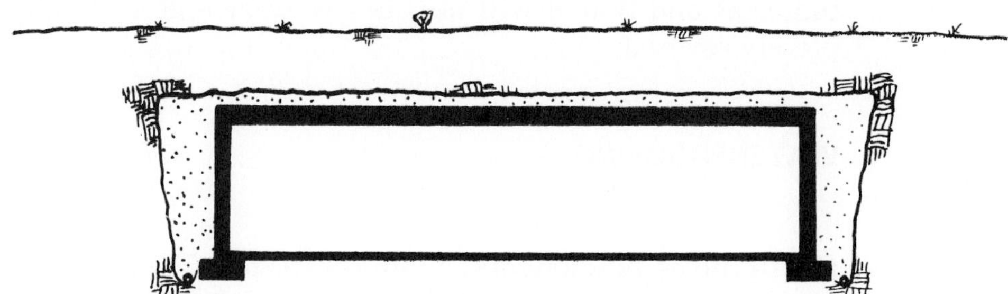

Figure 2-14 A Swedish or French footing drain carries away water that filters down from an encompassing gravel bed.

Wall and roof waterproofing must be accomplished before the entire job of graveling is completed. Sometimes the wall is done first. It is easier to fold the waterproofing materials over the edge of the footing when the tile and gravel are not yet in place. On the other hand, less harm may come to the surface of the wall covering if the drain pipes and some of the gravel are in place before tackling the exacting job of waterproofing the wall. The option is up to the individual builder.

Waterproofing materials are available from many manufacturers and in many forms. Most of those specifically designed for earth shelters involve asphalt, neoprene, or rubber as the base material. Installing them is a job for a recognized tradesperson in the specific field or one who is well self-educated on the subject. The waterproofing must be stringently applied according to the manufacturer's specifications. A leaky earth house is about as attractive as a leaky boat. Neither is necessary with today's technology.

Insulation on the roof may be coordinated with the waterproofing operation. There are many options to be considered when determining the use of Styrofoam on the concrete roof of an earth house. It takes varying depths of earth in different localities of the country to furnish adequate insulating and retention qualities for sheltering an above-the-earth house. The use of Styrofoam insulation on the top of the concrete can alter the amount of heat storage both above and below the ceiling (see later section on Owner-built Modifications—thermal comparison). This in turn can lessen the depth of total excavation that is required (Fig. 2-15).

A drainage envelope is arranged after the surface waterproofing is complete. In theory, this envelope can be a narrow, encompassing corridor of gravel which surrounds the sheltered walls and is topped off by a similar layer of gravel on top of the roof. In practice it becomes almost impossible to duplicate this arrangement as seen in an artist's view. It cannot be done with a bulldozer unless the entire cavity around the walls is filled with gravel. Bearing this in mind, it therefore is prudent not to excavate anymore yardage around a wall at the outset than is necessary to provide working space for the tiling and waterproofing tasks.

Surface drainage is the final consideration in an effective drainage system. So far the discussion could be centered around

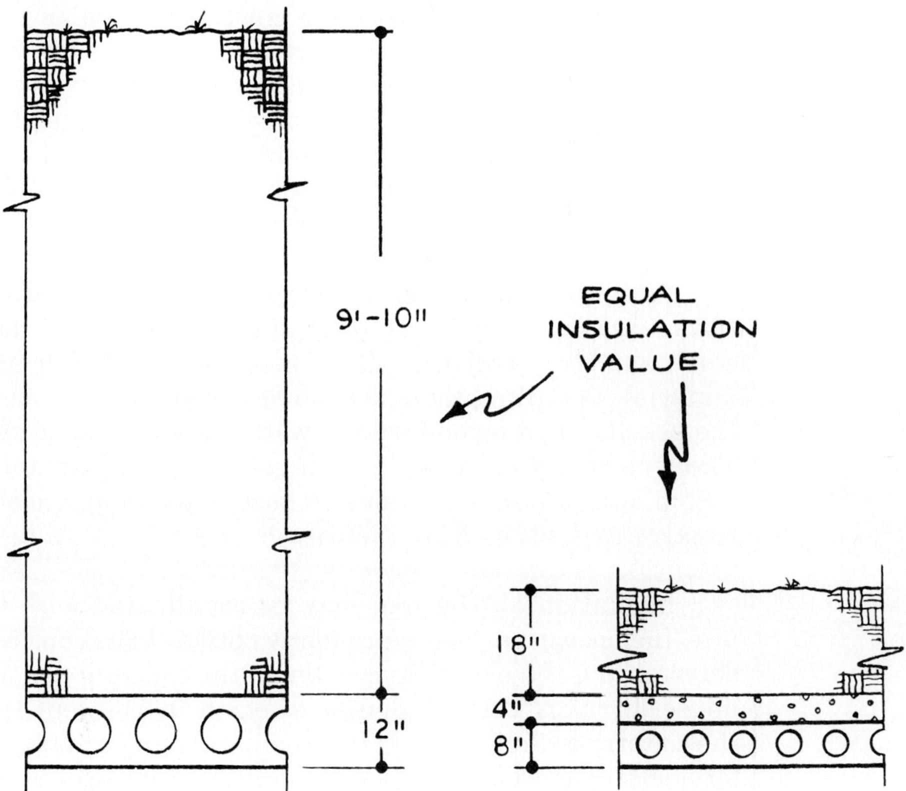

Figure 2-15 The roof-covering comparison shows how much less earth is required by using 2″ of Styrofoam insulation. However, that is not the whole story.

the topic of ground water handling only. Surface water should also be an integral part of the removal objective. It is obvious that nothing is to be gained by flushing a lot of rainwater through the underground drainage system if there is a better way to avoid such an overload. The final contours of the immediate vicinity are graded to form natural runoffs, miniature valleys, and swales. These will generally be U-shaped or broad arch-shaped depressions placed strategically above and behind the house. How many swales are needed and how deep they must be are dependent on how steep and expansive the watershed is and the rain-frequency character of the area. Adequate soil and a good ground cover of grass and shrubs will help keep erosion to a minimum. The contour directions should channel the water to distant points where penetration into the earth is no longer a menace to any part of the house.

ENCROACHMENT SITUATIONS

We are all familiar with industrial encroachment on old established residential neighborhoods. The shopping center takeover of the retirees' neighborhood and similar themes have been common drama plots for decades. Yet who would think that encroachment was a threat to an earth home? We tend to think of an earth-sheltered home as more isolated than a row house or even a subdivision. And rightly so, we should, for that is where the earth house shines. It requires a minimum quantity of acreage to escape certain elements of encroachment that might not be anticipated. For example, the earth house will usually face south and be dependent on the sun for a significant part of its interior light. That same source of energy, the sun, will also figure into the heating plan. With passive solar window collectors as a principle part of the heating system, the sun supply would be the main energy ingredient. Suppose a house of this type is situated close to an east-west roadway. The condominium developer comes along and up goes a six-story complex across from the hapless owner of the earth house. Without warning, the primary heat and light source in this family's home is permanently put in the shade.

A reverse problem is a potential hazard when an earth house comes into an established neighborhood. Unless there is plenty of room, the earth house may cause a watershedding problem for other properties below its level. Recognizing this potential problem, local civil authorities frequently reject a permit application to build in an established residential district unless full compliance with all ordinances and adequate space can be verified for a specific, engineered plan.

Resale feasibility is also a factor to be considered. Placing a house whose style is different from the neighborhood theme amongst the other houses will usually have a major effect on the resale potential and subsequently on the price that it will bring. It can be the best, the most expensive, the most maintenance free, or the most energy conserving house in the whole area but, like

it or not, it is out of place. Conversation pieces are great to talk
about but hard to sell for an amount near their value.

AESTHETICS

Before we get too unsold by the preceding remarks, let me hasten
to say that the facade of an earth home can reflect whatever homey
style you desire. The history of earth houses has gone down a
primitive—possibly illogical—path in terms of conventionality and
homelike attractiveness. The early conceptions, in our time, emit-
ted a cave-like impression around the exterior, were igloo-shaped
on the interior, and often clothed in fieldstone and rubble rock
throughout. Then came mid-20th century designs that took themes
from various nonhome-like objects much like Studebaker's jet air-
craft copy. In this category were round windows like the old diners
of the 1930s, pillbox tubes reminiscent of the World War II shore
defenses of Europe, and Quonset-shaped tunnels over which concrete was poured. Although these shapes were innovative and
structurally sound, they were such a drastic departure from what
people were accustomed to in housing that a trend never devel-
oped to any great extent. The waterproofing of that day also left
something to be desired in terms of reliability and permanence.
The general impression conjured up at the mention of a house in
the earth was one of darkness, dampness, and problems. Today's
technology has overcome the problems of the early earth shelters.
The earth-sheltered house can now be considered a viable alternative system of construction with many long-range benefits not
enjoyed by conventional construction designs. Why then has it not
seen a resurgence of interest among consumers?

Appearance, I firmly believe, is the answer. It is not the
assets of the system that are rejected, it is the nonconformity that
is hard to accept. In the years immediately after World War II, an
innovative engineer acquired an airplane hanger outside of Co-
lumbus, Ohio, and proceeded to manufacture completely prefabricated all-porcelainized steel houses. They were called the Lustron houses (Fig. 2-16). It was an amazingly maintenance free,
fireproof, practical, and attractive little house with a life expectancy far greater than wood. A number were bought and erected
throughout the land. The concept quickly died on the vine. Many

people thought it was the square steel panels (the siding), which set it apart from wood, that caused the rejection. The whole house could be cleaned in minutes by simply washing it down with water from a garden hose, but the siding was disparagingly alluded to by comparing it with the material used on filling stations. The few little Lustrons that came into existence so many years ago are still standing neat and clean despite the general rejection. So it seems to be with the earth house. Can the outward appearance be comparable to a conventional house if that is what the consumer wants?

Figure 2-16   A Lustron all-steel house built in the late 1940s. (Courtesy of Clarence B. Luvaas, Cedar Rapids, Iowa.)

POSITIVE DESIGN

With no reluctance, we can reject the concept that, because the house is mostly in the earth, it should contain cave-like characteristics or even reminders. Rather, we shall think of it as a conventional home with an alternative environment from the front on back. The earth is another form of siding and roof material, but the facade is to be like any other acceptable design. Take a point of view as if you are driving by the front of conventional houses.

What do you see? What do you want your neighbors and the world to see as they drive by your house? Can we produce an appearance that is in harmony with other houses? With a little imagination and ingenuity, this challenge can be met without compromising the basic features of the earth house. In a way, it is something like designing the facade of one of the units of a group of row houses.

FACADE STYLES

The French mansard roof style can be designed to give an impression of a conventional roof (Fig. 2-17). It can be extended on beyond the ends of the exposed front wall and turned back down the sides for a short distance. The ground grade level is terraced to match. The mansard completely hides the view of the earthen roof.

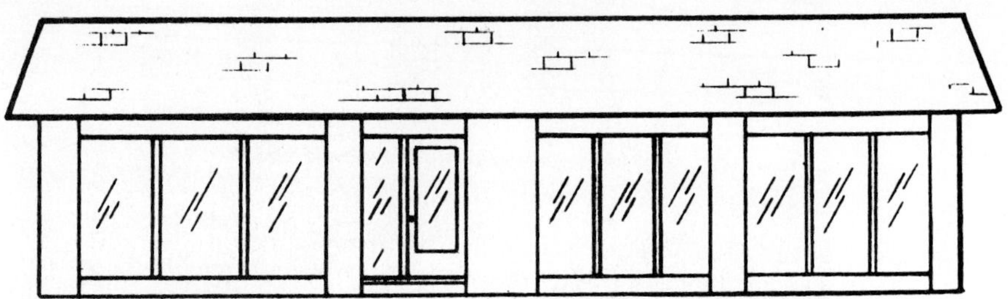

Figure 2-17 The mansard style facade gives a traditional appearance to this earth-sheltered house.

A gable end facade can be worked out with columns and an overhang to present a classic-traditional effect (Fig. 2-18). A suitable porch front is calculated to provide the correct summer shade and winter sun penetration. Pillars are located proportionately and the proper pitch for the roof is chosen (there are old books available that prescribe the standard profiles for authenticity). The roof is taken back to a point where it can be blended into the roof parapet.

An attractive variation of this design is to continue the facade roof rearward over the earth-roof area and place an entry on the backside. The covered space underneath provides a suitable

Figure 2-18 With a gable facade skillfully blended into the parapet, this design closely adheres to the classic Federal style.

and highly desirable outbuilding-type storage area. Conventional outbuildings, as such, are incongruous with the earth house as they seem to stick out of the ground and become focal points of attention. Large square footage inside an earth shelter for garden equipment and the usual miscellany of a home is an impractical expense. The gable-fronted earth-sheltered design will furnish a lot of space at a minimum outlay. The pitch of the roof and the overhang should be coordinated to sustain adequate height for earth coverage above the earth house wall area. The floor surface inside this created shelter can be simple gravel on top of the earthen roof. A ribbon footing out beyond the earth house wall will carry the bearing of the wood and composition roof. Intermediate support can be provided with posts, beams, and truss webs above the ceiling level (posts bear over partitions below). For a truly grand appearance, the concrete parapet is covered with drop siding which renders a two-story classical effect to the whole entrance.

Other styles are adaptable in rearranged form. The end of the gambrel design combined with knee-braced square posts is a real possibility for those who desire an historic early American flavor. This design, with the incorporated top storage area concept, will boast an enormous quantity of storage space in the loft. It will fit into a rural scene as well or better than a converted barn. It makes exceptionally good use of the area on top of a small earth home. Keep in mind that the face of the earth house is the long dimension, whereas the gable and gambrel are profiles usually found on the narrow end of a house. A wide front (say anywhere from 40' on) is probably not practical as the height will be disproportionately oversize compared to the facade below and will dwarf it unreasonably.

FLOOR PLAN PRINCIPLES

A conventional house plan uses the principle of clustering. Another term for it is the wagonwheel arrangement which stems from the central corridor hub. Though the rooms may all be rectangular, the principle is to group rooms in functional closeness and still maintain short direct routes from a central corridor. This arrangement devotes the least amount of wasted living space to corridors.

The objective in earth house planning is quite different. Though as much as possible of the conventional objective should be sought, there are other priorities that are paramount. The main one is natural light and ventilation. Though their housing origin may have started in caves, human beings have long since aspired to light and a feeling of space.

LIGHT AND VENTILATION

Let us assume that our floor plan criteria for the earth house requires natural light for each living-activity area with the exception of the bathrooms, clothes closets, storage rooms, and utility rooms. With this rule in mind, no room can be stacked behind another away from the window wall at the front of the house. Therefore a plan of strung-out rooms is where we begin our thinking. Next, we place the bedroom closets and the bathrooms on the rear wall. The pantry and storage space will go behind the kitchen and dining areas. The entertainment center goes on the back wall of the living room (better TV viewing and less exposure to direct sun rays). A compartmented entry is used to divide the living room from the dining area. Glass partitions permit light to pass through the foyer. Venetian blinds provide privacy at night or whenever desired (Fig. 2-19). This type of basic planning is simpler than planning a conventional house layout.

Ventilation follows the plan quite normally by traveling lengthwise through the house. It is simple to arrive at individual balance in the rooms by adjusting window openings. Generally, the end windows will be opened most frequently to create a lengthwise motion of fresh air. Intermediate-room windows will be opened to take in just enough air for comfort but not enough to break down the airflow throughout the length of the house. It is the manifold system. Varying air quantities and temperatures can be managed in each room by manipulating the windows to suit the needs of individuals.

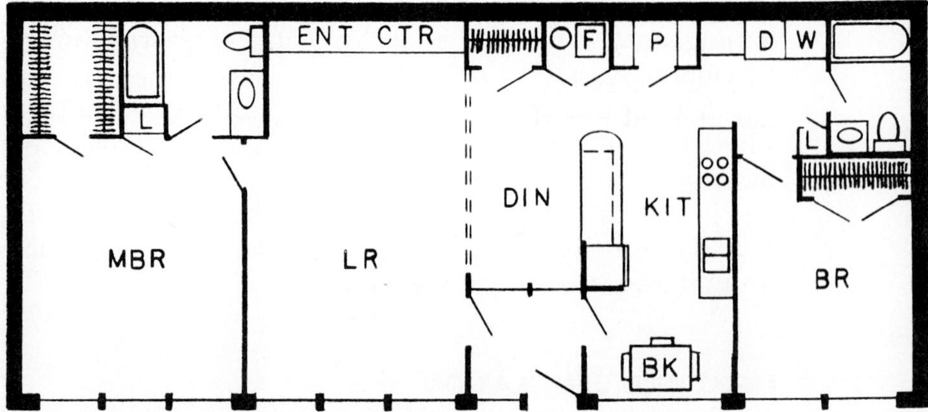

Figure 2-19 Light penetrates all of the living areas of this south-facing earth shelter plan.

EFFECT OF SOLAR HEATING ON FLOOR PLANNING

For successful passive solar heating of the earth shelter house, a large expanse of exposed glass is needed on the south-facing facade. In most designs this will dictate a full front of glass windows. Vertical windows will be all right as the collectors are the floor and other objects in the room. There has been confusion on this point (the proper angle of a collector); however, experience has taught us that no angle is needed on a passive glass wall. In fact, in some cases it is detrimental, as the heat is unmanageable and could lead to dangerously dried-out combustible materials in the rooms. By contrast, active solar collectors with absorber plates are most effective when angled to correlate with a specific latitude so that the sun's rays hit the collector as near to a right angle as possible most of the time.

A structural consideration is required of the designer of a passive solar-heated earth house. The supporting columns across the front of the structure need to be situated to bear the specific-imposed load. At the same time, the space between columns should be coordinated with the modular size of the window units. An uncoordinated plan can mandate custom-made window units at premium prices. The use of stock windows, necessarily of a narrower width than the opening, will require fillers of some kind, which will penalize the heat collection capacity. The glass area is smaller. More costly trimming and insulating results on both inner and outer surfaces.

9 OWNER-BUILT MODIFICATIONS

In this section we shall explore some real possibilities in design and construction which have potential for a novice or small-scale builder. These systems already exist and the combinations shown here are comparable to the tasks required in conventional house building. The purpose is to show that a lot of the earth-sheltered advantages can be incorporated into designs that do not require the large cranes and the massive concrete components common to the pure earth house. These alternative designs will require expertise and tools on a par with those expected to build a conventional one-story house on a full basement.

A thermal comparison between earth and Styrofoam insulation is essential to the understanding that underlies the following modified designs. It can be generalized, in crude proportions, that it takes about 10 times the depth of earth to equal one-part depth of standard insulation. This is not the whole story, of course, or few would opt for the deep dirt roof. For example, a shallow earth roof with 4″ of Styrofoam causes the whole house to be higher in the earth, and, consequently, it will lose a little more of its cooling zone toward the grade level. Also, there is the factor of delayed response to weather changes which is a little better with the full earth cover. The seasonal cyclic characteristic of the earth is more or less nullified as the earth depth is lessened below that of the frost depth for the area. For optimum seasonal cycling, a rule of thumb is to have as much earth above the roof as the official recorded local frost depth. Nonetheless, the advent of modern forms of insulation—and especially Styrofoam—have given us alternatives not heretofore possible. Since most of the heat gain in winter will come through the lower portion of the walls and tend to escape through the ceiling (as well as the front glass wall at night), the Styrofoam will provide a valuable resistance to this loss when placed on the upper part of the walls and the top of the roof deck (Fig. 2-20).

PARTIAL BERMED HOUSE

One of the simplest modifications that takes advantage of the earth's temperature is the berm system (Fig. 2-21). In its simplest form, a house design is created with south-facing, passive solar windows. Windows on the ends are wide, short in height, and placed as high in the wall as the smallest allowable header will permit. In the backside there may be no windows or openings. Earth will be contoured around the ends and sides up to a suitable exposure grade below the window sills. The wall structure can be made like an earth house or like the pressure-treated wood system for basements.

An insulation barrier needs to be carefully implanted near the top of the berm, otherwise the frost will eliminate a major part of the benefit from the earth around the top of the berm. Styrofoam is an ideal insulator for this barrier, as it is rigid, nondegradable, and highly effective per inch of thickness. Its Achilles' heel is the soft and destructible nature of the material.

Placement in the dirt must be carefully executed. Voids or sloppy joints will produce leaks and cause cold spots in the winter and hot spots in the summer. Note in the illustration how the ground barrier is pocketed between the wall barrier pieces. The beveling prevents water from entering at this junction. After a couple of pieces are in place, the dirt cover is carefully hand spread on top of the Styrofoam. It is not left exposed or incomplete until the fully prescribed depth of earth is in place (usually not less than 1') (Fig. 2-22).

Pressure-treated wood is used for the top plates, the thermal cripple studs, and the retainer sheathing, as these members are in close proximity to the earth at the top of the berm. The treated-wood basement system can also be used where one wishes to avoid concrete work (Fig. 2-23).

The berm minimum width at the top will be as much as the depth of the frost line in the area. Slope this surface, under the

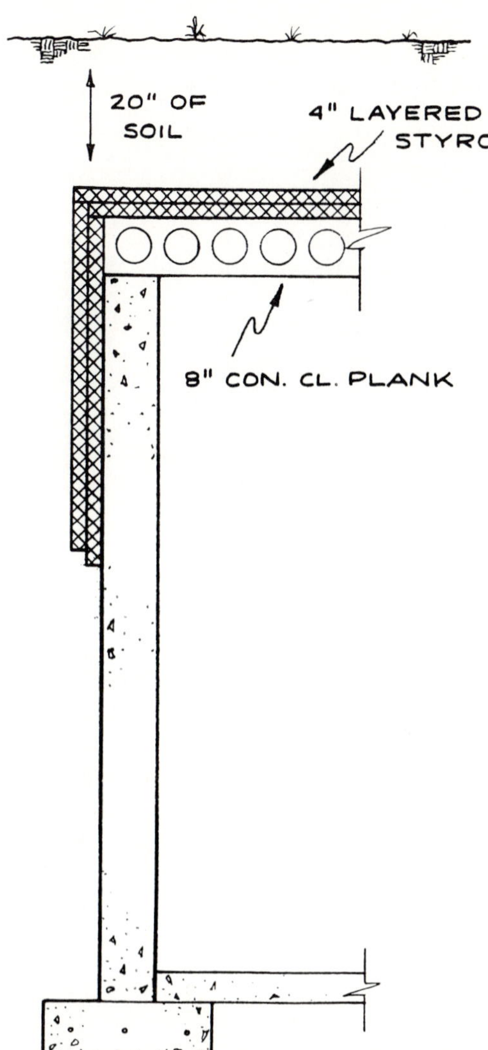

Figure 2-20 For both summer cooling and winter heating, Styrofoam on the top and halfway down the wall is more efficient than 2″ of Styrofoam covering the entire wall.

eaves, as much as possible so that rainwater does not find its way down the wall. Rain gutters are also good insurance.

The roof on a partial berm can be any style that pleases the owner. The only unique feature required, to coincide with the conservation objective, is a large capacity for insulation over the ceiling. For comparatively low pitches ($^3/_{12}$ to $^6/_{12}$), a thermal truss design is a good option if it is combined with a good insulation scheme and top-notch installation (many insulation envelopes are

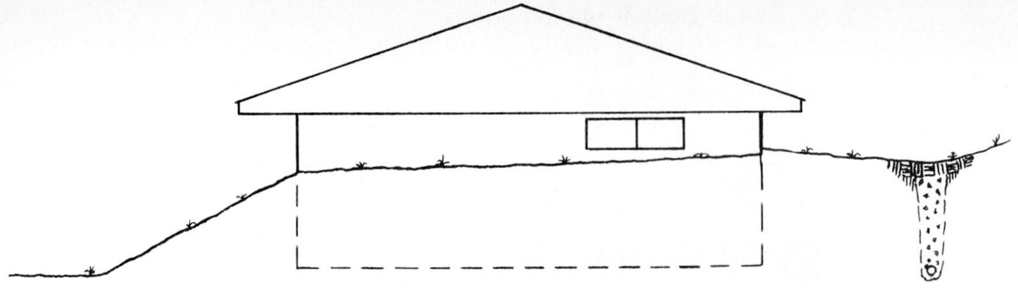

Figure 2-21 End view of a house with three sides partially bermed.

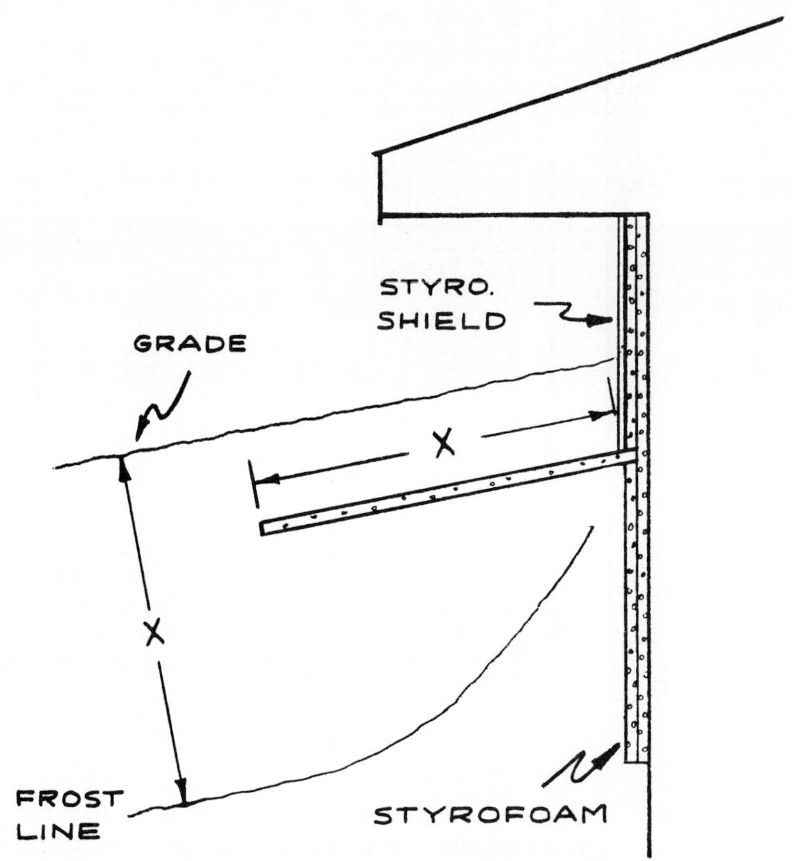

Figure 2-22 On a partially bermed wall, a below-surface insulation barrier will permit warmer earth temperatures to stay closer to the ground surface in wintertime. In summer, the cooler-than-air atmosphere will also remain higher on the wall at a time when the coolness is desirable. The exposed Styrofoam above the ground must be protected with nonferrous sheetmetal or a treated plywood guard.

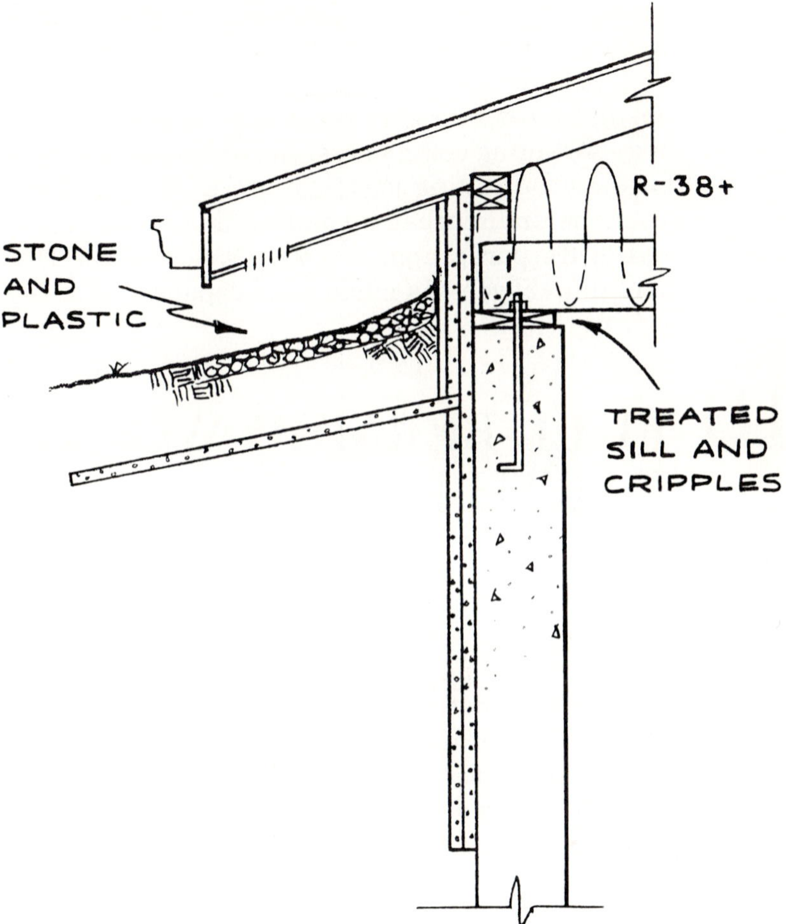

Figure 2-23 A higher grade line, conventional rafters, and thermal cripple studs will call for treated sills and cripples. Leave an air space at the ends of the ceiling joists.

defective due to careless installation). With very low pitches, layering of blanket insulation (the least costly form) is not practical with truss webs in the way all over the attic. Blown-in cellulose will be a better choice where working quarters are too cramped to do a good layering job with blanket fiberglass.

The first layer of insulation of the blanket type can be laid between the joists. It should be the same depth as the joists. Next, blow in a prescribed depth of cellulose to bring the total R-value into the 40-plus range. The cellulose will fill around the webs and any other neglected voids to give a tight envelope over the ceiling.

It makes a neater and less leaky job when the first course of insulation is laid between the ceiling joists before the electrical wire stringing commences. Insulation blankets of the same thickness as the ceiling joist size are used. The wiring can then pass over the undisturbed insulation in a straight line directly to each outlet. In paragraphs to come, we shall see how a conventional roof (fewer webs) is made with capacity for a high thermal-rated ceiling.

10 FULL-BERMED WOOD EARTH HOUSE

The ultimate system, one which can be built with hand tools (other than excavation), is now within the scope of the individual house builder. Modern technology brought us to this point. Good waterproofing materials, efficient insulating products, and wood that does not deteriorate underground are components that make it possible. Let us look into a system that combines much of the energy efficiency of an earth house, is made of wood, and is covered with a traditional-appearing wood and composition roof.

First we choose an appropriate lot, just as we would for a full-depth earth shelter. Then we make the plan. Next comes the excavation. At this point the structure becomes unique.

The depth of the footings and the floor bottom requires careful calculation because the amount of bulldozer work will want to be held to a minimum after erection of the house. The foundation bed comes next (Fig. 2-24). The comparison of this bed to the massive earth shelter bed may seem farfetched. Remember that the concrete footing of the earth house must support many more tons of concrete wall and earthen roof compared to the much lighter load imposed by an all-wood structure. Also, the footing is not the real supporter. It merely spreads the load. The foundation bed (the undisturbed earth below) does the actual supporting. In the all-weather wood foundation (AWWF) system, the defined footing area is a trench of compacted gravel.

Wall framing is largely conventional although some variations are notable (see illustrations Fig. 2-24 and Fig. 2-25). For

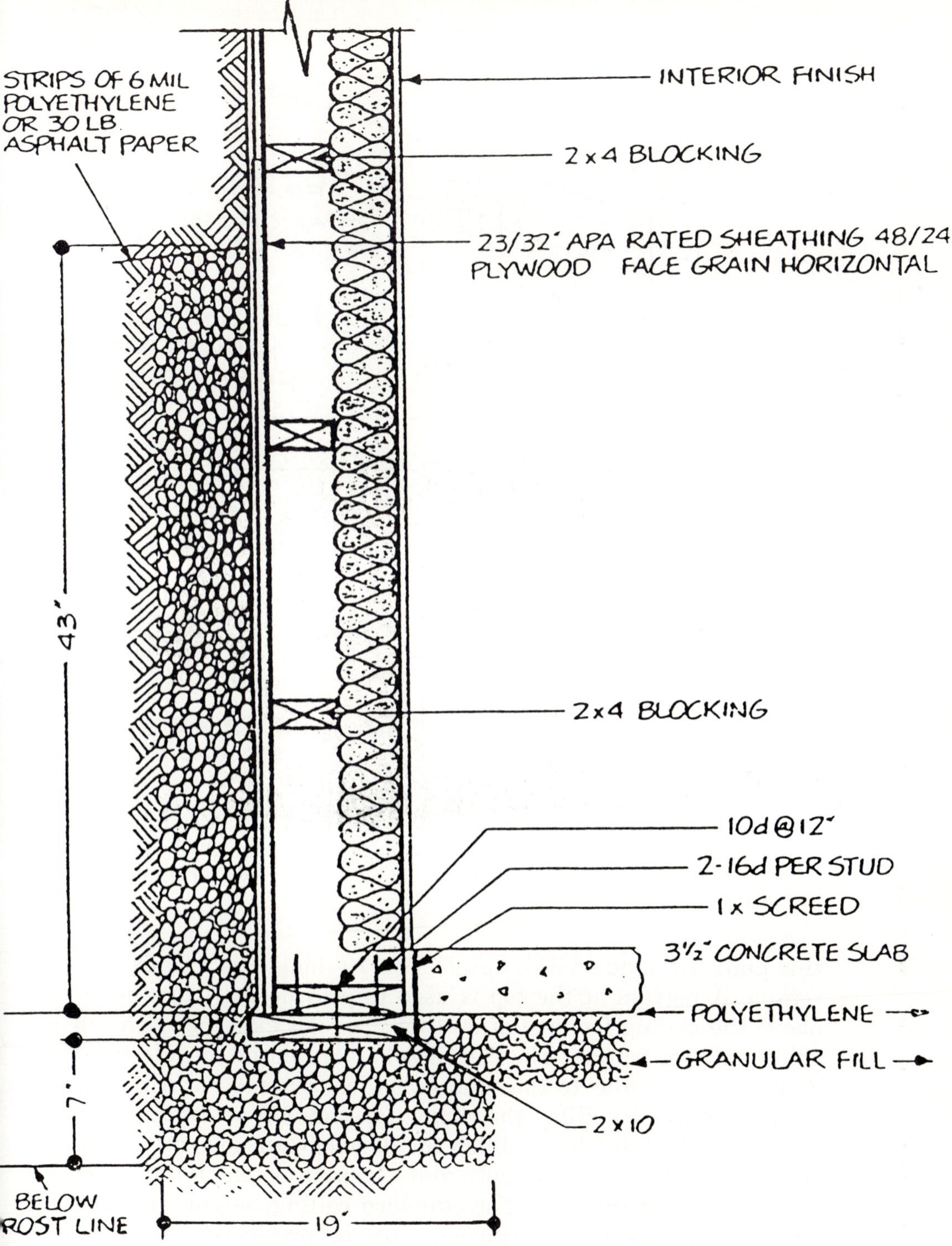

Figure 2-24 The all-weather wood foundation system (AWWF).

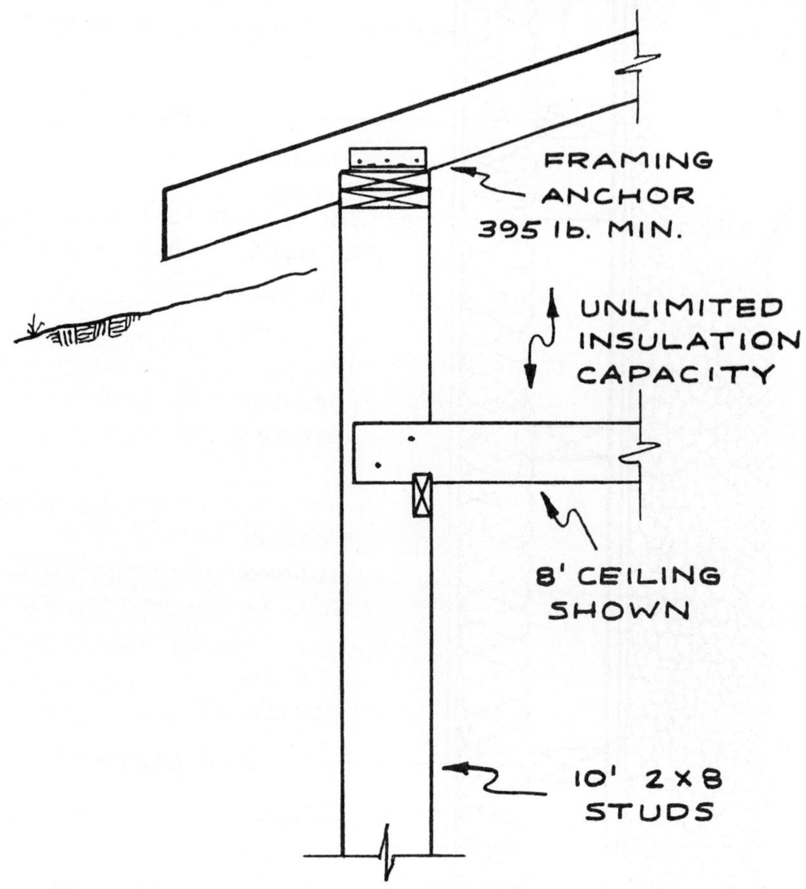

Figure 2-25 The permanent wood foundation system (PWF, also AWWF) is a viable alternative for building a full-bermed earth shelter.

this plan, 10′ studs will be used. The 10′ length is unique for a reason. A portion at the top is used to provide the extra height above the ceiling for insulation that does not exist beneath conventional roof frames. The ceiling joists are borne on inletted, 2 × 4 ribbons similar to the vintage balloon frame. For a regular 8′-high (nominal) ceiling, the ribbon top and bottom locations are carefully calculated to establish the dado cut, taking into consideration the concrete floor depth and a locking notch on the underside of the joist (if used). For standard ceiling height, the measurement for the ribbon location must be precisely coordinated with the length of conventional precut studs that will be used on the interior partitions. Ignoring this calculation will cause the height to be too great or too little to accommodate precuts, and in either case much custom cutting, and possibly waste, will result. None of the modular wall covering materials, such as paneling or plasterboard, will fit the height space without customizing.

The ceiling framework should be designed with three structural considerations in mind. One is to meet the outer walls at right angles with the joists wherever possible. Another objective is to keep the spans of the individual rooms to the smallest possible length. A general objective is to make the joists work for us as anti-spreaders and compression resistors to the earth pressures from the outside. Without a specific plan it is difficult to cite any rules other than referring to recognized span tables. Some generalities may help.

Full-length, one-piece joists will simplify the work. Many earth-sheltered designs are no more than 20′ deep from front wall to rear wall. With small, unexposed, partitioned-off areas at the rear, the joists may not span more than 12 to 16′ of unsupported area. In such a case, the girth size is determined from the table for the longest of the reduced clear spans and not upon the overall 20′ figure. A great advantage of one-piece joists running from front to rear is that the entire ceiling, when covered, performs as a box beam laid over on its side. For any part of the earth behind the back wall to push in the ceiling area, it must push all of the ceiling as a unit or fracture the ceiling into segments.

Notching the end of each joist will transfer part of the inward pressure of the earth from the stud to the joist and thence to the ceiling as a unit. A 1″ notch will be adequate as the end grain is very strong in the compression mode. Deeper notching is to be avoided as it will reach a point where the joist is reduced to a size level, for its span, that will require the next bigger sized joist.

Joists adjacent to the end wall (parallel) will perform a moderate support function if each is blocked to the ribbon joist (this joist is surface nailed and doubles as a ceiling backer board). Duplicate length blocks are cut if the end wall checks straight with a string line. If it is not perfectly straight, the opportunity is there to freeze the adjacent joist in a straight position. It is then used as your point of beginning (POB) for spacing all other joists that cross perpendicular partitions. To do this, each block will be custom cut to a length that holds the joist in a straight posture. Block out a string line tied at each end alongside of the joists. Nail the first block opposite a stud that is nearest to the center of the span. Place each block to come in the middle of each remaining space and opposite a stud. Push the joist into the proper alignment with the string each time and measure the distance the block will span. Continue the process until all blocks are in place. End nail the block to the freeborn joist with 16d common nails. Toenail the end of the block that meets the ribbon joist with one nail in the lower quarter of one side and another nail in the upper quarter of the other side (Fig. 2-26).

Higher than standard ceilings are obtainable when using 10′ studs. More than adequate room exists above the ceiling for an optimum R-40 to R-50 insulation when the ceiling is held to standard height. A 9′ ceiling is entirely feasible. That much more height plus the openness concept for ventilation and light may entirely alleviate any feelings of claustrophobia that may affect some persons.

Conventional stick-built rafters are a good choice for this

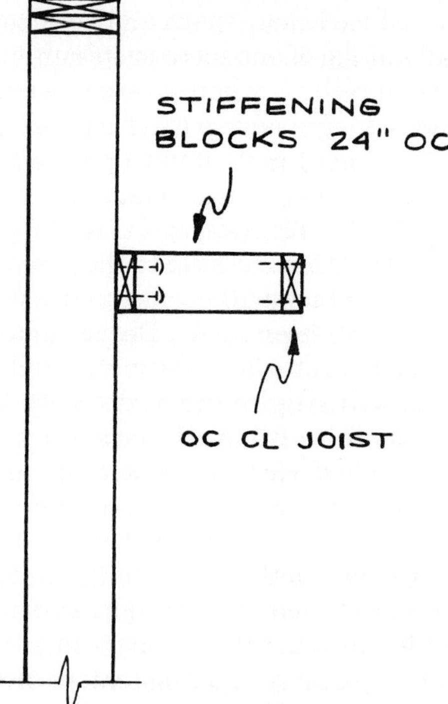

Figure 2-26 The end walls will be stiffened by using wood blocks on 24″ centering. Coordinate the block centering so that the ceiling drywall joints will fall on them.

modified earth shelter design. Because the rooms are spread laterally, and generally only one room deep, the full depth of the house will be in a narrow-to-medium depth range. No great spans will be encountered when the gables are on the ends. By opting for conventional rafters, no overall truss webbing will be present to interfere with the spreading of blanket insulation. Layered insulation of the roll blanket type will net the most material economy and can produce the best system. It takes some doing, and probably more time, to get it all laid properly. The stud-wall cavities are insulated first with blankets long enough to go past the ceiling level on up to the top plate. The first layer of joist-height, blanket-roll fiberglass is laid between the joists. The ends are curled right up the wall cavity on top of the first wall cavity layer. The wall cavities are now full from the ceiling up to the plate. The joist cavities are also full to the top edge of the joists. The wiring is run in. The second layer is placed perpendicular to the first (across the joists). Work from each side toward the middle. Compact the fiberglass snugly against each previous course and smooth the top edges. When you reach the last opening, custom cut a piece about 1″ wider than the narrowest point between the last course. Squeeze it in so the system is under uniform pressure (tightly mated along all the edges).

The AWWF wall design for bermed earth shelter construction calls for pressure-treated materials throughout those parts that come in contact with the earth or zones of undue dampness (see Figs. 2-24 and 2-25). The full-bermed AWWF system will use materials with the AWPB FDN stamp upon each piece (American Wood Preservative Bureau foundation grade). The footing boards, sole plates, studs, slab retainer, and sheathing will be AWPB grade.

The ceiling joist bearing ribbon, by definitive location, would not necessarily require FDN grade lumber as it is not in direct contact with the earth. However, due to its marginal proximity, the use of treated lumber would be considered quality construction.

The ceiling joists are another matter. Only the outer ends, on the rear wall, are near the earth environment. To butt the ends of the joists against the plywood sheathing is to make them vulnerable to dry-rot unnecessarily. This potential problem can be substantially eliminated by field soaking the joist ends with preservative and leaving a space of about 1″ to 1½″ between the end of each joist and the interior side of the wall sheathing. This will still leave plenty of space for good nailing. It does not affect the bearing as that is governed by the ribbon thickness of 1½″. Any amount that goes beyond that is irrelevant to the actual bearing. A small notch on the underside of the joists helps them to perform as lateral braces against the earth pressure from without. That pressure is also resisted by the conventional rafters higher up the wall. These two component assemblies, along with the added stiffness of 2 × 6 or 2 × 8 studs, will resist the inward stress of the earth, providing the correct grade of wood is used throughout.

The direction of force on an earth-sheltered house wall is inward, the opposite of that on a conventional, above-ground wall frame where the objective is to tie the walls in (prevent them from spreading outward). With the earth shelter, the objective is to hold the walls out and prevent them from being bent inward. The significance is that the attaching nails will be slanted in the opposite direction to create sheer stress. The nails should be pointed slightly outward on the ends of both joists and rafters where they are fastened.

Rafter anchoring to the top plates presents a unique situation since the ceiling joists are not on that level. The rafters cannot make use of the joists as ties across the building. There is no danger of the rafters pushing out the walls as the walls are backed with earth berming. There is a danger of the rafters displacing the fasteners and sloughing off the plates. Toenails to the plates are not adequate for the task of preventing the roof from spreading outward at the base. Two methods of holding the rafters in place are feasible and should be used together. Use metal anchor plates at the bearing base of the rafter seats. These can be galvanized sheet-metal anchors or angle irons. In addition to these anchors, a cross tie is attached to a rafter set and to the plate every 4′ on top of the plate.

A one-piece tie is much preferred as pieced-together ties are seldom stretch free unless there is a long overlap at the junction and lots of properly angled nails. Good nailing is of the utmost importance as the entire objective (preventing rafter seat slough-off and ridge sag) lies in the balance. The one-piece tie can be supported in the middle of its span by a simple, vertical 2 × 4 post which bears on a ceiling joist (Fig. 2-27). There should be no con-

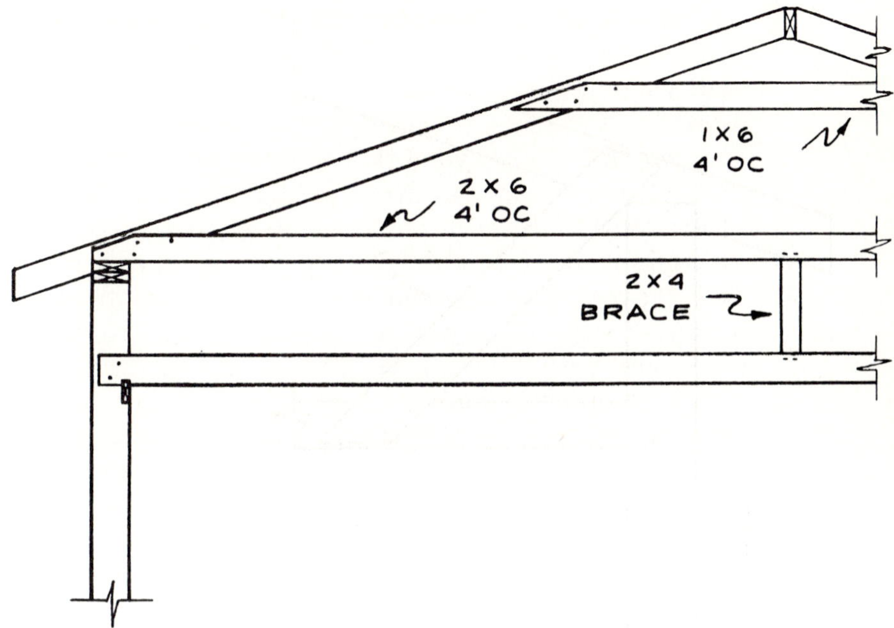

Figure 2-27 One-piece ties at top plate level will counteract the roofs inclination to spread at the bottom. These ties may be used at 4', 5'-4", or 6' intervals, depending on the size of the roof (a larger span will require more ties and closer spacing). Collar ties in the upper third are still required on 4' spacing.

fusion of the full-length ties at the plate level with rafter ties in the upper third of the peak of the roof frame. These upper ties are still a requirement (one for every 4' along the roof). The larger ties at plate level are replacements for the ceiling joists that do not exist at the usable level in this design.

An optional tie that is practical to use on every other rafter set is the *inverted knee brace* (web) (Fig. 2-28). It is simple and effective. It should be coordinated with the collar braces the same as with the span tie. As roof size increases in size and weight, it will be logical to increase the quantity of knee braces to one for every rafter-plate junction. Again, nailing procedures are of capital importance. The anti-spreading deterrent will be voided if the ends of the braces are split by poorly placed or incorrectly angled nails. Nails should be placed in the hooking posture, points from opposite ends angled slightly toward each other (Fig. 2-29).

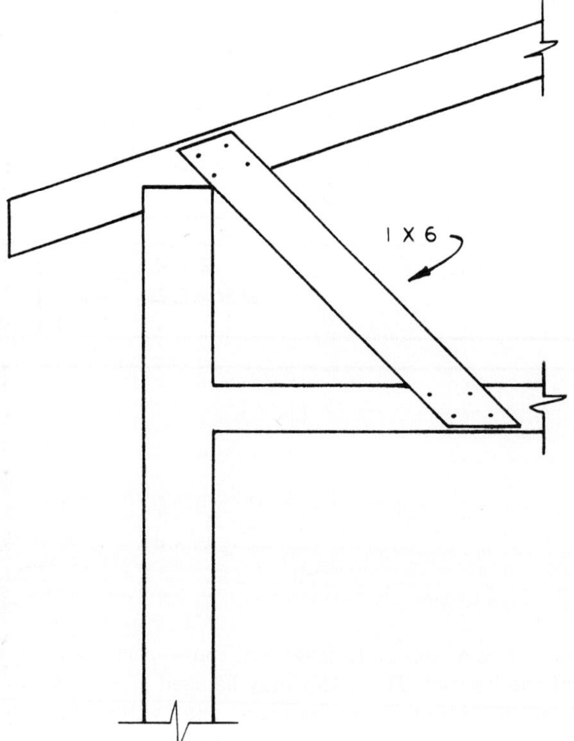

Figure 2-28 A 1 × 6 wood knee brace is surface nailed.

A comforting thought is that the large-size girth of the top plate makes it very stiff. Two 2 × 6s or 2 × 8s nailed together present a strong edge to accommodate the lesser pressures of the earth toward its berm top (Fig. 2-30). As the earth slants toward its highest grade level against the wall, the horizontal quantity of earth drops off, and with it, the quantity of lateral pressure. Another characteristic of humus type of earth is that it "settles in" and becomes stable and unmoving. When this occurs (usually after a full year of seasonal changes), the pressure on a wall diminishes to near nothing. Only a severe saturation by rain and ground water will recreate a lateral pressure situation. Gravel and sand fill, on the other hand, will continue to exert pressure on a wall because their nature is to collapse and move toward the gravity source via the easiest route. These characteristics may influence the quantity and type of backfill that is arranged in a particular earth environment.

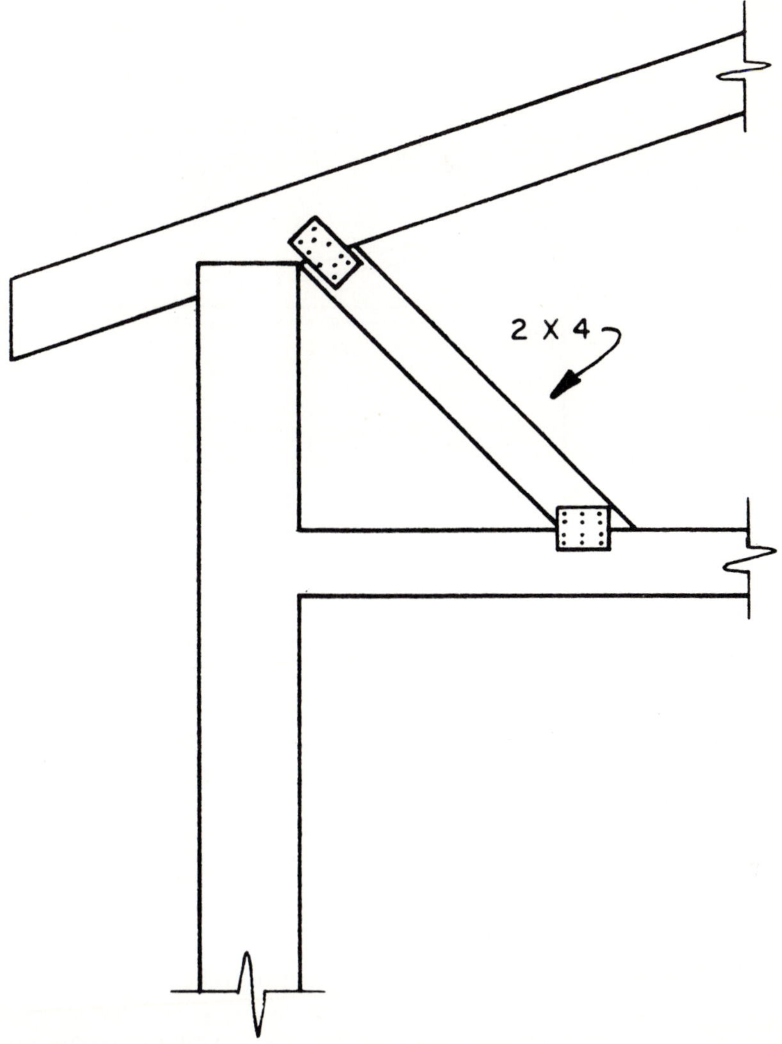

Figure 2-29 A 2 × 4 truss-type web brace is fastened with metal nail plates or glued and nailed plywood gussets.

UNIQUE-TYPE NAILS

Appropriate nails are required for underground fastening. In addition to the difference in nail angling, there are some rules about types. Whether wood is treated or not, ordinary steel nails

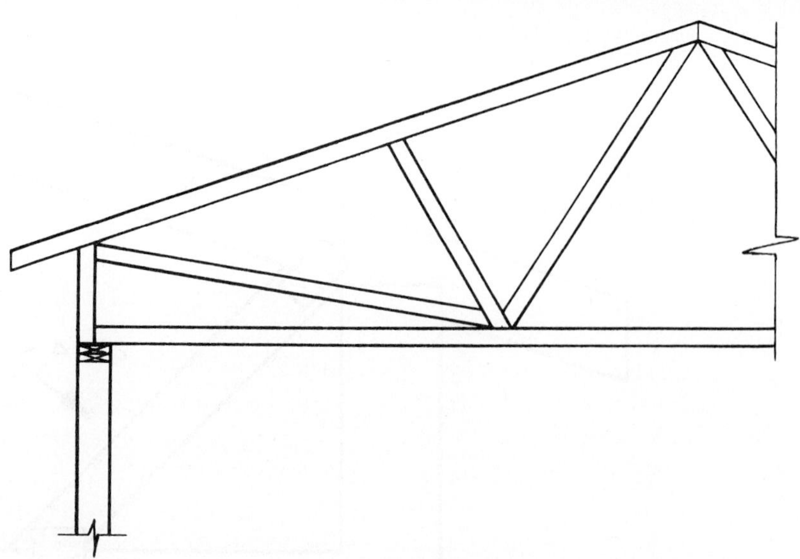

Figure 2-30 A raised truss is a viable alternative roof style for the full berm.

are prone to rust and early deterioration when used below ground. It is recommended by the American Wood Preservers Bureau (AWPB) that hot dipped galvanized or stainless steel 304 or 316 nails be used on all pressure-treated wood or other wood exposed to moisture. Aluminum or carbon steel nails may cause reactions with waterborne treatments and should not be used.

These nail requirements present another of those situations where a builder's knowledge or ethics are briefly exposed to examination. The informed and honest builder will follow the rules (pay the temporary initial extra cost for proper nails) and face the mirror each morning with high self-esteem. The practical feature of this type of reaction, for the contractor, is that business will be good. Few consumers will knowingly choose an inferior component to be placed in a structure as potentially permanent as an earth-sheltered home. These same consumers will be disappointed, disillusioned, and perhaps even irate when the construction of their home breaks down due to the contractor's ignorance or deceit. An up-front contractor, who points out the more costly but lasting essentials, will have a stable, confident clientele. Those who hide their profiteering habits in poured concrete (omitted reinforcing) and cheaper, inadequate covered-up materials will not suffer immediate embarrassment. But, somewhere down the line it will all come to light. One's good name is a precious coin with which to barter.

SUBFLOOR DRAINAGE

Interior floor drains are usually incorporated in an earth shelter type of structure (Fig. 2-31). Sometimes these are shown with a perforated, vertical pipe leading down into a gravel bed, the idea being to drain the floor. This type of design may work satisfactorily as long as the gravel drainage system remains comparatively dry. There are two potential problems with this drain. It sometimes emits undesirable odors of the earth that pass freely into the living area. It can sometimes be perceived as no more than a

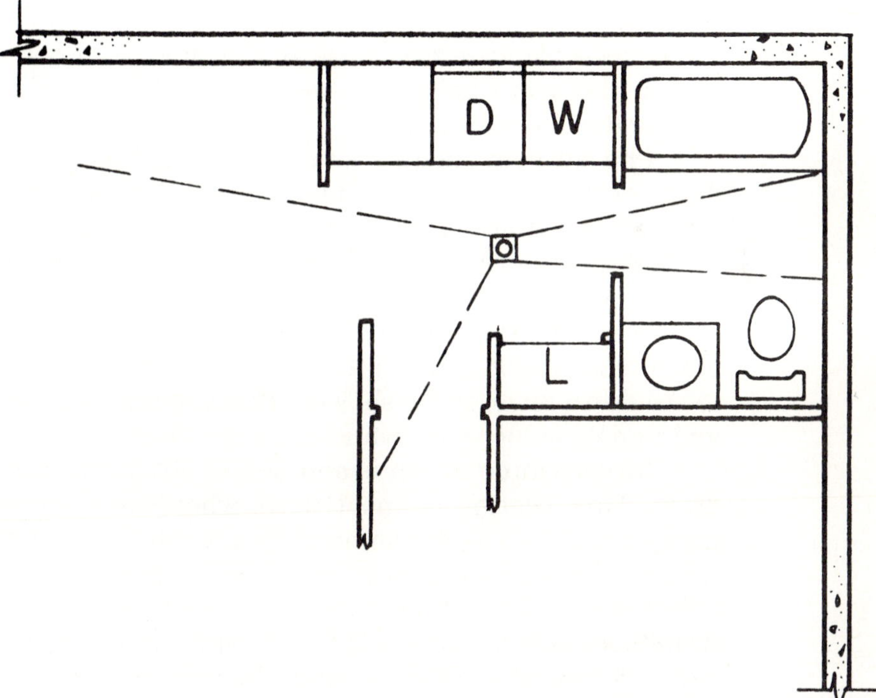

Figure 2-31 A floor drain with a floating ball valve, intended for draining the entire house, may be placed in an unobtrusive location. The entire floor should have an unnoticeable slope toward the drain.

humid or musty odor, but will conjure feelings of dampness or swampishness.

Flooding may never occur but if it does, just once, it may cause great damage to wall skins, cabinets, and furnishings. Such a flooding condition can take place when an abnormal amount of water is dumped on the drain system. A torrential storm or an unusually wet season can glut an otherwise adequate drain system. The ground and gravel bed are both saturated and the daylight drain plugs up (sand, silt, or rodents are frequent causes of plugged drain pipes near the exiting end). The water that backs up has to go somewhere. The open floor drain is the first exit it will reach. It will spew out until the water level inside the house reaches the level on the exterior subgrade level of saturation. This same condition is set up when an electric sump pump is the sole means of discharging ground water from the footing area. All it takes is an electrical failure—a common occurrence during storms.

A reverse flow valve is an answer to the floor drain situation. One type uses a flipper valve which closes the drain when water tries to move backward in the pipe. Another is a floating ball in the drain housing which is floated up to close the drain hole under the floor plate.

The shower drain provides an unobtrusive overall floor drain in the remote case of floor flooding. The shower floor (called a pan in conventional showers) is formed in the floor below the level of the bathroom floor. With all floor drains, the general slope of the floor must be consistently directed to the drain. Where the shower constitutes the only drain in the house, it means that the entire floor needs a tiny bit of sloping toward the bathroom and to the drain cover of the shower. This sloping must be very gentle and unnoticeable when walking on the floor.

An entrance drain is another acceptable location for a floor drain. This location is unobtrusive when the drain cover is relatively small and is surrounded by a ceramic tile floor covering. Locating an entrance foyer on the same level or lower is a good choice. The floor is slanted slightly toward the drain with the exterior door side a fraction lower than the interior door side of the room. In case of a water backup, the front door can be left open a little and the water will drain off provided the threshold is not higher than the floor. The tracked-in mud and debris from little feet (and big feet too) can simply be hosed out when the floor is ceramic tile and the walls are wiped dry quickly after hosing.

A sunken foyer that is one step down is advantageous in that no water will enter the living quarters provided the grade level in front of the entrance is properly slanted away (Fig. 2-32). In the case of the blocked drain, causing water to back up and out of the floor drain, the water is simply shunted outdoors by leaving the exterior door open a little. Remember, we are thinking only of a catastrophic type of deluge that may or may not ever happen or of a blocked drain. Even if either did occur, a properly built drainage system will usually take care of the water as most of it is handled by the slanted contouring of the yard surface.

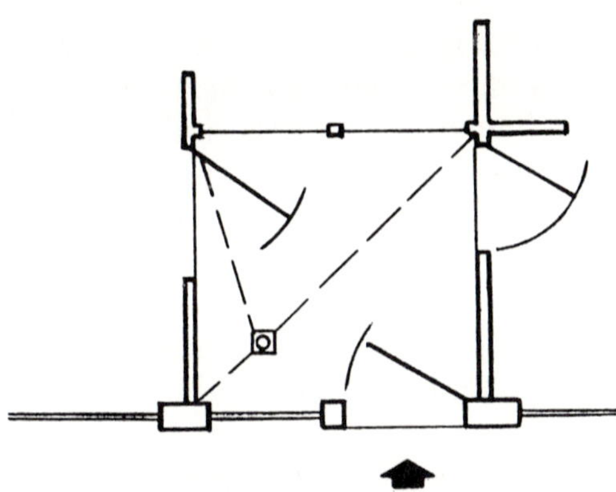

Figure 2-32 A sunken entrance (foyer) with a floor drain can serve as an emergency full-house drain if the floor is properly contoured.

BUTTRESSING LONG WALLS

Specifications given on the foregoing section views of earth-sheltered and AWWF modifications are not intended to be taken as acceptable for all sizes or all floor plan arrangements. These section views are general representations of a house plan up to a maximum depth from front to rear of about 24'. The exact depth and particularly the extended length across the face are not complete criteria upon which to base material sizes and quality grades.

The controlling factor in the earth-sheltered AWWF modification is the lateral span of each segment of wall that can be constructed before internal support is required. The question is, How frequently is a buttressing element (integral brace) needed along a wall? The total length of the back wall that retains the earth is of no importance. It could go on without limits. What we must determine is what wall span is feasible between supports. The ability of the wall to withstand the lateral pressure of the earth, as well as the compression load of the roof, is dependent on the size and grade of the materials and the spacing module of the studs. These elements are pitted against the localized composition of the earth environment around the wall (stable, shifty, and so on). A bearing wall, running parallel to the long dimension of the house, will hold out the end walls at some intermediate junction. Along the back wall several properly designed short partitions, at right angles, will brace the wall against the weight of the earth (Fig. 2-33).

A wall covering of sheetrock (the drywall system) may suffice as a skin for a partition box brace where there is enough of it. It leaves a lot to be desired, however, on short walls such as those found at the rear of the house. A rule of thumb is to use a piece of plywood sheathing on one side, or both sides, of any wall that is 4′ or less in length (this provides the same type of bracing as used at the exterior corners of the above-ground framework). Adjacent studs that will not have plywood bracing can be shimmed out with scrap strips of sheetrock or ripped shims from scrap 2 × 4s to form a surface over which the final covering of drywall goes. A small

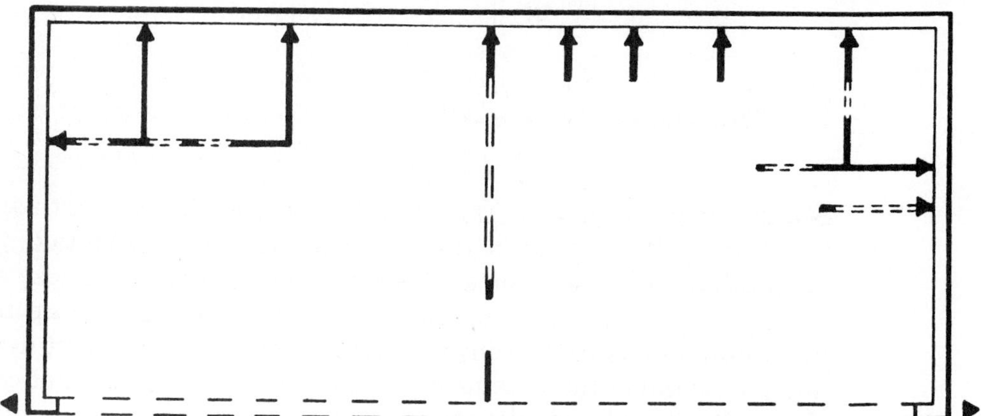

Figure 2-33 This skeletonized plan is shown in detail in Fig. 2-19. The partitions, shown crosswise, are walls that support the walls on the right and left end. Those shown in vertical posture serve as buttresses along the back wall. Continuous headers and the parapet provide resistance to inward thrust at the corners of the pillared and glassed front wall. Plywood sheet bracing is called for on most of these walls (the short ones in particular).

drawback of this technique is that the wall is now ½″ or 1″ deeper than standard. Should there be a doorway in the partition, it will require deeper jambs. When there are no openings, there will be no effect from the slightly deeper wall.

An inletted 1 × 6 diagonal brace is an alternative to a plywood brace. The length of the wall must be great enough to accommodate a brace from sole to top plate within the 45° to 60° angle range. The brace top will be next to the exterior wall, just short of the last stud in the partition wall. Use every perpendicular partition that butts the back wall in the role of a brace. This quantity of bracing will, in some measure, make up for the lost bracing potential created by long spans of windows on the front wall.

Partitions (box braces, in effect) that tie across a building help the wall on both sides to be rigid. This is why a partition that runs straight through is so much better than one that zigs and zags from the front to the rear wall. By modularly placing a front-to-rear partition, the ceiling joist above will become a substantial tie across any perpendicular corridors (it must be well fastened to the top plate by careful nailing into the backer board which is flush with the top plate on one edge). The bracing of the back wall is then shared with the front wall.

Sole plate nailing takes on a special meaning when a framed wall is called on to serve as a box brace. With a slab floor, the partition will likely be nailed to the floor with a powder cartridge gun. Normally, these concrete nails are driven vertical to the surface to assure that they do not angle off and fail to penetrate. In the brace wall, it is advantageous to have just the slightest bit of angle. Slant the gun handle ever so slightly toward the exterior wall. This will incline the nail point toward the direction of lateral compression on the exterior wall. The nails will resist better in this posture.

CONFIDENCE IN TREATED LUMBER

The credibility of treated lumber is remarkable. It offers a broad spectrum of possibilities for the carpenter-builder. The prognosis for the life of pressure-treated wood underground is 100 years. Several 2 × 4 × 16″ boards were buried in 1938 as a living test.

To date, over a half-century later, these boards show no sign of deterioration from termites, fungus, or any other source. The 100-year life may be a modest prediction.

CONCLUSIONS FOR THE CONSERVATION BUILDER

Full earth-sheltered homes and modified systems have undergone many changes. New and currently available materials make self-building possible. We have only touched the surface in this book. Those who are seriously interested in the full earth shelter concept are encouraged to carry the quest further. An excellent resource text that will help you take that next step is available from The Underground Space Center, 11 Mines and Metallurgy Building, 221 Church Street S. E., Minneapolis, Minnesota 55455.

As of the late 1980s, there is little, if any, known reference available in the realm of the modified solar and berm house outside of this book. Nonetheless, the principles of PWF (permanent wood foundation) are abundant, proven, and practical. The design principles described in this chapter adapt the PWF earth shelter system into a practical structure that can be self-built by those who are capable with tools and will follow specifications. For more detailed information, with specific load and grade tables, contact the American Plywood Association, P.O. Box 11700, Tacoma, Washington 98411. Many other sources of information are listed in the bibliography accompanying the APA booklet.

The principles of superinsulated, above-ground frame walls are found in Part 4. By placing the double-wall house on a PWF basement, the best of both worlds can be achieved.

REVIEW TOPICS

1. Describe what "seasonal lag" is and why it can be used to advantage in the earth shelter design.
2. Describe what is meant by "temperature differential" and give some examples.
3. List and explain several advantages of the earth shelter house.
4. Explain the importance of proper earth shelter orientation.

5. Discuss all the aspects of drainage in the earth shelter concept.

6. Why is the orientation to the sun so important with the earth shelter?

7. Explain the meaning of COP.

8. Explain the term "nosebleed" in an earth shelter. Describe a thermal break and tell where breaks are needed in the earth design.

9. Describe how excess water can be eliminated from around the foundation and floor of the earth shelter.

10. Explain how to contour the earth around an earth shelter that is excavated into the south face of a hill at a location below the hilltop.

11. When considering a plot of ground for an earth shelter, the word "encroachment" may come up. Discuss this term in relation to the desirability of the location.

12. Describe some designs that are applicable for earth-sheltered houses that will blend with traditional above-ground houses.

13. Describe the differences to be found in the floor plan of a modest-size earth-sheltered house and an above-ground house.

14. Describe the objectives to be sought in relation to light and ventilation.

15. Describe the effects on the floor plan that will be exerted when solar heat is sought as the primary source of heat.

16. What is meant by "partial berming"? Describe this type of shelter.

17. Describe a one-story, partial-bermed, superinsulated structure using the AWWF system—the house that can be built with regular construction tools and no cranes.

18. Ceiling joists perform as bulwarks to hold out the walls in an AWWF system. In a conventional house, ceiling joists hold the walls from spreading outward. Explain this difference.

19. Explain the difference between nails used above ground and those used on pressure-treated lumber underground.

20. How does a reverse-flow valve work in a drain line below the slab floor? How does a float-ball in a floor drain stop the water from reversing and flooding the floor above?

21. Explain how to buttress long rear walls with concrete or with wood integrally.

Part 3

Use
of Solar Energy

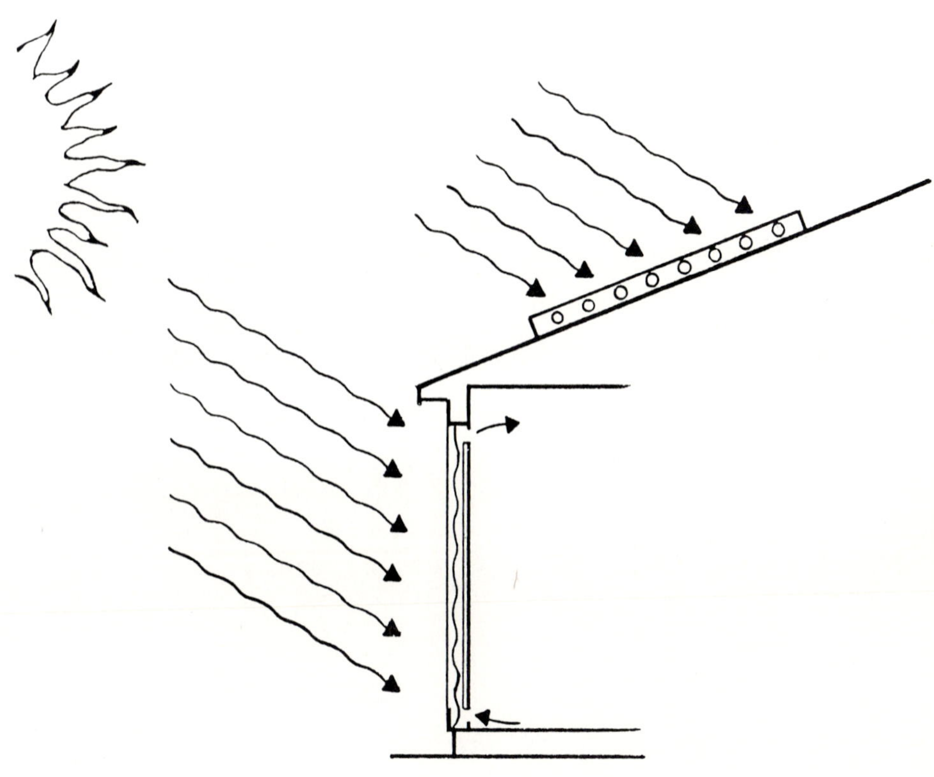

11 SOLAR COLLECTORS

The second most constant element we can use to make a home comfortable is the heat from the sun. There is comfort and security in knowing that "the sun always comes up." Unfortunately, it does not always shine on us. At one time the author lived and built in Colorado. For six years, the sun shone at least a part of every day. At another time, he lived in another area where the sun broke through an average of 56 days a year. Other construction experiences took place in Iowa, Michigan, Arkansas, Canada, and Europe. In all these areas of the world, there was benefit to be gained from the sun's heat regardless of whether the sunshine was constantly visible.

The infrared rays of the sun, when diffused by clouds, will emit about one-third the amount of heat that reaches earth on a clear day. Heat, radiating toward the earth, though unseen, can be collected and stored in a home to a certain degree. The feature of the sun that makes it less constant than earth-temperature energy is that when your side of the earth is in the shade (revolved away from the sun) there is no potential heat gain on the shaded side. Therefore, the solar supply potential is limited to daylight hours. Unfortunately, in the winter when we have the greatest need of heat, the days are the shortest. Despite these limitations, if the solar heat that is free to all can be harnessed and stored economically, it is a proven, long-lasting, and profitable utility saver for the home owner.

Collection and storage are the two key factors in a viable system. Insulation, of a proper quantity and quality, and a tightly sealed structure will retard heat loss to such an extent that little or no auxiliary heat is required to make it over the cold cycle (the sunless hours). It then behooves us to create enough collection capacity and thermal mass (heat sump) to slow down the cooling-off period of each 24-hour cycle.

ACTIVE SOLAR SYSTEMS

Collectors in the active category are those that require mechanisms and controls. There are many designs and variations on the market and just about any price bracket you would choose to explore. A general characteristic of the fluid-media collector is that a large quantity of plumbing is inherent to the system. Since the circulation of fluid is through collectors exposed to outdoor temperatures, it must be freeze-proof. Antifreeze lowers the usable heat factor a little but is not a significant deterrent to the system's validity.

Circulation pumps are required in more sophisticated systems. Smaller units rely on the heat-rise principle. Safety valves are there to eliminate the potential of an overheating explosion. Bypass and draindown valves are present to facilitate emptying and flushing the system periodically.

Designing an active solar collector heating system is a job for an engineer in that field. During the fuel crunch of the late 1970s and early 1980s, many articles appeared in periodicals on the subject of conservation via a solar system of heating. Some of these were feature write-ups with detailed illustrations depicting plausible system designs. In fact, some of these amateur and homemade structures were experimental and unproven.

A recommended, authoritative reference is *Solarizing Your Present Home,* edited by Joe Carter, Rodale Press, Emmaus, Pennsylvania 18049.

Another significant reason why early solar systems did not attain full acceptance was due to inadequate materials used in their construction. A good book aimed at this factor is *Solar Heating Materials Handbook,* by Homann, Darnall, and Lindeman; AnaChem, Incorporated, Albuquerque, New Mexico 87100.

PASSIVE SOLAR SYSTEMS

A passive solar system operates primarily without the aid of mechanical or electrical controls. Carefully designed, it will blend with the house and not appear as an add-on. As an auxiliary to a mainline heating system, the collectors may simply be windows placed in strategic locations on a south wall. Several characteristics of the passive solar system make it especially attractive to the energy-conservation-minded person, also to those interested in long-term savings in utility costs.

- Simplicity of design
- Unsophisticated materials
- Site built
- Few or no moving parts to break down
- Home owner maintenance
- Free energy supply

The simplest form of solar collection is to use ordinary windows in quantity, and at a proper orientation, to turn living areas into collectors. Double glazing is the best compromise for permitting radiation to enter the house while providing superior retention of heat throughout the sunless hours (Fig. 3-1). Single glass will admit a little more radiation but will lose disproportionately at night. Triple glass provides greater insulating value but impedes radiant penetration too much. Tall windows, and as many as practical, will be placed on the south-facing wall. Fewer windows, and smaller ones will be used on the other sides of the house. This will affect both the floor plan and the choice of building lot that is suitable.

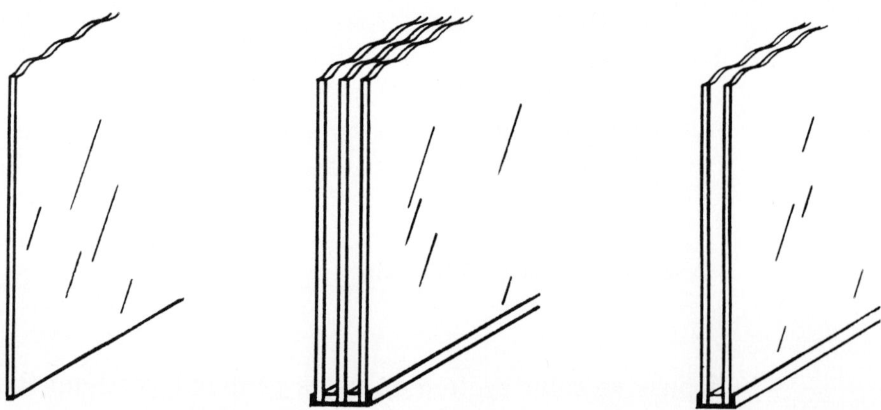

Figure 3-1 (a) Single-pane glass is inadequate for retaining solar heat at nighttime. (b) Triple Thermopane glass has the highest R-value for heat retention. (c) Double Thermopane permits penetration of solar heat best and retains the heat fairly well into the night.

The range of the sun's angle in summer and winter dictates the eave overhang that is important for maximum winter heat gain and for adequate summer shade (Fig. 3-2). Generally, a horizontal plancier depth of 30″ will be an average for houses between the thirtieth and fiftieth latitudes. This figure represents an economical size for plancier covering skin cut from 4 × 8′ sheets (32″ is the perfect module for making three pieces without any waste). In the wintertime, sun rays penetrate about 8 to 10′ into a south-facing room. All solid objects touched by the rays will act as absorbers until they are no longer in the sunshine path. Then they begin to give up their heat at a rate dependent upon the quantity and quality of the house's insulation factor. Figure 3-3 shows the five temperature zones in the United States in relation to recommended minimum insulation R-values (left table). The table on the right ranks the R-value of specific depths of various types of insulation.

Door types have a significant effect upon the heat retention effectiveness of the house. Doors and windows comprise the greatest square footage of heat loss potential in the house. An insulated door is about four times as resistant to heat loss as a wood door. Add a storm door and the combination becomes about the same as that of a frame wall with 3 ½″ of glass fiber insulation. Through-

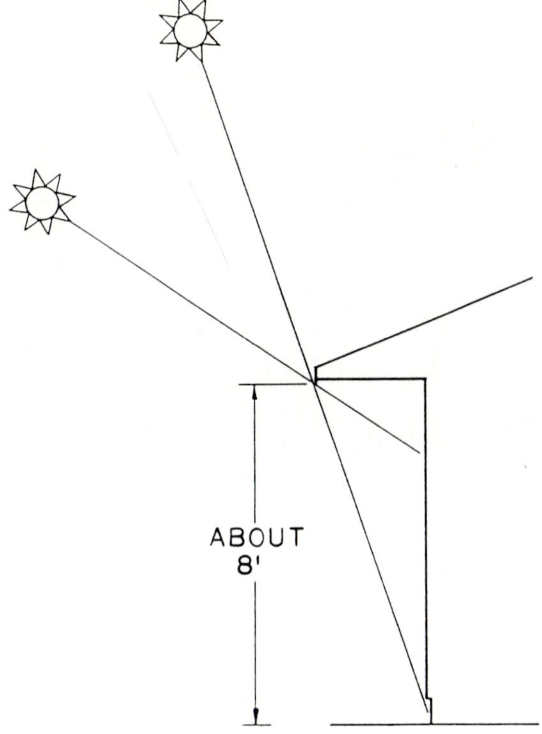

NORTH LATITUDE (DEGREES)	SHADOW HEIGHT (FEET) WIDTH OF OVERHANG (FEET)					
	3	4	5	6	7	8
25	1.1	1.5	1.9	2.2	2.6	3.0
30	1.4	1.9	2.4	2.9	3.4	3.8
35	1.8	2.4	3.0	3.5	4.1	4.7
40	2.1	2.8	3.6	4.3	5.0	5.7
45	2.6	3.4	4.3	5.1	6.0	6.8
50	3.0	4.1	5.1	6.1	7.1	8.2

Figure 3-2 Measure on your section plan from the bottom of the facia level, down the wall to a point where you wish the shade to cover. This is the desired shadow height.

out any house designed for thermal conservation, there should be an attempt made to balance the insulation factors in a coordinated proportion (Fig. 3-4).

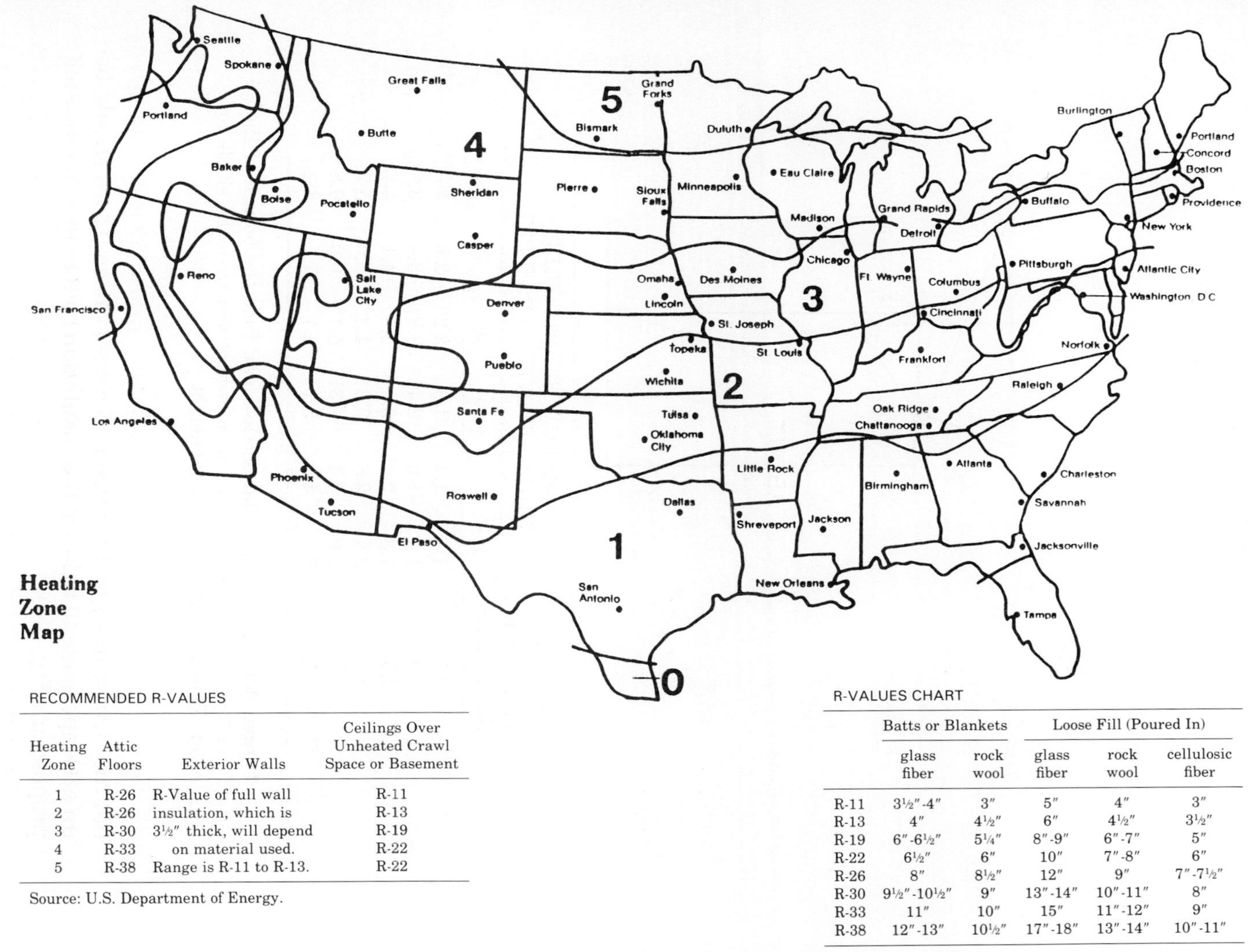

RECOMMENDED R-VALUES

Heating Zone	Attic Floors	Exterior Walls	Ceilings Over Unheated Crawl Space or Basement
1	R-26	R-Value of full wall	R-11
2	R-26	insulation, which is	R-13
3	R-30	3½" thick, will depend	R-19
4	R-33	on material used.	R-22
5	R-38	Range is R-11 to R-13.	R-22

Source: U.S. Department of Energy.

R-VALUES CHART

	Batts or Blankets		Loose Fill (Poured In)		
	glass fiber	rock wool	glass fiber	rock wool	cellulosic fiber
R-11	3½"-4"	3"	5"	4"	3"
R-13	4"	4½"	6"	4½"	3½"
R-19	6"-6½"	5¼"	8"-9"	6"-7"	5"
R-22	6½"	6"	10"	7"-8"	6"
R-26	8"	8½"	12"	9"	7"-7½"
R-30	9½"-10½"	9"	13"-14"	10"-11"	8"
R-33	11"	10"	15"	11"-12"	9"
R-38	12"-13"	10½"	17"-18"	13"-14"	10"-11"

Figure 3-3 Match your latitude and shadow height to find the required overhang on the table in Fig. 3-2. *Example*: For a latitude of 35° and a desired shadow height of 5', the width of overhang is 3'.

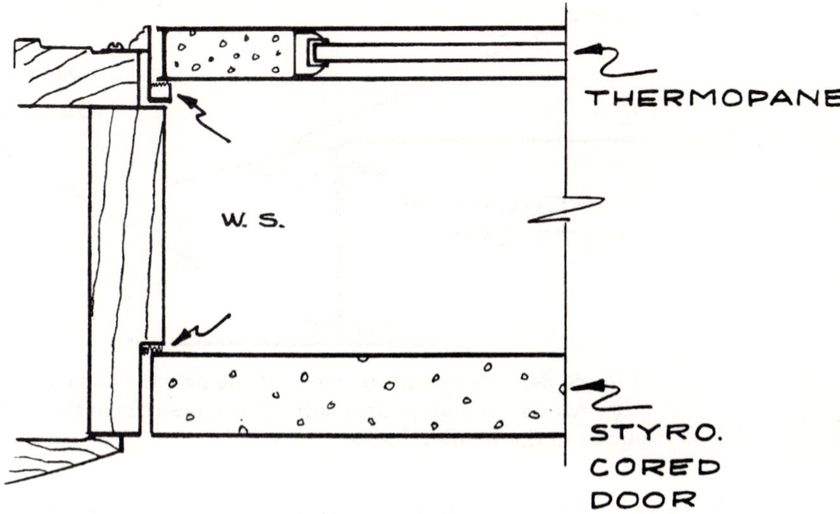

Figure 3-4   A combination of an insulated exterior door (a Thermo-paned and insulated storm door) and full weatherstripping will provide an R-factor comparable to R-11 fiberglass.

GREENHOUSE COLLECTORS

The solar greenhouse gets its name from early use as a heated space to start garden plants ahead of season. When outdoor planting time came, the started plants were transplanted in the garden. A jump of several weeks could be made over the conventional way of sowing seeds. The same principle is used to bring auxiliary heat into the living quarters of a house.

In winter, when the sun is low in the sky, the radiant waves penetrate deeply into the greenhouse and deposit their heat. Ducts with fans will distribute the warmth into other selected areas. The warm air in the collector room rises and is drawn to the interior from high-on-the-wall openings. The cool air below is drawn back into the collector room through floor-level openings with or without blowers. Thus a natural distribution and circulation pattern is set up. The electric fan(s) may be controlled by a thermostat that turns them on to accelerate the air movement when more heat is desired and turns them off to reduce the rate of movement (Fig. 3-5).

In summer mode, when heat gain is undesirable, the collec-

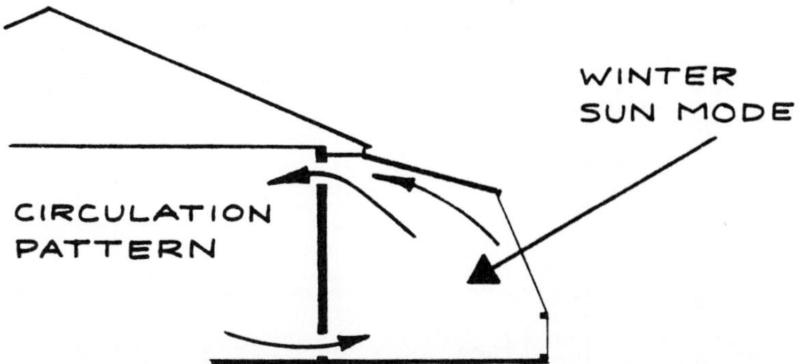

Figure 3-5 This diagram generally depicts the basic greenhouse collection and circulation principle when the sun is in its winter arc and angle in the United States.

tor room must be able to discharge all unwanted heat. First, it is desirable to have hardwood shade trees that shade the collector glass expanse at all hours of sunlight. Trees that provide shade in the summer and shed their leaves in the winter are ideal. They even add coolness to the area under each tree. The best plans, however, sometimes go awry. A crucial tree in the shade role may die or be destroyed by a wind storm. Even though trees are planned as an element of the solar system, it would be folly to rely solely on their shade as protection against the overheating of a collector in the summer season. A carefully planned overhang, that operates effectively both winter and summer, should be coordinated into the plan. In addition to this fixed method of control, there are manual controls to be considered. Windows on the north side of the house and windows and vents in the collector room are opened to create natural cross ventilation. A power vent fan in the ceiling of the collector room will effect a complete air exchange in a matter of minutes. Controlled by a thermostat, this arrangement will automatically keep the room temperature at a level not in excess of the current outdoor temperature (Fig. 3-6).

TILTED OR VERTICAL GLASS

Early greenhouse and storage room collectors were mostly built with tilted glass at an angle that would receive the sun rays as nearly perpendicular as possible (actually, the angle is constantly

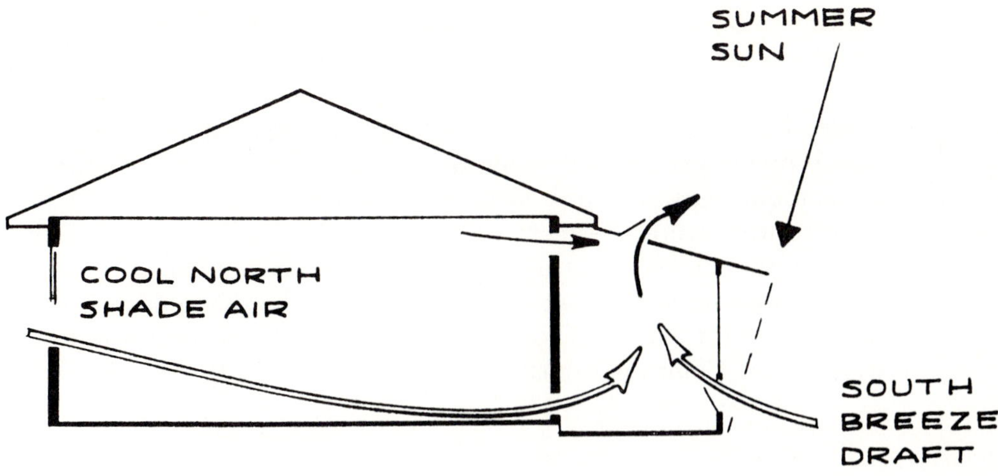

Figure 3-6 A permanent overhang, low intake windows, and a roof vent will circulate the hot air out during the summer months.

changing). The sun angle in wintertime is said to be approximately whatever the latitude is at the building site. This is a broad generalization stemming from December 22.

Common practice has taught us some costly lessons. Angled glass in a window wall is more difficult to seal against rain and snow. It is more prone to damage from falling limbs. Slanted glass walls are more costly to build. The designs with slanted glass are seldom in harmony with tradition and frequently give the look of an add-on or retrofit.

The most important lesson to remember is that a slanted-glass wall collector is more difficult to regulate in the off-season than a vertical-glassed one. Early two-story, slanted collectors were the main culprits. Temperatures in some designs would reach alarming heights toward the apex of a narrow greenhouse-type collector. Wooden components became tinder-dry, and there was concern about spontaneous combustion. The negatives that go with the slanted-glass wall outweigh the slight solar advantage. For south-wall, home-heating room collectors, the vertical wall is the current standard. Any less solar potential from the vertical glass can usually be recouped easily by adding a few more square feet of glass.

Reflected-heat gains can be realized by providing a reflective surface ahead of the windows. Additional sunshine bounces off the reflective surface and passes through the windows to be absorbed within the room. The width of the surface (distance out from the wall) sets a limit on the amount of reflection that takes place. Using the winter sun angle (about 32°), it is possible to figure out approximately how far out a reflective surface should be to make optimum use of the reflection principle (Fig. 3-7). Reflectors may take the form of insulated shutters, hinged at the bottom and closable in the night and at off-season times.

A masonry patio or a wood deck will provide a designer reflection source. The surface will work most efficiently when it is a light color. Colors other than white will absorb the radiation at

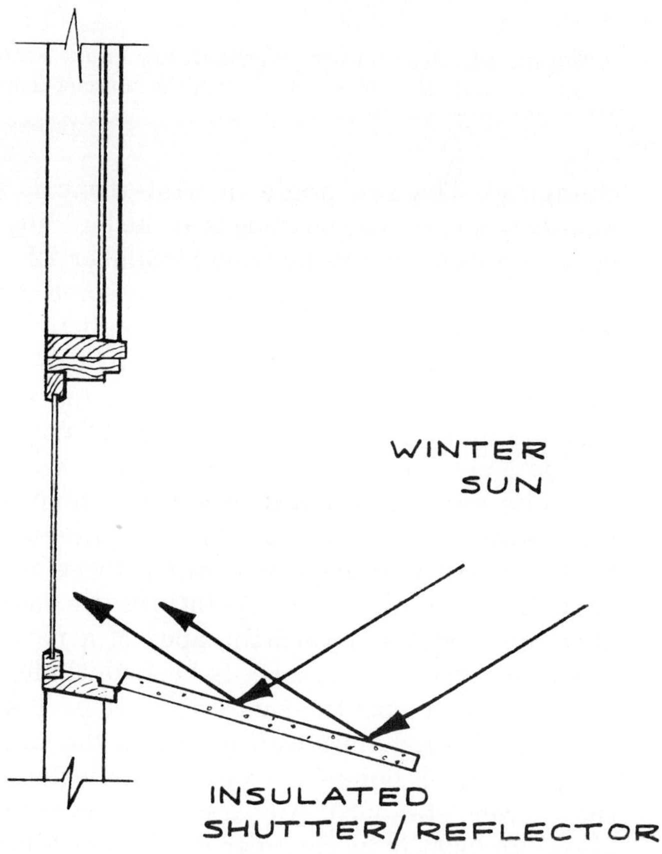

Figure 3-7 Integral, insulated shutters are opened during daylight hours to serve as solar reflectors.

different rates. The darker the color, the more it absorbs and the less effective it will be as a reflector.

A solar wick will occur where a reflector slab contacts a slab-floored house foundation that does not contain a perimeter insulation barrier (Fig. 3-8). Most slab-floored houses currently being built have a Styrofoam barrier between the foundation and the floor. This will insulate the foundation from the floor but will not isolate a reflector slab from the foundation if it is poured up against it. One way to avoid this wick is to bury a treated 2 × 4, on edge, between the foundation and the slab reflector. The top edge of the 2 × 4 is flush with the surface of the slab; in fact, it can be used during construction as the concrete ground-board from which to level the concrete with your screed, and then it can be left in permanently. It should be nailed to the foundation with cement nails so there is no tendency to ease up and out from ground water.

A greenbelt between the foundation and the reflective slab is another alternative. Some form of low shrubbery is attractive. Unless there is some shade on this belt from eaves, it may be difficult to raise any greenery in the summertime as the glare and heat that reflect back will burn out most types of floral adornment (Fig. 3-9). An alternative is to cover this area with ornamental stone.

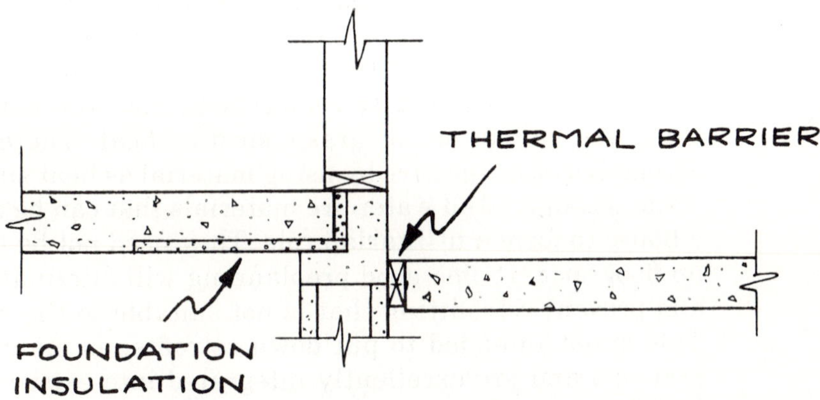

Figure 3-8 Heat, in an interior slab floor, will conduct outdoors in wintertime and be lost at night ("the wick effect") unless an insular break is in place. Coolness will bleed out during air-conditioning months.

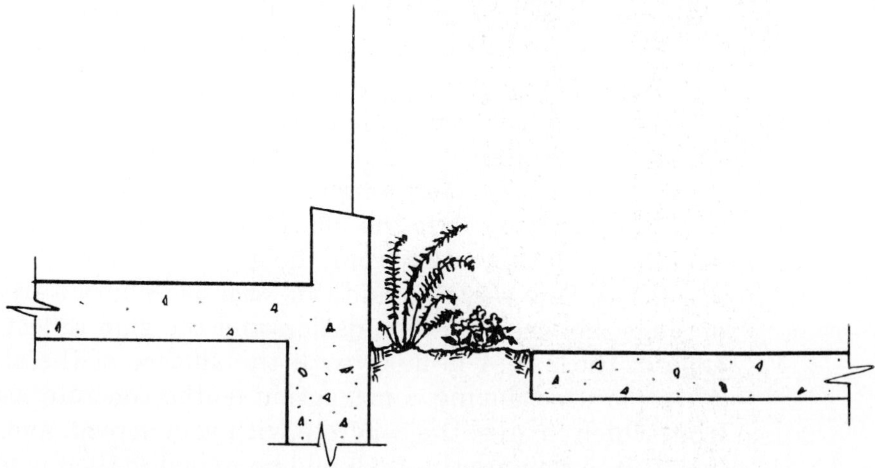

Figure 3-9 A floral greenbelt will stop outdoor slab heat from conducting into the interior floor slab if it is protected in some way from solar burn out.

12 SOLAR STORAGE

The basic solar wall does its work during the sun's visible arching period of the day. As a major source of heat for a house, this would normally leave us without any heat for about 17 hours. To fully exploit the potential of the sun, we must store as much heat as possible. It is puzzling to comprehend how you can store something you cannot see or grasp, such as heat. There are ways to accomplish the objective by using material as heat sinks or sumps. Rock, masonry, and water are materials that can be designed into a house to form a utilitarian role. They need not be ugly nor take up floor space. Some good preplanning will eliminate the pitfalls and prevent retrofitting that is not suitable to the original plan. This is not intended to put down retrofits, as many designs are practical and are excellently integrated into existing structures. In fact, a retrofit project is most exciting and challenging, especially when the result is coupled with the resurrection and restoration of a classic old house which otherwise was untenable.

HEAT STORAGE BIN

A heat-sump storage bin is one way to accumulate and store the produce from a daylight solar collector (Fig. 3-10). The heat from the collector (whether an active or passive type) is drawn by a fan through ducts to the storage area where medium-size rocks absorb it. The heat is taken from this stone sump by gravity or by fan force and directed into the various rooms as desired (much the same as a gravity or forced air furnace). Cold air returns take the distributed air back to the solar room and the cycle continues. With a well-correlated collection and storage facility it is often possible to store enough heat during the production period to carry over the nighttime hours. It works best if the massive glass collector surface can be isolated at night. If it is a partitioned room, such as a sun room or greenhouse, it can be shut off easily by closing the insulated passage doors. The heat from the sump is then circulated through the conventional heat exchange ductwork

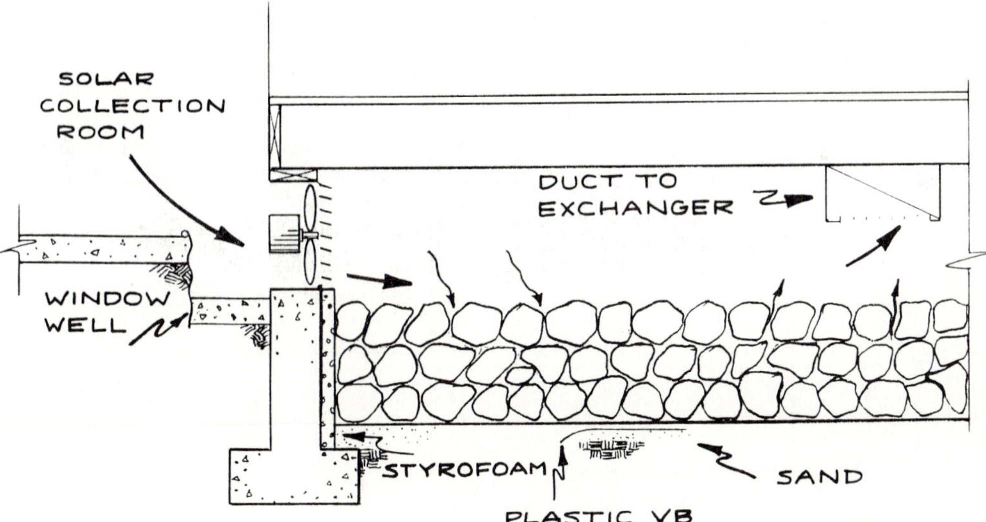

Figure 3-10 A crawl space can be designed into a heat sump storage bin. Stones, that can be placed by hand, make up the retention medium. A thermostat coordinates the intake fan and shutters. Walls and floor are adequately insulated.

by the cold air return fan. Where the window collector is an integral part of a functional living area such as the living room, then some means of insulating the windows after sunset is needed, otherwise the heat sump contents will be circulated a few times and quickly lost out the window area.

MASONRY STORAGE WALL

A thermal storage wall is a popular and simple expedient for extending the potential usefulness of daytime solar accumulation (Fig. 3-11). Solid masonry units provide better heat retention than

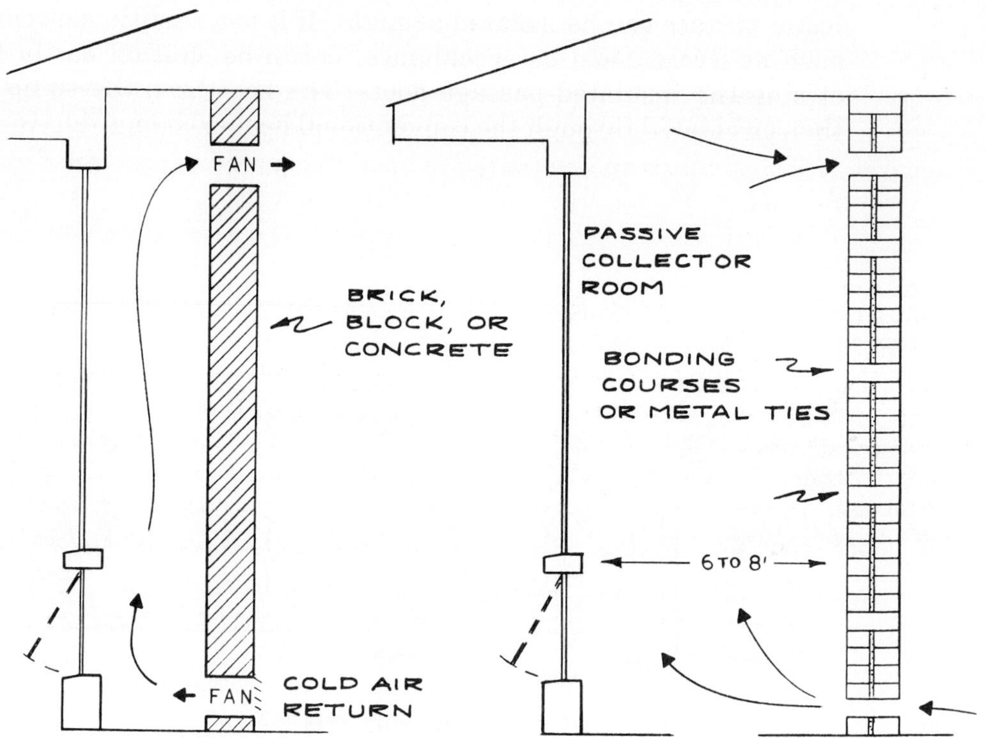

Figure 3-11 Interior masonry walls serve to store heat into the night. (a) A solid wall with register openings at top and bottom. Thermostatically-controlled fans circulate the air. (b) A collector room with a passive storage partition. Intake ducts are provided by omitting brick units in the first course. Heat ducts are made in a higher course near the top.

hollow core types. Solid bricks or poured concrete provide design options. Blocks are more aesthetically acceptable in a stack-bond formation than in the structural staggered mode.

The solar storage wall is placed inside the glass collector surface in a position that will guarantee the greatest amount of direct exposure to the sun rays coming through the glass in the winter. Some arrangement is needed to insulate the windows at night, otherwise the daytime gain will be rapidly lost through the glass. This could entail insulated interior shutters that need swinging room. An objective may be to make enough depth available to be able to use the space for some living function while still keeping a significant part of the wall exposed to the sun's direct rays. The wall does not depend entirely on radiation for heat as the hot air in the room will also convect into the wall. Where sunlight radiates on a portion of the lower half of a storage wall, there still is great potential for increased absorption near the top because the radiant heat is conducting upward in the material mass of the wall.

Distributing the heat from the storage wall is accomplished through openings like those in a greenhouse-type collector. Cold air is circulated back into the collector corridor through openings at the bottom of the wall along the floor line. Squirrel cage blowers are placed in these cold-air return ducts to draw the cold air back into the collector room.

A completely passive cool air return arrangement can be worked out attractively by laying the first course or two of bricks across the bottom of the wall with brick-width voids between each brick. These spaces will be about the same as the brick depth dimension. The cool air that collects at floor level will return through the miniature corridors to the heat side of the wall and gravitate upward while being reheated. A matching row of voided courses is placed near the top of the wall to permit the hot air to pass through into the living area, thus completing the heating cycle.

Where more light is desired in the room on the interior side of the heat storage wall, the wall may be free-standing and only as high as desired. The space above permits all of the heat that is generated to roll over the top. There is an inherent problem with this design as there is no way to control the heat. There are no registers to close and no automated fans to shut down. On very warm sunny days the system may suffer from overkill. It will then require some manual balancing such as opening windows in strategic locations. Another alternative is to have a system of exterior shutters which block the sun from the collector windows but do not exclude the light. Slant-louver awning types are a common solution to this problem. Shutters on the interior side of the windows will not exclude the heat. In fact it will build up excessively between the glass and the shutter. A completely tight shutter will virtually turn each window unit into a box-type collector without a discharge.

The ability to either discharge excess heat or store it in a desirable place is a basic tenet of collector design. Many times it can be handled with no more sophistication than a window fan or a ceiling discharge fan. A ceiling fan with a reversible rotation motor can often be called upon to do double duty. With too much heat, it is used in the exhaust mode. At night it may be reversed to bring in desired warm air from the attic. This condition is most effective where a roof has dark shingles.

The color of the storage wall is a significant factor to its absorption rate. Light colors reflect. Flat black is the best absorption color but is rarely an acceptable choice in the decor of a space used for multipurpose activity. Flat paint of the darkest acceptable shade is a good choice. A shiny (gloss and high gloss) finish causes a mirror-like reflection that turns away absorption. The dark painted part of the wall need only go as high as the highest point on the wall that the sun will shine on directly. Light colors may be used above this line with no detriment to the absorption. In nonheating season this dark color may be lightened with temporary coverings or painted over for the summer.

TROMBE WALL

Trombe wall is a term generally used to describe a combination comprised of a glassed-over wall surface with a space between of about 4″ or more. The wall surface is used to generate heated air from the sun's rays that are trapped behind the glass. In turn, this heated air is shunted from the trombe wall collector to desired locations directly or by ductwork. It is in effect a retrofitted or designed multipurpose use of an existing wall. When that wall is stone or masonry, as in many old period homes, the added factor of the superior media retention of stone is of great benefit. Not only do we enjoy the effects of the solar collection feature but also the benefits of after-sunlight retention in the stone sump of the wall. With a little imagination and some ingenuity, just about any south-facing stone, masonry, or brick wall can be fashioned to serve as a trombe heater.

HEAT STORAGE MEDIA

Two construction materials—water and masonry—come to the foreground of consideration when discussing storage of heat for later distribution. From a practical construction standpoint, masonry is by far the most adaptable. One can design it to be situated as load-bearing for structural integrity, or one can insert it purely as a heat utility element with some accompanying virtues such as a sight barrier wall, a partition, or a decorative monument. Water, by comparison, is obviously nonsupporting and therefore entails some type of permanent container.

Heat retention qualities of materials may be compared in two ways. One is by weight, the other is by volume. For example, a pound of water can store about five times as much heat as a pound of brick. By volume, however, water will store about twice as much as the brick. These factors will lead us to a specific study of which media is best for a particular house plan. Certainly a negative objective is to avoid large masses of either water or masonry that serve only a utilitarian purpose a fraction of the year (the heating days). Another consideration is the weight that may require additional foundation support. A final factor lies in the cost of water storage units. Most of these are only obtainable from commercial manufacturers. There are many attractive systems available at a price. Unlike other more conventional building supplies, you cannot walk into the local building supply outlet and walk out with a kit. Again, it is one of those payback considerations where the two-to-one savings of the media may warrant the initial added expense.

CENTRAL HEAT BACKUP

Auxiliary heat backup is usually needed with a passive solar system. Where a solar window wall and storage sump wall system is the primary source of heat, it will be advantageous to have an auxiliary forced-air heating system with full-house hot- and cold-air ductwork throughout. The thermostat is wired to run the auxiliary air exchanger (the central cold-air return blower) until no more heat remains to be used in the storage wall. Then the auxiliary furnace (gas, oil, or electric) takes over until the storage wall is regenerated by renewed radiation from the sun.

13 DOMESTIC HOT WATER CONSERVATION

It is quite easy to overlook the significant cost of providing hot water for the home. In the past half-century or more the water heater has emerged as a separate facility. Prior to then, in many homes it was typical to heat water in receptacles on top of the cooking stove or in a siderigger well. Furnaces might have had a coil of water line pipe running around the inside of the firebox which was heated by the fire in the winter. When gas became a common fuel, this coil was modified into a small vertical heater encased in a cast iron shell with its own little gas burner at the bottom. This opened up the potential of instant hot water in the summer as well as winter. Early models were extremely limited as there was no storage tank. Later a storage tank was added but insulation was yet to come. Today's water heater, with its large storage capacity, its automatic controls, and high intensity insulation covering is a far cry from the old days. The modern water heater has literally changed the hygienic habits of most people from what they were before hot water was so easy to obtain.

The cost of DHW (domestic hot water) does not show up separately on a utility bill if the heating fuel is the same as that being used to heat the house. Therefore the DHW cost often escapes attention. In most households it is possible to save considerably on the cost of water heating with a few nontechnical adjustments.

CONVENTIONAL ECONOMY MEASURES

Thermostatic control of the water temperature can be set wherever one wishes to have it. The thermostat is usually set at the factory for a maintained 140°. This "scalding temperature" is seldom necessary in a typical family home where water use is intermittent. On an electric water heater the thermostats may be set to somewhere between 100 and 120°. On gas and oil fired water heaters the arrow can be set just below "warm" and adjusted up or down as desired after some trial use. A savings will be realized and no discomfort (no difference) will be felt as most of us temper the too-hot water with a mixture of cold water at the mixing tap or shower head. The savings comes largely from the nonuse times when the thermostat no longer has to sustain such a high temperature (Fig. 3-12).

Electric water heaters have the thermostats next to the exposed end of the heating elements. These are to be found under the cover plates on the side of the heater shell. Be sure to throw the correct breaker in your main electrical service entrance to the off position before removing the cover plates. There will be insulation covering the element head from view. A safe way to expose the wiring contacts and the thermostat dial is to move the insulation aside with a popsicle stick; then jump a ground and a hot wire with a simple pocket current tester (available anywhere) to be certain the current is off. Ground wires (negative) are usually white or green. Hot wires (positive) are black, red, and blue. Now you can turn the dial indicator arrow to a lower temperature. A little experimenting will net the setting that proves satisfactory to all.

A timer is another means of saving. This little electrical switching device can be set to turn on and turn off the power to the water heater at several different times of the day and night. The settings can be fitted to the family needs. For example, if both parents work and the children are in school, there is no need to maintain a high level of hot water generation throughout the hours when no one is at home to use it. The stops that are fastened to the timer face are set to switch on the heater a half-hour or so before the family demand begins and to switch it off when the needs stop. The small cost of the timer ($20 to $25) will be recovered in a short period of time. The reduced running time will

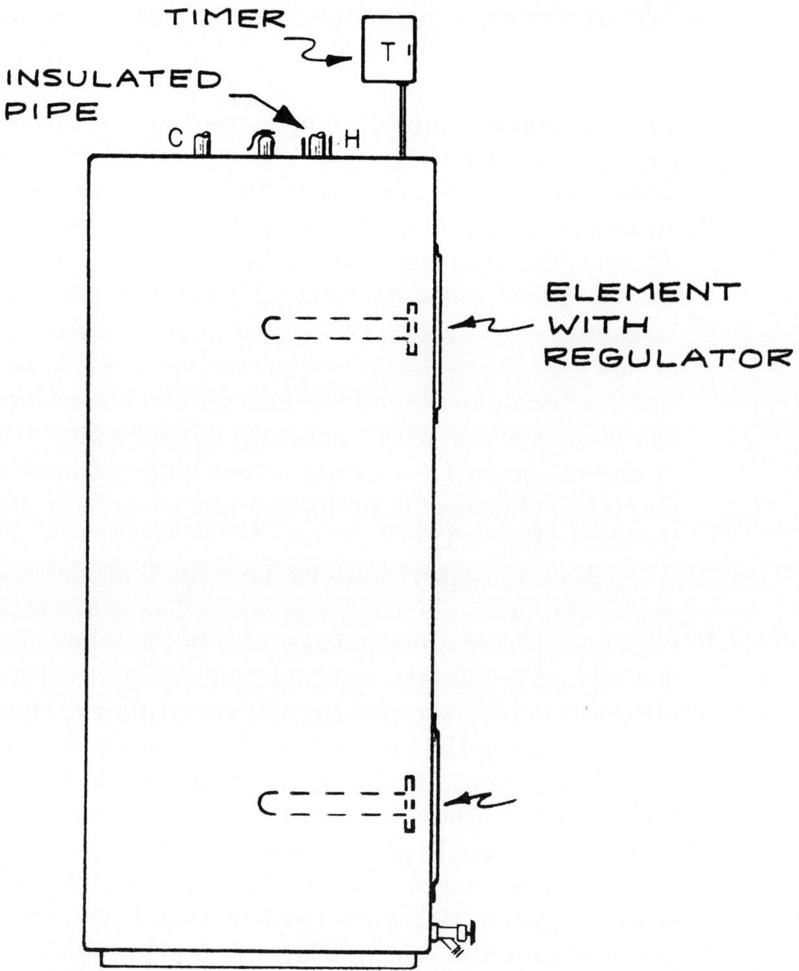

Figure 3-12 Economy measures on a conventional water heater involve installing and setting a timer and adjusting the temperature of the heating elements.

also prolong the life of the elements and the heater as a whole. For example, when the heater is shut down for about six hours at night and six hours during the day, there is a potential for significant energy savings as well as a longer life expectancy for the water heater. When special times of demand arise, it is a simple matter to switch the timer to the "on" position manually without interrupting the cycle settings.

Superinsulation provides another means of upgrading the

efficiency of some water heaters. During the transition period from uninsulated heaters to totally insulated and metal-clad heaters, there was a great market for insulation kits to cover the bare, galvanized steel storage tank. Most modern heaters are well insulated and protected with an outer shell of enameled sheet metal. There is a simple test which will indicate whether your heater could use additional insulation. When the elements are on, run your bare hands over all of the surface of the outer metal covering. There should be no warmth felt. A warm area, or spot, indicates a heat leak. General warmth over a large area or all over the shell is cause to apply another insulation blanket to the exterior of the heater. A vulnerable spot is behind the element covers where the insulation is sometimes not spread back adequately over the thermostat.

Pipe insulation is also a consideration that may net a long-range savings. A plumbing layout that has long lines of pipe from the hot water heater to the first takeoff and from one outlet location to another will have costly loss of heat in the hot water lines. When a hot water tap is used intermittently, the hot water that stands in the pipe after the outlet is turned off cools down quickly. Copper and PVC pipe lose significant heat during the transit of the hot water, as well as during the dormant period. Inexpensive pipe insulation can be purchased in glass fiber rolls or synthetic foam tubes. The latter will do a more permanent job when properly fused at the joints with solvent. An added bonus to this installation is that it practically eliminates the pipe dripping syndrome that occurs from condensation. At the minimal cost involved, you may wish to insulate both cold and hot pipes to eliminate heat loss and dripping.

Heater elements themselves can sometimes cause a loss of efficiency. After a few years of normal use, an element begins to succumb to rust and oxidization. If a person pays no heed to the condition by conducting a periodic sight examination, the element loop will at some point in time rust through and no longer work. Some consumers will inspect and usually replace the elements every two or three years as a preventive measure against an untimely breakdown. It is also rationalized that the cost of replacing an old element, whether defective or not, is well worth the trouble and will be recouped by new elements which give off heat at their maximum efficiency.

Replacing an element is a simple job of taking off and replacing. All power to the heater must be shut off during the operation. The water is drained from the tank by connecting a garden hose to the drain tap at the bottom of the tank and placing the discharge end outdoors. Obviously the discharge end of the hose must be at a lower level than the tank bottom. The two cover plates are removed in the same manner as for resetting the thermostat. Detach the wires from the head of the element and make mental or graphic note of where each color will go on the replacement. Unbolt the element and withdraw it straight out through the hole. Replace it with the new element, being sure to place the correct wattage unit in the correct hole. A 2500-watt element is the sustaining element. The 4500-watt element is characterized as a fast recovery element. Some tanks have both elements in the 4500-watt size. When we think of 9000 watts of electricity as the equivalent of 90 100-watt light bulbs—which would light all of the rooms in 15 six-room houses at once—the reality of the cost of hot water is more explicit. Other combinations of wattage may be found in your water heater. Unless you have a constant shortage of hot water, it is logical to stay with the original element combination of wattage. Should you desire to change, the advice of a certified heating expert may be a valuable service to seek out.

Sediment accumulation is another enemy of economy in the operation of a water heater. Many water sources are not as pure as could be hoped for, especially in rural settings where wells are the source. Contamination which clogs a heater comes in several forms such as lime, calcium, and iron. These types of solid matter make use of the water heater tank as a sump. They settle to the bottom as sediment. One time the author removed a lower element and found it encrusted with hard matter and burned through in one place. A flashlight inspection into the hole revealed that the element had been completely submerged in sediment. After screwing off the drain tap, through which the sediment would not pass, two pails of scale and sandy particles were flushed out. The encased element had obviously been overworked for a long time before it gave up. The tank was heated, largely by the upper element only, throughout the period of sediment submersion. Regular draining, at least once a year, might have prevented this breakdown (Fig. 3-13).

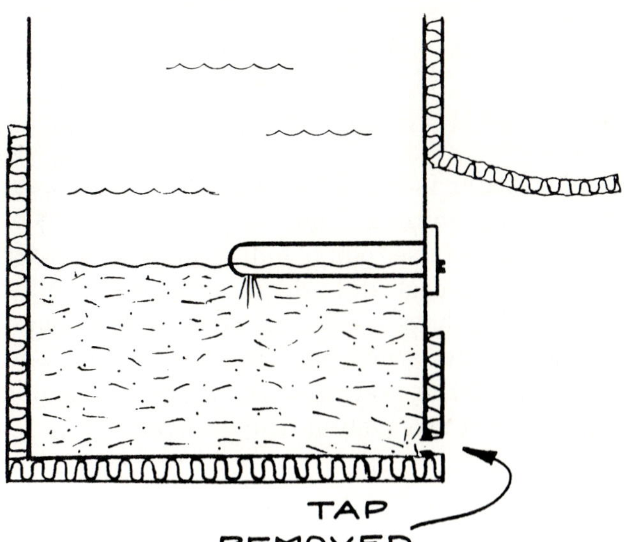

Figure 3-13 A water heater's lower element that becomes submerged in sediment is a candidate for early burnout.

Flow regulators present another low-cost containment potential. It is no challenge at all for a youngster or an adult to empty a water heater while taking a shower. By contrast, RV travelers are famous for effectively showering with a mere gallon or two of water. The most miserly technique is to wet down, turn off the water, and soap up. Then turn on the shower and rinse in a minimum of water. Now, believe me, I am not advocating that we do away with shower therapy and certainly not that our habits of hygiene be lessened in quality. But for those who are economy minded or have five or six little ones to run through the shower every evening, the flow regulator may be an answer to your prayer. The flow regulator fits on the tap or shower head and simply cuts down on the volume of water that can pass through. Anyone who has taken a shower under a perforated gallon can hung from a branch knows that you don't need 45 pounds of pressure or 5 gallons per minute to get clean. A flow regulator for a shower head can be found at any mart, building supply company, or plumbing supply store. Actually, many people prefer the spray-like discharge better than the searing blast that a nonregulated head can produce. The economy is realized forthrightly in the reduced volume of hot water used to accomplish the same results.

14 SOLAR-ASSISTED WATER HEATING

Solar heating of domestic water is similar to solar air heating except that it always involves plumbing. There are many brands of commercially made collectors in use today. A drawback to greater proliferation is the high initial cost and added labor required for installing them. Nonetheless, these collectors warrant consideration after a long-range feasibility study has been made. The do-it-yourself person can duplicate the results with readily available materials including the core of the system, the absorber.

FLAT PLATE WATER HEATERS

A flat plate absorber, as its name implies, is much like a thin radiator housed in a shallow box. This collector is found lying flat on a properly sloped roof or mounted at a carefully determined angle to the sun. Cold water is introduced at the bottom of the absorber, heated through the glass by the sun, and discharged at the top from whence it travels to a hot water storage tank. There are several basic absorber storage designs.

A coil of pipe is probably the simplest absorber that can be made at home. Black plastic pipe is coiled on a piece of flat-black painted plywood with a couple of inches of space between each coil. The pipe is held in formation with pipe straps at third points or quarter points. Styrofoam is sandwiched under the plywood for insulation. Sides may be made of treated 2 × 4s or 1 × 4s encased in aluminum flashing. The top is double-strength glass or clear plastic. The absorption characteristics may be improved by using black painted corregated aluminum under the coil (Fig. 3-14).

Rectangular absorbers provide a choice of two pipe feed alternatives. The simplest is much like the coil system where the water goes in one end of the pipe, travels the full length, and emerges out the other end. In a rectangular box this single transit route is accomplished by forming the pipe in a serpentine pattern. This pattern provides flexibility in shaping a collector box to a specifically confined space. The absorber is usually made of hard

Figure 3-14 The simplest solar flat-plate water heater can be fabricated from a coil of black pipe. It is suspended on a black background in an airtight collector box. This design will not drain down. Some arrangement must be provided to prevent freezing—such as locating the heater in a temperate sun room.

copper pipe. Each turn is made with sweated (soldered) elbows. The copper pipe must be thoroughly cleaned of oxidization and flux before painting it flat black. There are types of flat black paint made specifically to absorb more heat. Check with your paint store expert. It is advisable to construct the collector box so that the glass can be removed periodically for repainting of the absorber and also for replacement of a broken pane. It is important when designing the disassembly feature that we adhere to the airtight and waterproof objectives of any type of collector (Fig. 3-15).

The manifold absorber has some advantages over the previous examples. This design uses a larger distribution pipe at the entry and discharge ends of the absorber. In the coil and the serpentine absorber, the water comes in cold and leaves hot. When water is drawn off slowly at a tap in the house, the temperature in the pipe will vary considerably from one end to the other. The discharge end will continue to be very hot while the entry end will be cold until there is time for it to warm up. The manifold arrangement permits a portion of hot water to be drawn off the top of each circuit that extends between the cold and the hot manifold. The cold water entering the bottom manifold simultaneously is drawn part way up into each of the individual circuits. The recovery time is reduced due to the added convection contact points of the cold water with the hot water that is still in the top part of the absorber. The manifold pipes will be larger size than the joiner pipes. The size will depend on how many takeoffs are made (Fig. 3-16).

Copper pipe comes in three thicknesses: K, L, and M. K is the thickest, L is next, and M is the thinnest. L or M are usually used for absorbers. Hard copper comes in 10′ and 20′ lengths. Soft

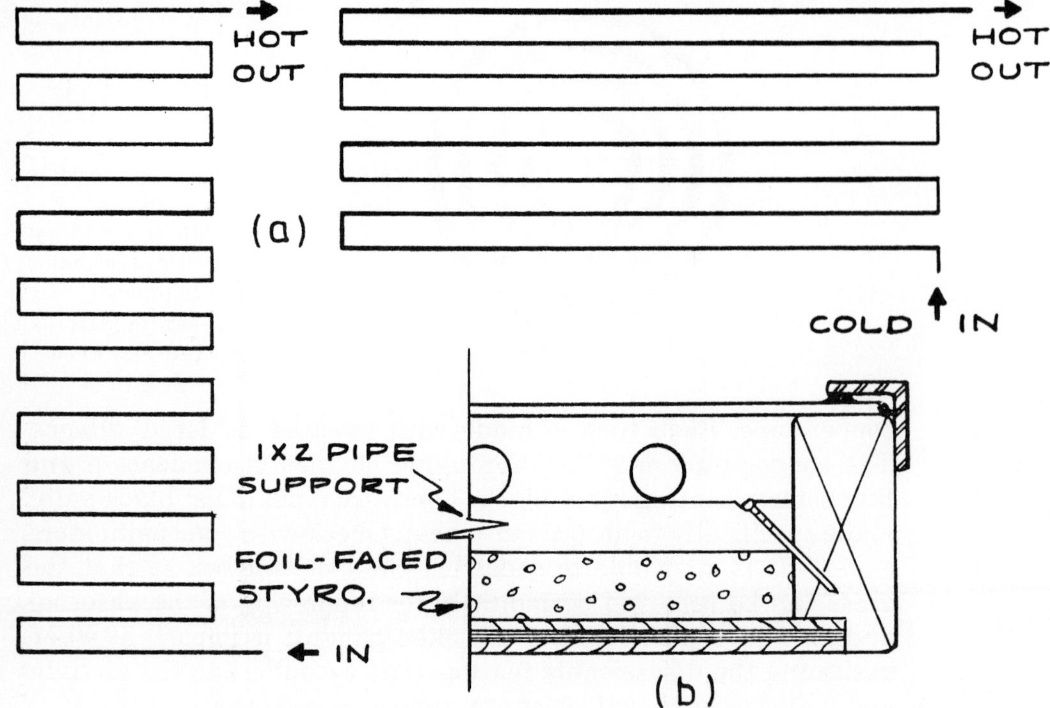

Figure 3-15 (a) The rectangular, serpentine pipe layout can be adapted to many different shaped spaces for a solar water heater. (b) A cross-section view of the materials in a flat-plate water heater. Pipes must be horizontal for drain down purposes.

copper is difficult to use in a collector because the bends cannot be made sharp enough without crimping (flattening) the pipe. Too much box space results from using wide-arched bends.

Soldering is a fearsome task for many. There are rules which assure success without strife.

1. Clean the copper with steelwool or plumbers' sandpaper. Make it shine wherever you want the solder to go. Remember the inside of the elbows and tees.
2. Flux both parts and assemble.
3. Heat the pipes, not the solder (solder will melt long before the copper is ready to fuse).
4. Touch the solder to the pipe. Do not melt it on with the torch. If the solder does not flow, heat the copper some

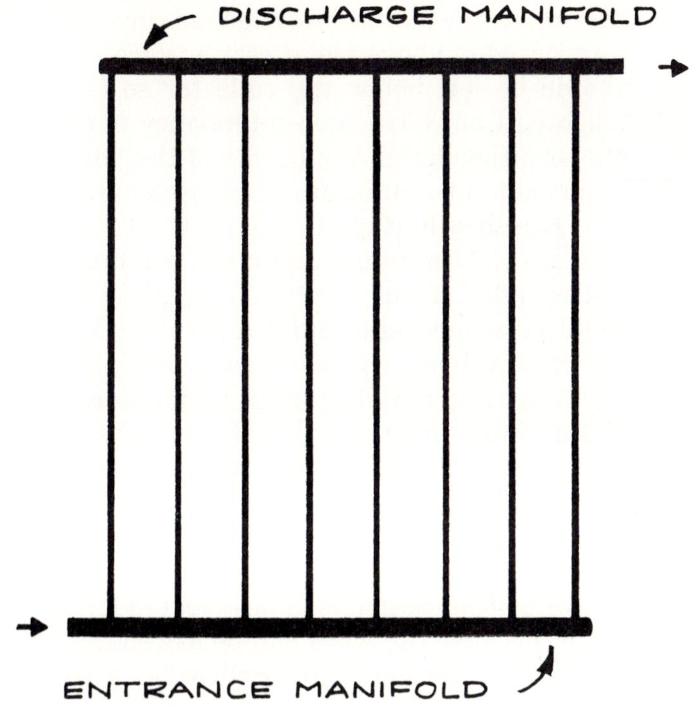

Figure 3-16 A manifold pipe arrangement will discharge and recoup rapidly.

more. When the copper is hot enough, it will suck the molten solder down into the joint.

5. Immediately remove the heat as soon as the joint is full all around the pipe.

6. Wait until the solder loses its sheen before moving the assembly.

MOUNTING THE FLAT PLATE COLLECTOR

Mounting a flat plate system of collectors on a roof is a handyman's niche. Specifics are not required herein as the job falls in the custom category for each roof. Some general principles should be kept in mind to avoid future problems.

Most flat plate collectors will involve a tilted angle to face the sun in the most advantageous way. This means standing each unit on edge above the direct surface of the roof. Enough space should be left below the collector so leaves and other airborne trash will not have such a tendency to collect on the uphill side. On the other hand, the profile of the box that is presented to the wind should be maintained as low as practical.

Bracing materials should be of a waterproof and rustproof character. Aluminum angle iron is a favored brace material. It is lightweight, strong, and fairly easy to work (much less effort is required when using hand tools than when working with steel). No rust problem will exist to stain light-colored shingles. Many hardware and building supply companies now stock short lengths of aluminum in a variety of shapes (this may be an expensive way to buy it). Only aluminum, stainless steel, or heavily galvanized bolts should be used to fasten the braces and collector to the roof (brass is an option also but is usually too expensive to be considered).

An easier option is to use treated lumber, redwood, or cedar—easier because the wood can be sawed and fabricated on-site with little effort. By using bolts with flat washers, a moderately successful job can be accomplished. Such an economy arrangement will not compare, however, to a long life expectancy mount made of metal.

Unless a roof is facing directly south, all four mounting legs could be unique in length. As a rectangular box is rotated away from parallel with the roof, each leg takes on its own particular length. It is feasible to position the collector parallel to the roof so long as its direction is not more than 10° away from due south at high noon. This will simply mean that its reception angle is improved a few minutes earlier in the morning or sustained longer in the afternoon, and it will be shortened on the opposite end of the sunlit hours. In such a case (collector parallel), the leg braces on the bottom of the box will match each other, and those on the top will match each other. The attachment angle at the bottom of the legs will be identical on all four. This condition makes for much less customizing—particularly in dealing with compound angular cuts where the base plates meet the roof. When the collector box is parallel and level, the feet of the braces will be at simple, uniform angles to the vertical legs.

Cosmetically, the entire positioning of the parallel system appears to have continuity and looks less like an afterthought. Taking this under advance consideration may encourage the designer or home planner to begin by searching for a proper-facing lot. When the lot orientation is fixed but large enough, there is still the potential of revolving the house orientation to gain the exposure angle desired. As we move from the large rural tracts to the very limited and restricted city lots, we begin to close out the feasibility percentage for solar orientation. Setback regulations and parallelism restrictions often cancel out the potential for a good exposure. Only where streets run east and west will there be choices with full facing potential. Even there, the owner may wish to mount collectors on the rear roof only. This cuts the lot choices in half for all rectangular house plans, because only north-facing lots will qualify. Angled streets, cul-de-sacs, and north-south running streets are often adaptable to house plans that have a wing which runs within 10° of east and west along its roof line. Collectors can be mounted on the south-facing roof of the wing.

Surface mounting through shingles creates a potential for "trouble in River City." It is necessary to violate the hard and fast rule that all rain-carrying materials must be laid in a shedding posture. Here we are faced with having to bolt something to the surface of a roof that will stand up to high wind storms and driven rain without causing a leak. Let us see how we can work ourselves out of this dilemma.

First let us go for a philosophy that the fewer holes made in the roof, the better. One solid anchor bolt to hold each leg will be the goal, provided each bolt can be made adequate for the purpose.

The mount bases may fall on a rafter or in between. Where they fall on a rafter, we will use lag bolts (a lag bolt is a very large screw with a square head by which it is driven into a predrilled pilot hole with a wrench). A lag bolt, of adequate length, will penetrate deeply into the rafter and provide a good anchor. Bolts are not recommended for anchoring over a rafter, as a hole would have to be drilled completely through the rafter. This would substantially decrease its bearing capacity (weaken its ability to support the imposed load). Lag bolts are readily obtainable only in ferrous metal (iron). After seating an iron fastener, even though galvanized, the head should be encased in roof cement which bonds to the brace. As long as this covering is in contact, the iron head will not succumb to rust, and the roof will be protected from ugly stains (Fig. 3-17).

Mount bases that fall between joists will require a wood

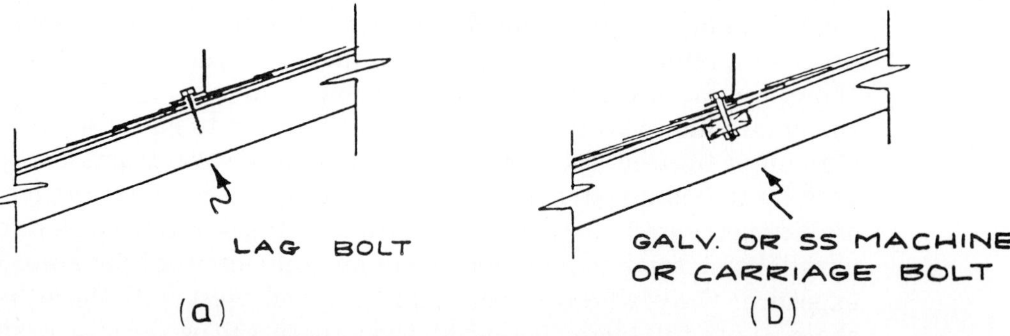

Figure 3-17 (a) Lag bolts are used when the bracket hole is directly over a rafter. (b) A wood block, end nailed to the rafters, backs up a carriage or machine bolt.

backup block under the sheathing and bolts with washers under each nut. Thin sheathing on currently built houses is not an adequate anchoring base to withstand the pressure that may be exerted on the collector from wind. In most cases, the installer will have a choice of where to position the collector so that anchoring will be into rafters or between them.

Flashing the leg braces is one way to overcome the water danger to the roof. There are two ways to watershed the base of the braces so that the holes will not leak. One commonly practiced method is to lay a bed of roof cement where the leg base will contact the roof (around the bolt hole). Particularly where this method of sealing is used on white and light-color shingled roofs, the brace bases are traced in their exact position while aligned by temporarily inserting the mounting bolts. The cement is carefully contained within the perimeter of the tracing so that no great squeeze-out will occur. An adequate amount is required so that a gasket-seal effect takes place (the pressure of the bolting down will spread the cement and form a waterproof seal). Any excess that squeezes out is progressively removed with a disposable tool such as a popsicle stick. This careful approach will eliminate the unsightly marring of the roof. It is something of a traumatic boo-boo to step in a glob of black cement and then track it across a white roof. There is no cleanup remedy short of replacement of every defiled shingle. Collectors on dark shingled roofs do not present quite such a hazard from black cement (Fig. 3-18).

The metal flashing technique is a little more time consuming but will prove superior over the years. Water will run off the smooth metal surface of flashing more rapidly than from a com-

Figure 3-18 This set of flat plate collectors can supply a major portion of the domestic hot water needs year-round. The solar collector may also provide an effective auxilliary source of energy to assist a hot water space heating system. (Courtesy of Oren Atchley Co., Inc., Fort Smith, Arkansas.)

position shingle surface. The water will not have the opportunity to soak in under the collector feet. Installing the flashing is done in the same manner as septic and air vents are flashed. A piece of flashing metal is cut to a length of about 4 to 6″ longer than the foot of the leg plus the distance to the bottom edge of the shingle above. The width will vary depending on the width of the footplate. The width will then be within a range of about 6 to 8″. The upper part of the flashing is tucked up under the shingle above the mounting leg. The upper edge must not be exposed in a shingle gutter. Move it away from the gutter or make the flashing piece a little longer so that it will slide up higher than the top of the gutter and be under the next-higher tab (Fig. 3-19). Steps for installing the flashing are

1. Cut each piece of flashing metal to an adequate size.
2. Position the flashing and indent the hole position.
3. Punch or cut the hole out.

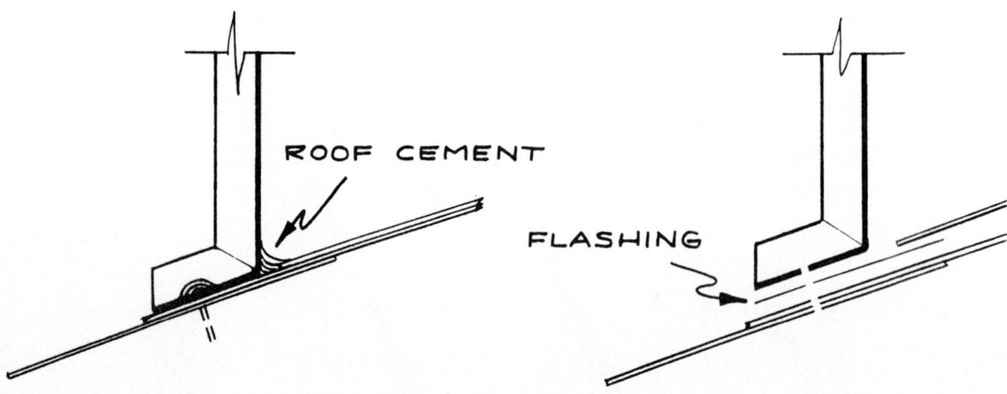

Figure 3-19 Waterproofing legs to a roof surface.

4. Spread a light coat of cement over all the underside of the flashing.

5. Spread cement on the shingle in a donut around the hole and within the area that will be covered by the flashing (use the same care just described to minimize squeeze-out).

6. Position the flashing and hold it in alignment with an inserted bolt.

7. Nail the flashing in four places: each lower corner and below the tab of the shingle that is lapping over the top of the flashing.

8. Put a dab of cement over each nail head and smooth it out to bond and seal the head with the flashing metal. With dark or black shingles the entire flashing may be lightly coated with cement to make the flashing less reflective and noticeable.

9. Position the collector and align with the bolts.

10. Trace around the feet of the mounting legs and seal as described earlier for direct application on shingles.

Periodic inspections will help to prevent a breakdown. Close visual examination of the exterior parts is a worthy routine. Check all the cemented areas for voids and breakdown of the cement. Baked out and shrunken weather cracks reveal areas that will require a maintenance job. Regrout all such areas with fresh cement. Inspect under the roof for signs of leakage. Do not concentrate only in the area of the bolts and backup blocks. Water frequently runs across a sheathing joint and emerges several feet from its entrance point. Water-stained wood will give cause for serious investigation. In spite of the cautionary notes regarding surface mounting, a well-done job will net many years of economical water heating.

BREADBOX COLLECTOR

The breadbox collector is another choice for a home-built design for either air heating or water heating. The name comes from the shape which employs a box with a slanted front. The front is glassed and receives the sun's rays at the optimum compromise angle for hot water the year around.

Water containers may be as simple as one tank or as complex as several in series. The cold water is routed through the breadbox system into the conventional water heater. In limited sunshine areas, the breadbox functions as an auxilliary and provides free hot water to the indoor tank whenever it can. In areas where the sun shines most of the time, the breadbox may be the main provider, and the conventional heater provides backup service. The latter case is one where the thermostatic controls on the heating elements can be set at their lowest levels so that they rarely come on during the daytime. With a timer in the line, little or no cost is incurred for daytime water heating except on stormy or sunless days.

The box is constructed of sturdy lumber as it must survive the rigors of the outdoors as well as support the weight of many gallons of water. The exterior of the box will be weatherproofed as well as the house itself. The sides and bottom inside the breadbox are tightly insulated to hold out the cold and keep the heat in the hot water. The infiltration impregnability of the box and the R-rating quantity of the insulation are most important during the nighttime. It is then that the hot water will give off its heat to the outdoors unless it can be contained in an airtight box that is well insulated (Fig. 3-20).

The heat absorption rate is greatly enhanced by painting

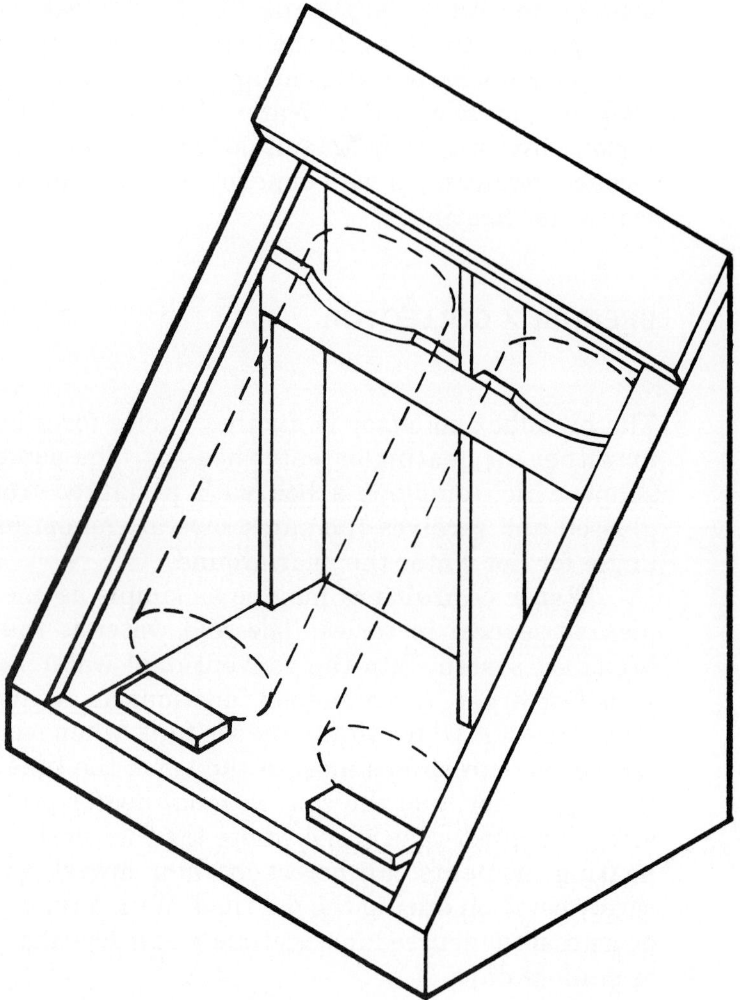

Figure 3-20 The breadbox solar water heater maximizes the sun's angle in wintertime (shown without insulation or top-glazed cover).

the water tank(s) flat black. The interior of the box can be adapted as a reflective surface to gain considerably more sunshine. A curved stainless steel sheet may be curved under the tank(s). The sun rays will reflect from the mirror-like curved surface of the stainless steel onto the underside of the tank which is otherwise in the shade. The extra exposure and the heat from the stainless metal will contribute to a quicker and greater absorption rate (Fig. 3-21).

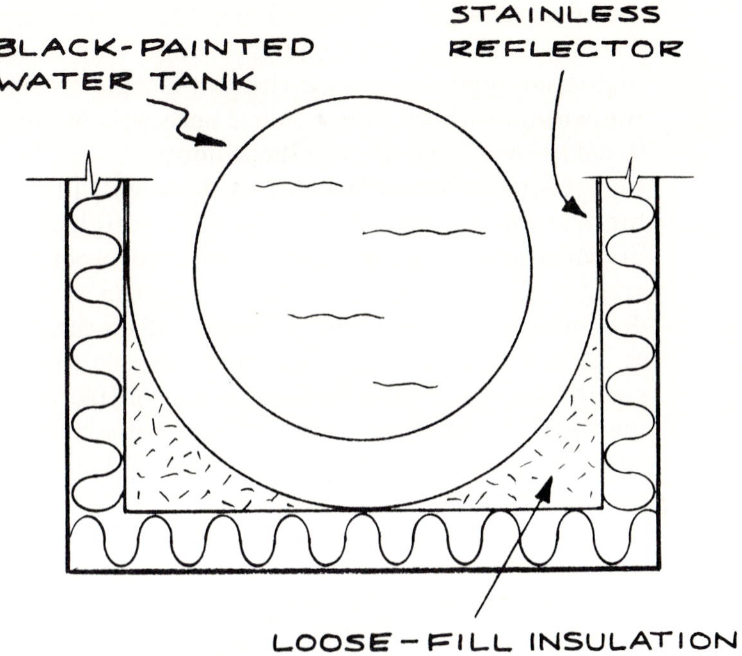

Figure 3-21   A section view of a water tank in a solar collector box.

Air heat can be introduced to the box as an auxiliary contributor of heat for the water in the tanks by adapting a collector system similar to a flat plate air heater (see Part 4, Section 19). Corrugated aluminum sheet metal is used to line the box. For a tilt-faced breadbox, the corrugations of the metal are placed parallel to the tank(s) and curved in a radius around the back corners of the interior. This system will be prone to overheating in the summertime on peak temperature days unless cold water is frequently and consistently being drawn into the tank. A regulated air temperature thermostatic relief valve is required in the box surface to prevent overheating.

A manual system of protection against overheating is to install hinged shutter doors. The shutters furnish other advantages for residents who are frequently gone from the house several days a week or take extended vacations away from home. In the closed position, the sun is effectively blocked, and the water heating function is shut down. The shutters also protect against windstorm damage and unnecessary weathering of the materials surrounding the glass. In northern climates or anywhere that deep freezing is characteristic in the winter, the shutters must be of an insulated type, otherwise the tanks may freeze and burst, since the water in them is not hot. There will be no heat in the water to carry over through the dark hours.

A sandwiched insulated door will fill the requirement for high intensity insulation and light weight. An inch or more of Styrofoam for the core and ¼″ weatherproof plywood for the covering makes a feasible design. A solid (no window), insulated steel door makes a good shutter. Such a door can frequently be found at surplus centers at a fraction of new cost. Bear in mind that the size of the door may influence the entire dimensional requirements of the collector. Also, it is extremely important to consider what the position of the shutter door will be when it is in the open position and how to weatherproof it in that position.

A final protection against freezing, which does not require constant attention, is the use of electrical heat tape. The heat tape has its own little temperature sensor which automatically permits the current to flow when the temperature approaches freezing. When the danger is over, the sensor breaks the current and stops the heat. A 110 to 120 outlet, permanently installed in the breadbox, is needed. To guarantee nonfreezing, a tape that is long enough is required. The tape should be secured in some way to the unexposed side of the tank. No part may cross another or come in contact with another. The tape should be removed in summertime as its life will be severely limited if exposed to the high temperatures during the collector's working hours. This is a good reason for constructing the glass face of the breadbox so it can be readily opened at least twice a year.

The glazing on the slanting face of a breadbox heater is carefully installed to be as airtight as possible. The most efficient glass will be double pane (Thermopane is preferred, though two panes set in butyl or silicone will suffice). Many fine collectors have been made from surplus sliding, patio door glass.

Lightweight angular flashing will be required all around the top edges where the glass rests on the sides. The side flashing pieces will be standard 90° angles. The top and bottom edges will require custom bent angles to match the pitch of the cover (Fig. 3-22).

Arrangement of tanks is optional. Squatty, large diameter tanks can be stacked vertically. Smaller diameter tanks of greater

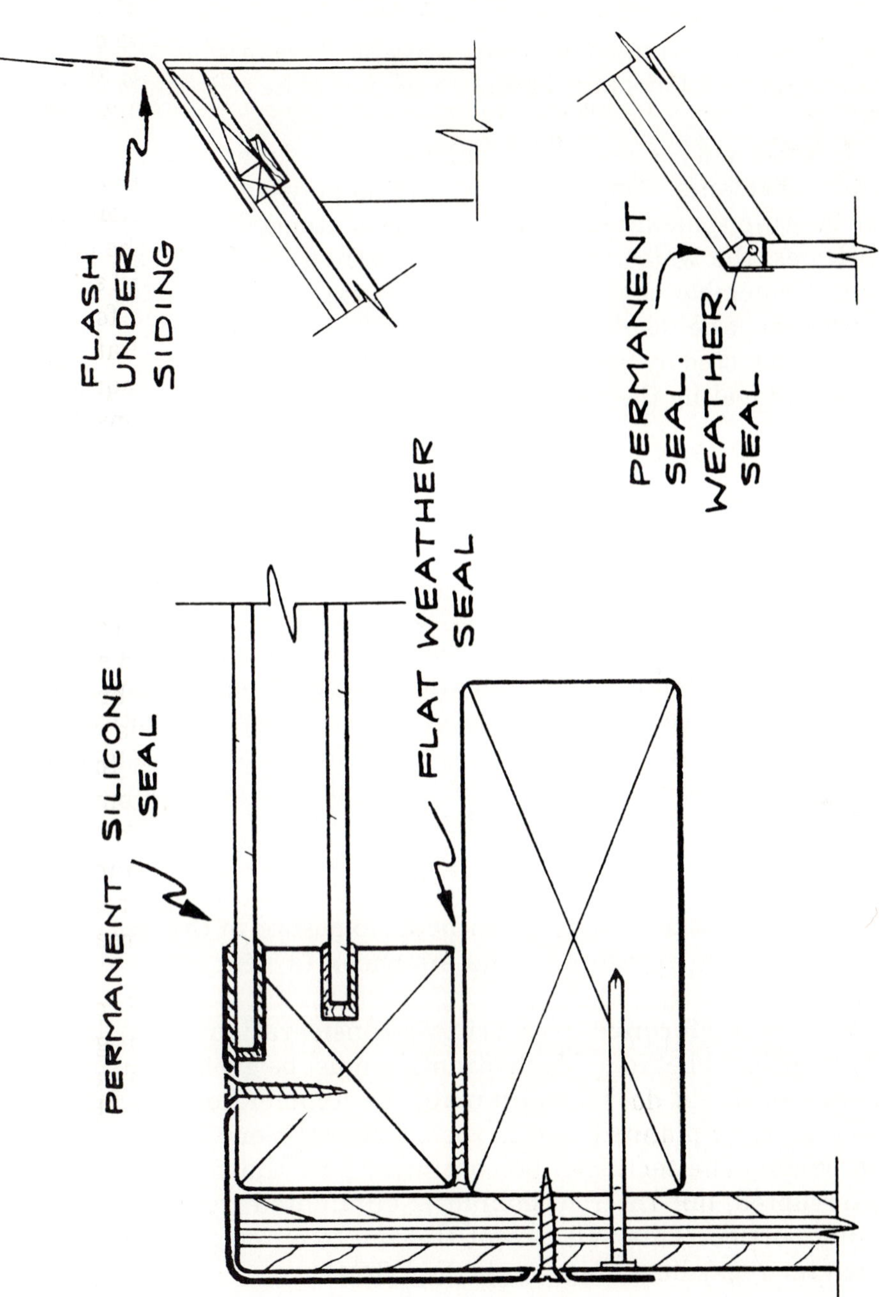

Figure 3-22 The glassed cover of a solar water heater must be as weather-tight and airtight as possible to retain both water and air heat around the tank. (a) The flashing is semi-permanently attached to the glazed-frame sides and lower edge. A rubber, or vinyl, gasket renders the glass top removable for cleaning and maintenance. (b) Top and side section views. The rubber seal surrounds the opening between the window frame and the breadbox sloping top.

height may be arranged side by side. Regardless of position, the multiple tank arrangement still presents a choice of series or manifold (parallel) hookup similar to the flat plate roof heater (Fig. 3-23).

Bypass valves and inline valves are useful at repair times, flushing incidents, and at times when one may want to drain the solar heating system and leave it empty (extended vacations). At such times, the water is channeled directly to the fuel-fed water heater. Remember that any supply pipes exposed to freezing temperature must be insulated and protected with heat tapes. A heat tape can be tested by placing the thermostat bulb in a refrigerator freezer and feeling the tape for signs of heat.

VERTICAL INTEGRAL SOLAR WATER HEATER

Aesthetics are frequently a roadblock to efficiency systems. So it is with the breadbox. Some folks would rather pay the difference to just not have that funny-looking thing protruding from the side of the house. There is an alternative. A vertical box is practical if it can be oriented to enough exposure. There are many places where it can be designed into a new house plan. On a south-facing wall, it can be incorporated into the end of a closet that meets the wall at right angles. A house so situated that a corner is pointed toward the south is another good candidate. The heater is built into the corner and receives a southeast exposure in the morning and a southwest exposure in the afternoon (a very efficient arrangement).

Eave interference is a critical consideration with these types of enclosed heaters. Much attention must be given to an eave overhang so that it does not eliminate the summer heating potential. A carefully planned void in the overhang is one way to treat the problem. The facia can be continued past the collector area uninterrupted, but the roof behind is eliminated from the overhanging portion. This will permit the sun to enter both summer and winter regardless of its angle (Fig. 3-24).

An integral solar air collector is described and illustrated in Part 4. It is a design that can be installed at the time the house is being framed. It is also possible to build this collector as an add-

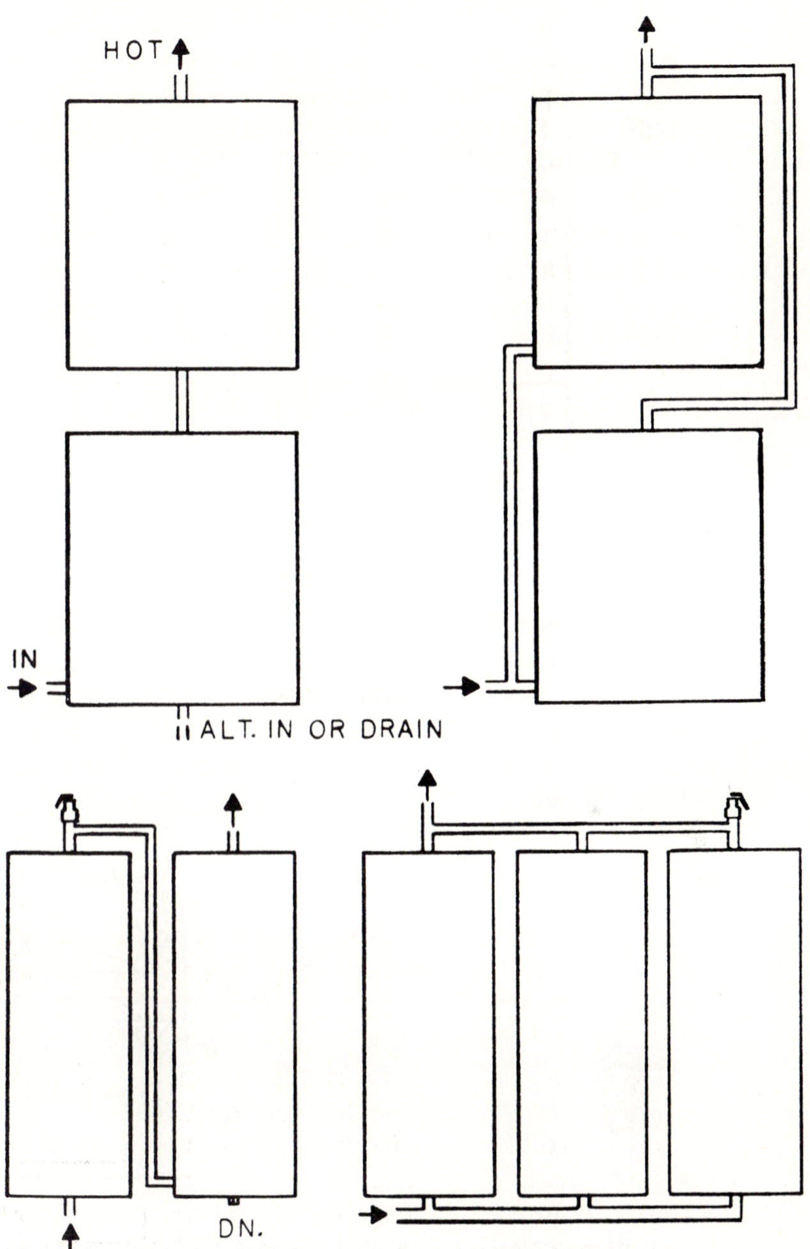

Figure 3-23 (a) Vertical and horizontal tank arrangements in series. (b) The top diagram is in parallel arrangement. The bottom diagram is the manifold system. All of these setups will drain down by use of a plug in the bottom or a drain valve in the intake pipe.

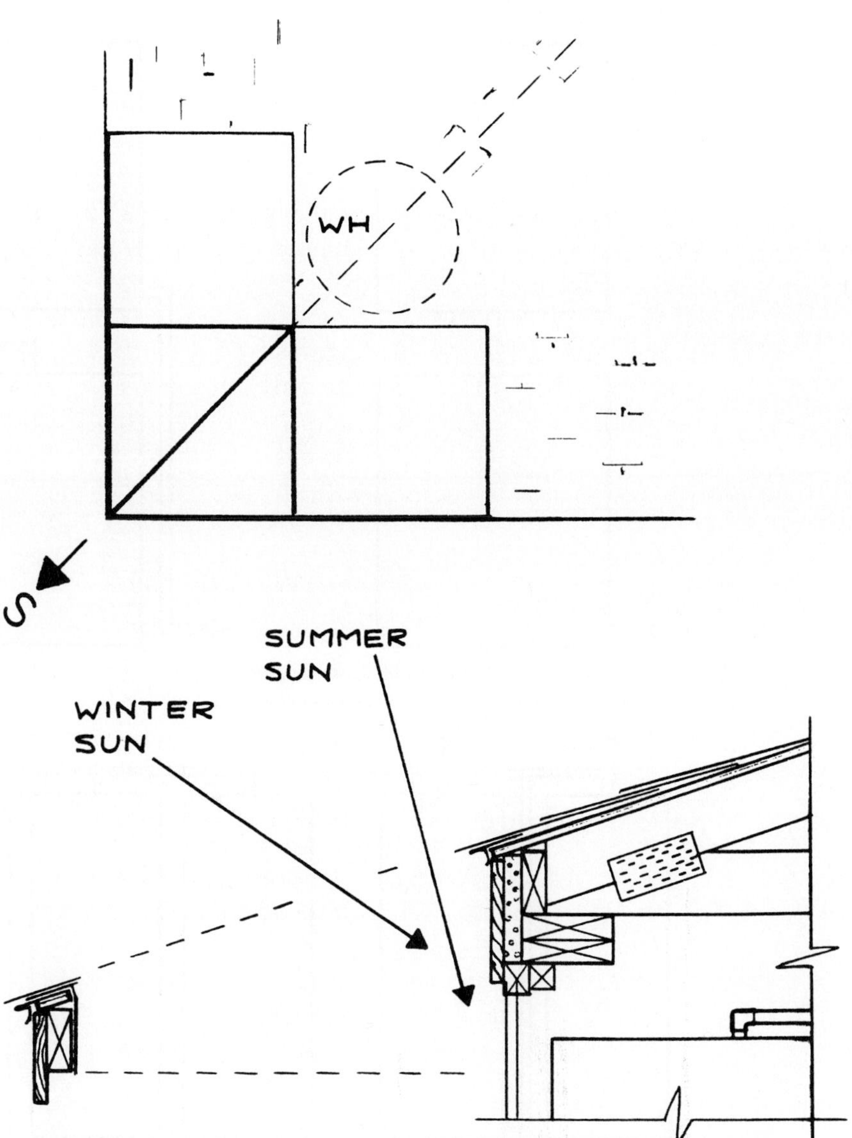

Figure 3-24 (a) A top view diagram of an exposed hip roof overhang. All exposed top and side surfaces (rafter tails) should be weather protected with shingles or flashing. (b) A section view showing the added sunshine exposure gained by the technique.

on box collector at minimum cost using locally available and non-sophisticated materials.

EFFICIENCY CONCEPT

Like the other forms of conservation construction, solar use will only reach a point of efficiency when an overall concept is adopted. Like a boat that leaks, it will only be moderately successful unless all the elements affecting the whole are considered and dealt with in the initial design. Things—such as proper orientation to the sun, complete and adequate full-house insulation without voids and leaks, and proper doors and windows—are all integrated, vital parts of a solar system's success.

REVIEW TOPICS

1. Explain how solar rays are beneficial even on cloudy days. How does the absorption rate compare to sunny days?
2. Describe the differences between an "active" and a "passive" solar system. State the advantages and disadvantages of both.
3. Explain the necessity for a discharge-venting system when windows or collectors are used to heat a house.
4. Explain the importance of a proper eave overhang to the successful use of solar heat. What is the ideal length of the eave for any location?
5. Describe the characteristic shape of a "greenhouse" collector.
7. Tilted window glass is most efficient for collecting solar heat to the interior environment. Despite this optimum feature, slanted glass has given way to vertical glass for a number of reasons. Discuss these reasons.
8. Explain how a reflective surface can add appreciably to solar intake. Tell about the different types, what they are made of, and how they are positioned for effectiveness.
9. What is a "greenbelt"? What problem exists with an improperly coordinated greenbelt?
10. Discuss the advantages and disadvantages of a heat storage bin (sump).

11. Explain how a masonry storage wall can be designed to move hot air into the living area and return cool air to the solar side of the wall, actively and passively.

12. State the best mediums for storing heat and list them in descending order.

13. What is a trombe wall? Where is it likely to be used (constructed on a house)?

14. Domestic hot water ranks next to full house heating as a utility cost in conventional fuel heated homes. Discuss several measures that can be taken to hold down the cost of domestic hot water in a house of this type.

15. Explain how at least one of the types of passive solar water heaters works and how it can be built.

16. Explain how to install a roof-mounted collector. Cover all the aspects of securing the legs to the roof and flashing the bases.

17. Describe fully a "breadbox" solar water heater. Include an explanation of different tank arrangements.

18. Explain how an integral solar water heater can be designed and built into the corner of a house. Comment on the orientation of the house and the eave overhang treatment.

Part 4

Super Energy-Saving House Design

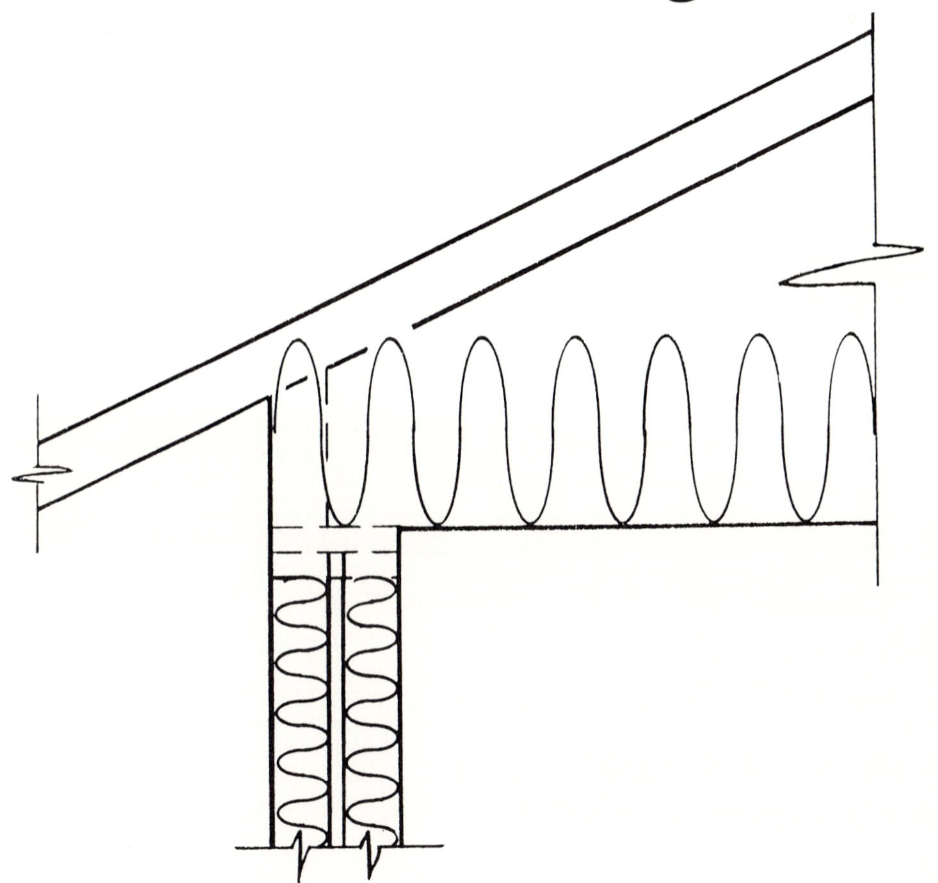

15 THE DOUBLE-WALL FRAME

The double wall, as designed by the author, is comprised of two wall frames, each made from 2 × 4 studs. The walls sandwich a ¾″ core of 1 × 4 diagonal and horizontal braces and spacer blocks. The headers are a unique design. The system is copyrighted against graphic reproduction but may be used in construction by a builder. Structurally, the framework is much stronger and more rigid than a conventionally framed single wall. The reader will readily see why as the descriptions unfold.

DOUBLE-WALL SECTION VIEW

A cross section is probably the best graphic view with which to begin the understanding of the double-wall conception (Figs. 4-1 and 4-2). From the sole plate to the top plate, there are subtle differences from a conventional wall frame. Basically, the double wall is comprised of two single walls attached together to form a nominal 8″ exterior wall frame. Placed on top of an AWWF (all-

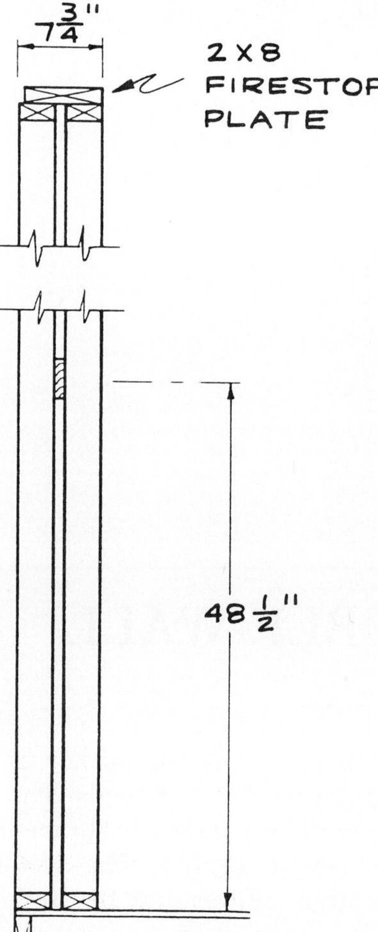

Figure 4-1 A double-stud wall, the heart of the system.

weather wood foundation), this plan provides an integrated energy-conservation model that can be constructed by family and small team builders (Fig. 4-3). With an exposed south basement wall, the house may be nearly independent of the need for fossil fuels when solar collection is used.

Sole plates of the double wall are conventional 2 × 4s. A small, nominal 1″ block is placed between the plates every 2 to 4′ as nailing progresses on the sole of the inside wall component. The purpose of this gauge is to maintain a uniform depth at the base of the wall. The block is placed on edge or end with its ¾″ thickness separating the soles. It is merely a spacer and is removed after the sole is nailed at any point.

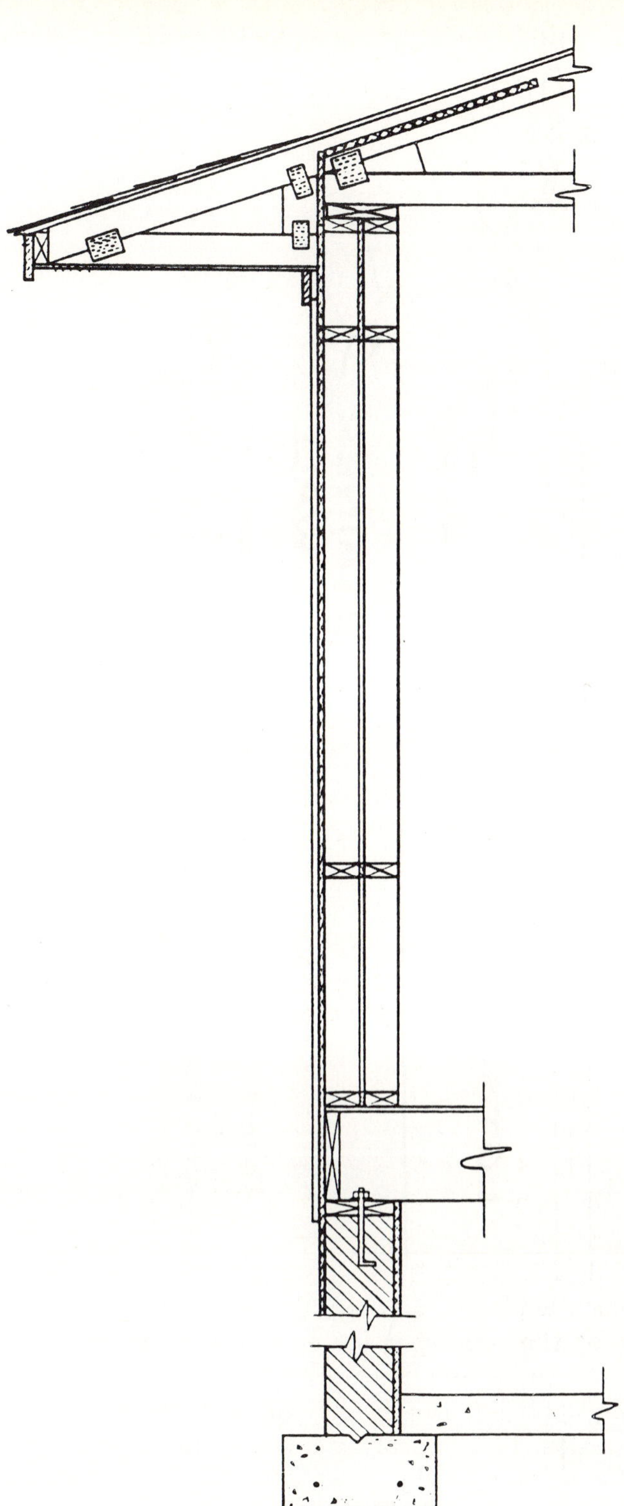

Figure 4-2 A full double wall section view with a conventional foundation.

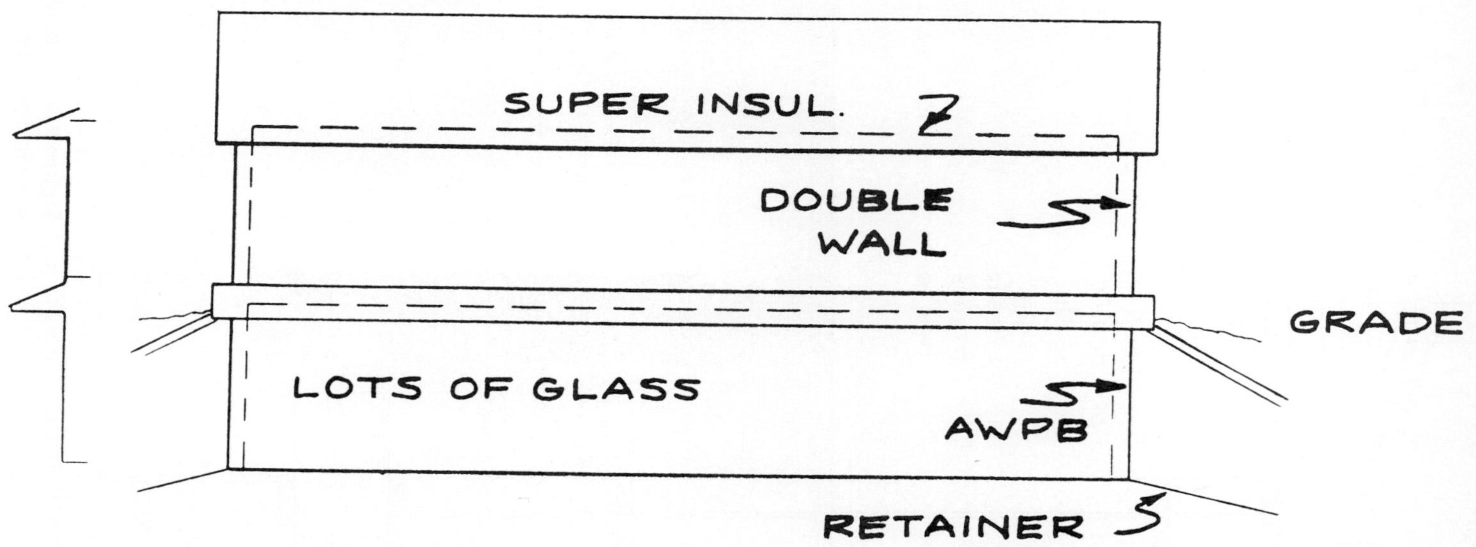

Figure 4-3 An optimum combination of systems for a conventional-appearing house contains the AWWF system for the lower story and the double-walled, super-insulated design for the grade level story with the two-story exposed side facing south.

Rough window sills (Fig. 4-4) are comprised of a single 2 × 4 in each wall segment. This creates two pieces at each window on a common horizontal plane with each other. There is never a need for double sills in the conventional stacked manner. Therefore, no more material is expended in a double-wall rough sill than in a single wall with double rough sills. The double-wall rough sill varies only in that the two pieces are side by side instead of stacked.

Window and door headers are a complete departure from the conventional uniform double 2 × 12 type. The header is a hybrid of a plywood boxed header. It is boxed in the shape of an I-beam. The surrounding framework is of the old cripple stud type with a flat 2 × 4 on the lower edge. A solid piece of ¾″ plywood is sandwiched between the frames (Fig. 4-5). It is cut to a 12¾″ height. The header is sandwiched between the lower member of the upper plate, the surrounding studs, the lower flat 2 × 4 nailer, and the OC cripple studs (Fig. 4-6). It fills the space normally occupied by a double 2 × 12 (11¼″) plus an additional 1½″ of height

Figure 4-4   The rough opening is spaced apart with a 1 × 2 surround nailed to the outer wall before raising the inner wall. (Courtesy John C. Frost.)

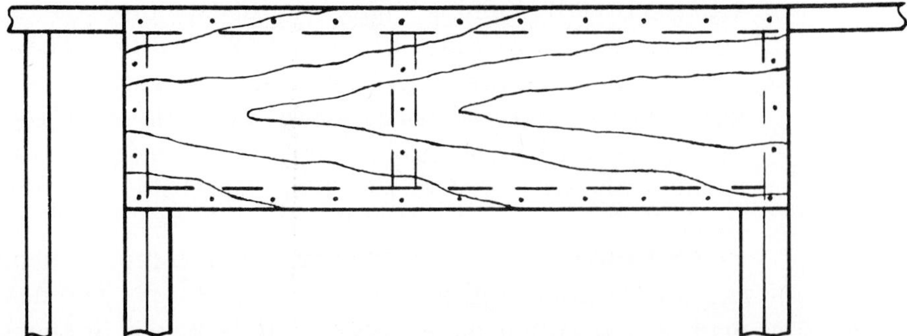

Figure 4-5 The plywood-sandwiched headers are glued and nailed to the interior side of the outer walls before the interior walls are erected.

where it goes up between the lower half of the double top plate (Fig. 4-7). A conventional 2 × 12 header is 3″ longer than the rough opening, as it bears on top the 1½″-thick trimmer stud on each end. The plywood header in the double wall is 6″ longer than the rough opening width of the window or door (Fig. 4-8). Its ends are sandwiched between the full-length stud posts of the opening framework. Note the section view in Fig. 4-6. This hybrid header will carry any conventional roof load to a span of 8′.

Headers over 8′ and up to 12′ can be designed and built as a combination I-beam and box beam. In addition to the sandwiched plywood, a plywood header is glued and nailed to the exterior in place of sheathing over the opening. The design may use vertical cripples in the boxed part or it may incorporate diagonal-bridging-type webs (Fig. 4-8). The plywood pieces will have end joints when

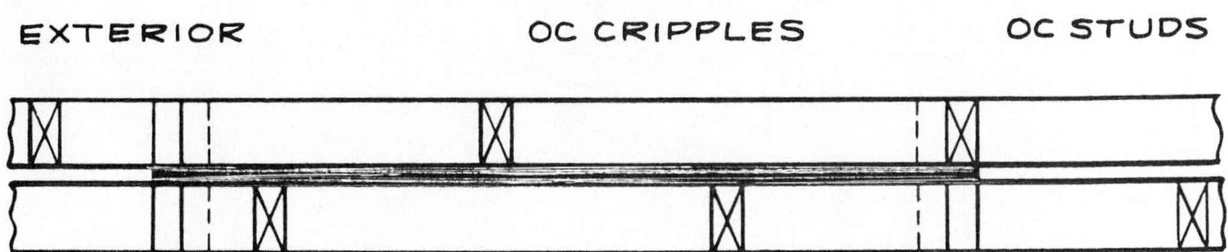

Figure 4-6 A top view of the sandwiched header before the top piece of the double plate is installed.

INNER FRAME IN PLACE

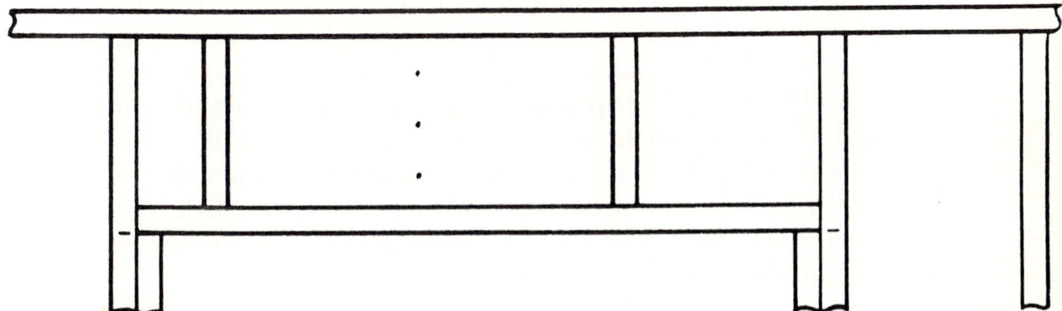

Figure 4-7 A face view of the sandwiched header. Note the invisible lines indicating that the header extends onto the full studs to which it is nailed and glued.

the header exceeds 8′ in length. The joint is purposely staggered so that the exterior ply joint is at the opposite end of the header ply joint. A 12′ header, for example, will have a vertical butt joint 4′ from one end of the sandwiched pieces. The plywood header on the exterior surface will have the joint toward the opposite end. Generally, spans from 8 to 12′ may be carried on boxed headers

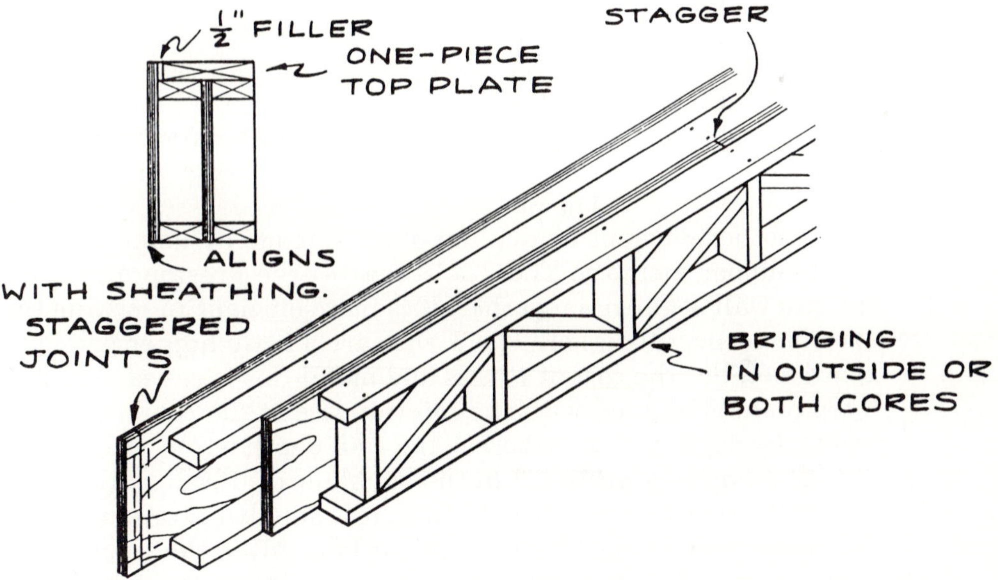

Figure 4-8 A header-boxing technique for headers over 8′ long.

as described, which have only cripple studs in the core. From 12 to 16′ the box should hold well-fitted cripples and bridgework. Beyond these lengths and for exceptional loads, an engineered design should be sought.

The double top plate (Fig. 4-9) may be made in a conventional manner with two 2 × 4s on each of the walls. If constructed in this manner, a 1 × 2 continuous spacer strip will be required around the perimeter of the exterior wall. It is flush with the top surface of the double plate sandwiched between the two walls. Its purpose is nonstructural. It is required as a firestop.

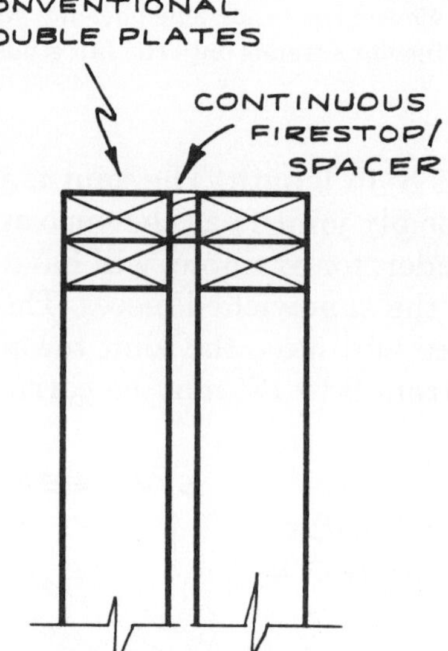

Figure 4-9 Conventional top plates on a double wall.

Another efficient double top plate is made by using a 2 × 8 for the upper member. The 2 × 8 creates the firestop and holds the two wall segments together. It is more efficient in locking the exterior corners together. The 2 × 8s are a little higher priced in board feet, but the cost of 1 × 2s and metal ties is saved. The 2 × 8 top plate is aligned with the interior face of the combined wall frame. Its depth is 7¼″, whereas the wall depth is 7¾″ (Fig. 4-10).

Bracing is simplified in the double wall. Because the bracing forms a core between the frames, it is simply surface nailed to the inside face of the exterior wall frame. After the inside wall frame is raised, the existing braces are nailed to the studs from the outside. If desired, a 1 × 4 horizontal band may be installed

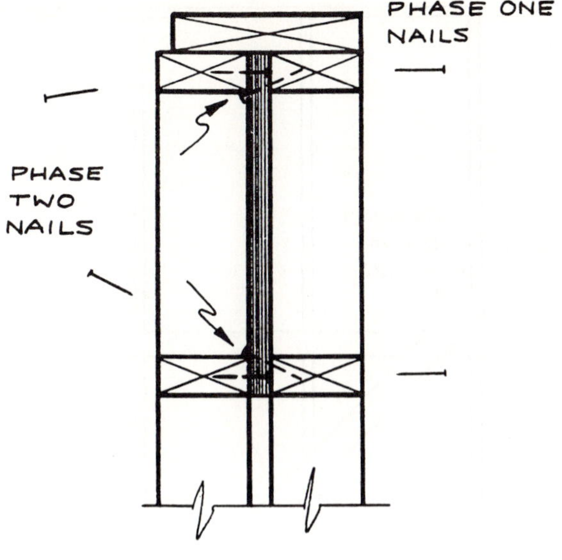

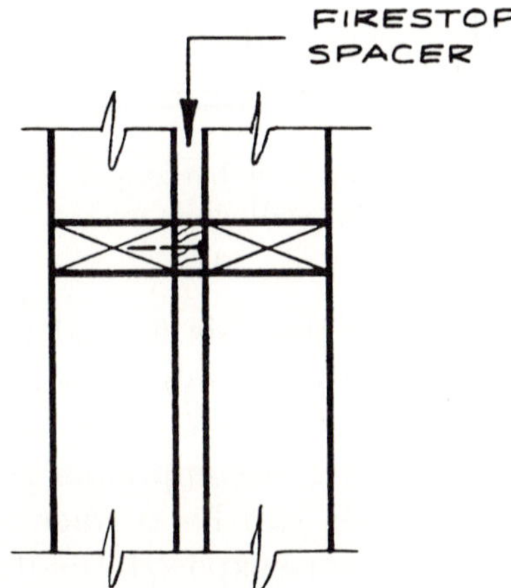

Figure 4-10 A 2 × 8 top piece on the double plate provides the cross-tie and firestop function.

between the inner and outer frame (Fig. 4-11). It is placed 4′ above the floor level. The band serves several good purposes. It stiffens the studs. It holds them in perfect alignment (plumb, straight, and correctly spaced). It ties the inner and outer walls together to form a superbly strong wall.

Studs in the double-wall design may be placed farther apart. Both the inner and outer wall frames will have their studs on 24″ spacing centers. The studs are staggered from one frame

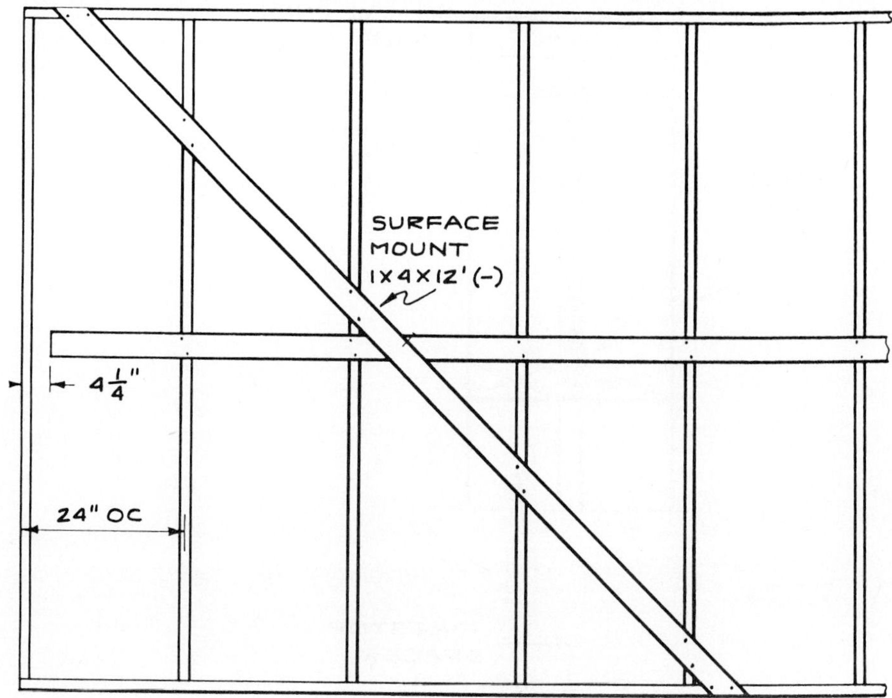

Figure 4-11 Diagonal wind bracing and horizontal spacer bracing is nailed to the inner surface of the outer wall while making the wall plumb.

to the other so that, in reality, there is a stud every foot (Fig. 4-12). The exterior studs are on even-numbered spacing (0, 2, 4, 6, 8', and so on). The inside frame studs are spaced at 1, 3, 5, 7, 9', and so on. The staggered formation accomplishes several positive objectives. The braces and bands can be surface nailed to both walls, since the nailing locations are exposed. Insulating blankets in each wall are staggered, which breaks up potential infiltration spots (no cold electric outlets). Wiring requires little or no drilling, as the wires are simply passed between the walls.

MATERIAL SAVINGS

A theme of quality in both material and workmanship has run through this book. It may seem strange at this point to receive advice advocating the purchase of cheaper materials. The case in

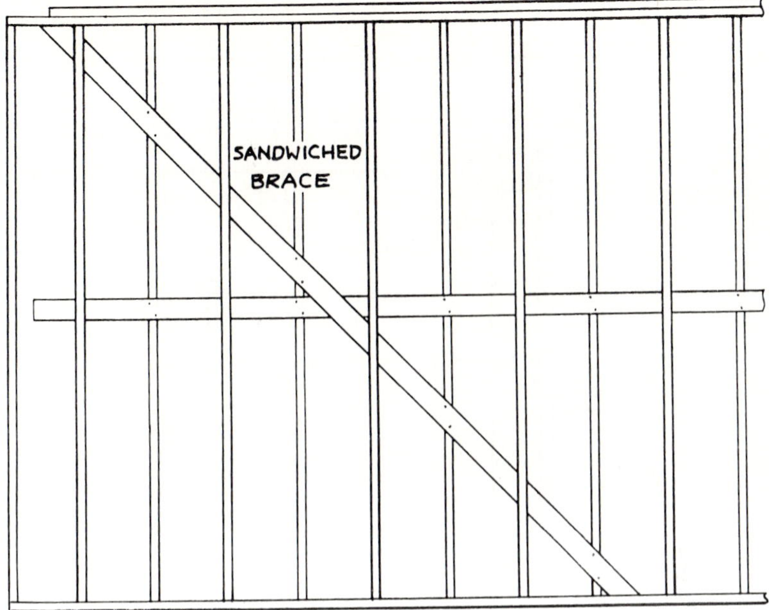

Figure 4-12 Braces, sandwiched between inner and outer walls, accommodate open-surface nailing due to their staggered stud formation.

point does exist with the double-wall design. The author was pleasantly surprised to find that studs costing as much as 40% less than others could be used successfully in the double-wall frame. It would seem logical that making two walls would cost twice what one wall would cost. It does not come out that way. The wider spacing (24″ instead of 16″) saves a stud in each 4′ of linear wall. The outer wall does not require extra studs to form internal backing corners at intersections or corners of the external walls. A small square block centered behind the braces connects the inner and outer wall and provides rigidity (Fig. 4-13). Another 3½″ × 3½″ block may be placed at the bottom on top of the sole and a third block at the top if desired, although they are not essential. In the final accounting, after a track record of several pilot houses, it was concluded that the only excess expenditure was the cost of additional insulation. Since the objective was to create the space for this least costly form of insulation (fiberglass blankets), the pay back was assured by advance planning. More rationale for the economy of the double-wall concept will follow as the construction technique is explained.

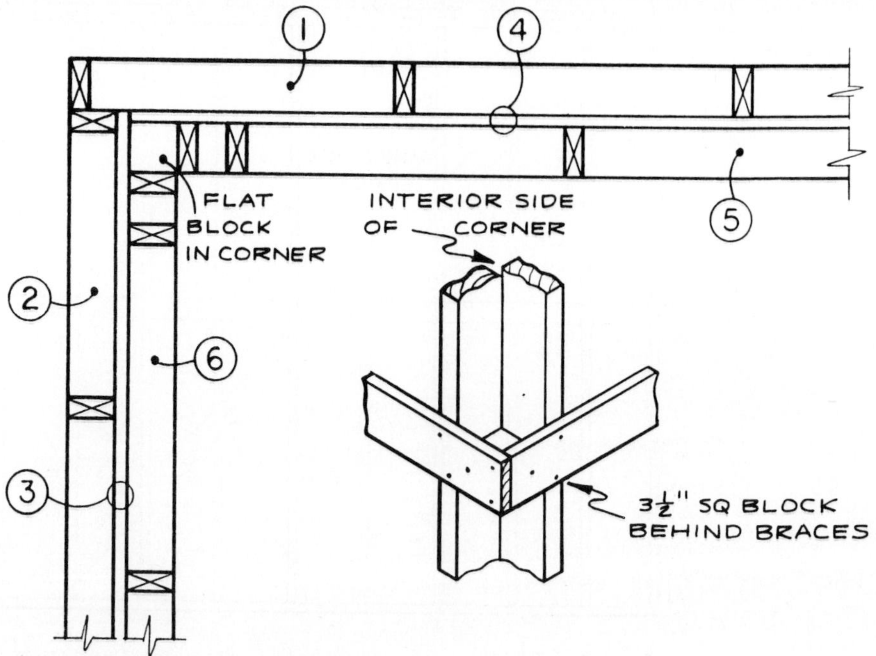

Figure 4-13 The top view section shows the corner and common stud positioning. The numbers indicate the assembly order.

DOUBLE-WALL FRAMING PROCEDURE

Phase 1 · The outer wall is constructed first. It is assembled on the floor adjacent to where it will be raised. Construction progresses as with a conventional wall with a few exceptions. Only one stud is placed at each end of the frame. All common studs are placed on 24″ centering. A window rough sill is made of one 2 × 4 only. A flat 2 × 4 is placed on top of the window and door trimmers. Between the lower top plate and this flat 2 × 4, a cripple stud will be put at each 24″ OC spacing mark. No second top plate or headers are installed yet. The frame wall is now raised, plumbed in two directions, and braced.

Phase 2 · Diagonal corner braces are nailed from the top corners to the sole. The preferred angle is 45°. A brace should not be steeper than 60°. Where a window or door interferes at a corner, the brace may be moved to the other side of the opening or a K brace used (Fig. 4-14). A 1 × 4 brace will have two 8d common or 8d coated nails placed into each stud. Offset the nails from the center-line of the stud so that they do not enter the stud in the same grain line. Place each nail at the farthest corner of the diagonal coverage over the stud Fig. 4-15. Aim the point of the nail toward the center axis of the stud. At the sole and top plate, stay away from the ends of the brace at least 1″ to avoid splitting. Hold a straightedge along the flat vertical surface of the stud when setting the first nail. Push the stud to the straightedge. A 6′ level is a good tool for this purpose. Do not squeeze the level and stud together, however, as this will bend the level and not accomplish the purpose of fixing the stud in a straight line. Check the spacing at 4′ above the floor after the brace is nailed. Each stud should be centered on 24″. It may be wise to recheck the plumbness of the corner before commencing this permanent bracing, to avoid polarizing a wall full of parallel but bowed studs.

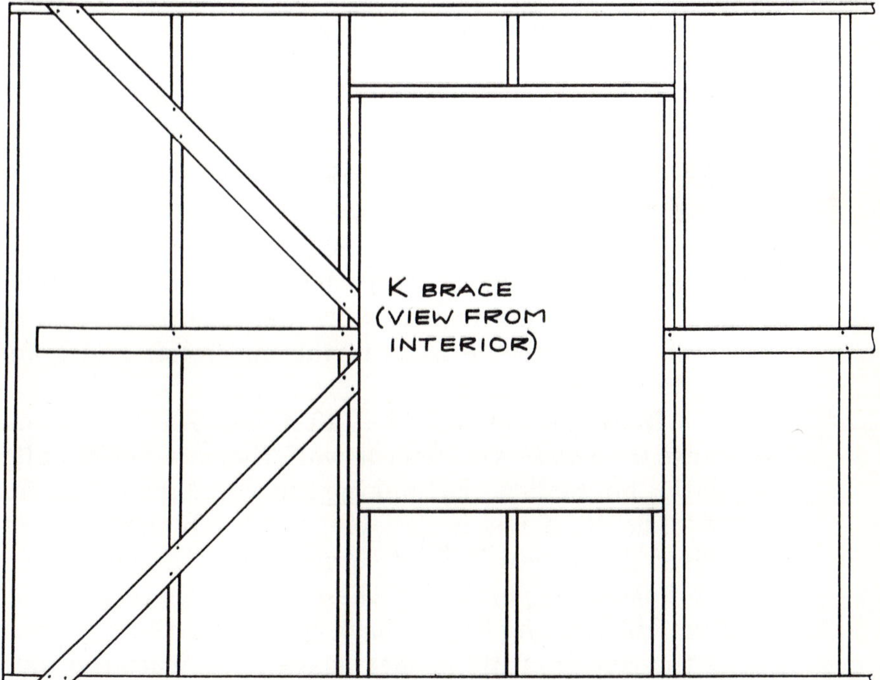

Figure 4-14 This K-brace is shown looking out from the interior.

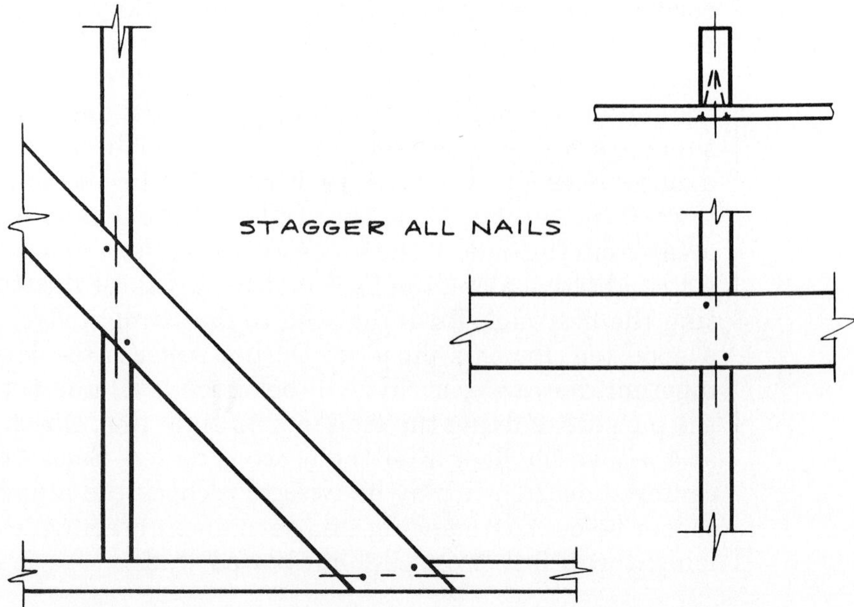

Figure 4-15 Proper nail angle and position are important to satisfactory bracing.

Next, nail the bands across the studs halfway up the studs (Fig. 4-16). Strike a chalk line where the top edge of the board should be. Strike the line from where the board will start to where it will end. Cut the end of the band at an angle to butt against the diagonal corner brace. Nail the ends first. Pull each bowed stud into straightness, testing with a straightedge, and nail through the band. Place the nails in the upper left and lower right segments of the coverage.

Headers are installed after the bracing is completed. Because the headers stiffen the wall, they are not installed while the wall is on the floor. By making the wall rigid on the floor, it would be difficult, if not impossible, to plumb the frame after it was raised. Set a nail in each corner of the ¾″ plywood header. Hold the header in place. Tap these four nails in only far enough to form an indexing hole at each corner. Mark an up-pointing arrow in the center of the header board to indicate the top edge. From the exterior side of the frame, draw an outline with a pencil around all the rectangular openings covered by the header. In other words,

Figure 4-16 Braces are nailed to the core faces of both external and internal wall frames.

trace all around the 2 × 4s. This will outline all the areas where glue will be placed. Take the header board down. Place it in a horizontal position. Apply glue in a continuous bead on all contact areas that have been outlined (Fig. 4-17). Spread the glue with a finger or a small stick. Tube adhesive may be used in a caulk gun. When two workers are available, the other person will be applying glue to the faces of the 2 × 4s in the wall frame where the header will contact. Place the header back on the frame (Fig. 4-18). Seat the four nails in the indexing holes and drive them home. Place nails at 4″ intervals on all contact points. Seven or 8D coated or box nails are adequate with the glue system. Larger nails are detrimental spaced this close together because they split the 2 × 4s. This is a case for many small nails that contribute to

Figure 4-17 Apply glue to the frame surface that will be in contact with the plywood header and to the traced locations of these structural members on the header.

Figure 4-18 Headers being nailed to the inner face of an outer frame after the glue was spread.

an all-over contact of the plywood with the structural framing members.

Surrounds are nailed around all the window and door openings. Flush the edge of the 1 × 2 with the rough opening. These 1 × 2 fillers will be on the interior edge of the trimmers and the rough window sills (Fig. 4-19). Where a table saw is available, the least costly fabrication of these 1 × 2s is to rip them from utility-grade precut studs. Set the saw fence for a ¾″ cut. The stud will net four 1 × 2s at a cost considerably lower than that of mill-cut 1 × 2s.

Where double 2 × 4 top plates are to be used on both the inner and outer walls, the firestop 1 × 2 will be nailed on next. The uppermost 2 × 4 top plate will probably have already been installed while the wall was lying on the floor. The 1 × 2 may also be nailed to the top plate while it lies on the floor.

After all exterior-wall components have been assembled and raised, the inside frames of the double wall will be assembled. The layout of stud locations is different. The soles and top plates are

Figure 4-19 Surrounds are nailed around all sides of all openings to provide the firestop requirement.

cut to butt snugly against the edges of the erected frame spacers. Spacing for studs is then laid out at the midpoint between the outer wall studs. Hook the 100' tape measure to the building-line side of the outer wall. Make adjustments if the outer frame is inset. Mark all the odd-foot locations. Place two marks at each stud location. The marks will be ¾" before and ¾" after the odd-foot marks. For example, a mark is placed at 11¼ and 12¾", 35¼ and 36¾", 59¼ and 60¾", and so on. This places a stud midway between each of the outer frame studs, which are on 24" even numbers. Remember to take the sheathing thickness into consideration where the inset frame technique has been practiced.

Partition intersecting studs are placed in the inside frame only (Fig. 4-20). Also, the blocked double-corner stud will be required on the inside frame only. A full stud can be saved at the corner by use of 3½ × 3½" 2 × 4 squares instead of three blocks and an extra stud. As shown in Fig. 4-21, a block is placed on the sole in the corner. Another is placed under the top plate. A third square block is placed midway up the corner behind the studs. Since these blocks are trapped behind the corner studs, only one 10d box nail is needed to hold them to the plates. The center block is held with one nail through each corner stud and a small nail through the end of each brace.

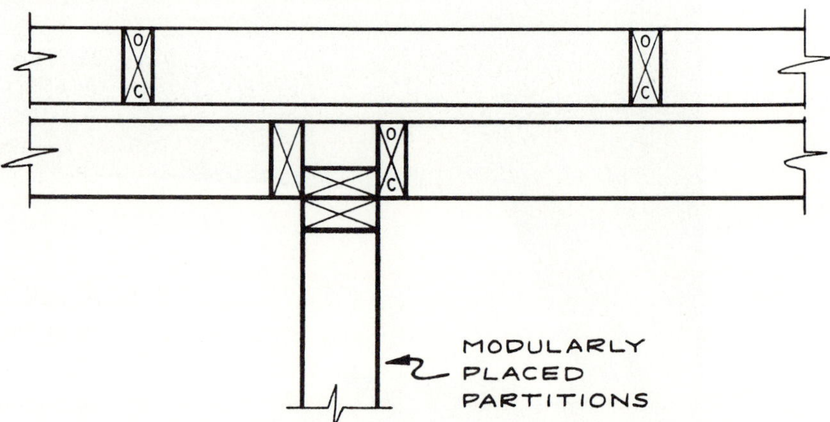

Figure 4-20 Partition intersection studs are integrated with the inner frame only. This eliminates any possibility of lost heat by conduction and leaves the outer frame stud space open for full insulation.

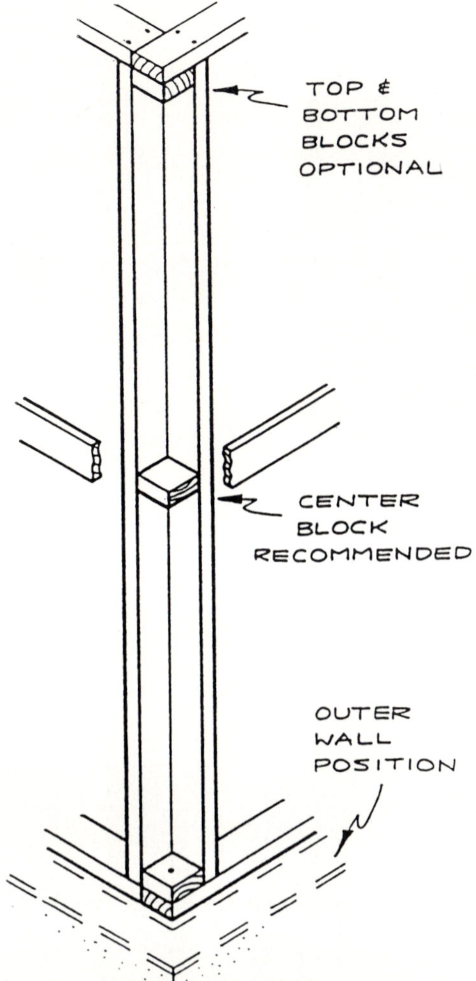

Figure 4-21 This view of the exterior side of the inner wall frame exposes the little blocks that may be used to tie the corner studs together in proper alignment.

Raise the wall frames in an order that will interlace the corners. For example, raise the two end frames of the outer walls first. Second, raise the long outer walls. Follow this same order with the inner walls. The corners will be interlaced as seen in Fig. 4-22.

Nailing the sole is perfected with the use of a couple of 1″ gauge blocks (¾″ thick; Fig. 4-23). Cutoffs from a brace will serve. A chalk line is snapped on the floor where the interior edge of the sole will be. Use the gauges between the soles where the nail is

Figure 4-22 Raising the inner frame in sequence.

being driven to prevent the sole from being driven closer to the outer wall than it should be. If the outer wall curves in, do not parallel and reproduce the error. Omit the block and lay to the chalk line. Any gross error in the outer wall should be corrected.

Figure 4-23 Sole plates are gauged apart with little 1″ nominal (3/4″) blocks until nailed permanently to a chalk line.

Drive each nail over, and anchored into, a floor joist. Since the joists are on 16″ centers and the common studs are on odd-numbered 24″ centers, there will be no studs over the joists in the inner wall. On the other hand, there will be joists under every other stud in the outer frame, those which are on 4′ modules. This knowledge helps locate joists quickly. Added to the visible joints in the ends of the modular sheathing, which tells where a joist is, there remain only the 16″ intermediate joist locations, which can be identified quickly with a tape measure or framing square tongue.

Frames with double 2 × 4 top plates will benefit by having metal ties across the top plates. A small sheet metal tie can be snipped from band iron, or ties can be purchased for the purpose. Place a string line along the inner or outer plate. Space it out away from the plate with an equal-thickness block at each end. Bring the plate with the string line into perfect straightness and secure it with braces to the floor. Interior bracing from the top plate of the outer wall, which is holding the wall plumb, will not interfere with the construction and raising of the inner wall because the stud centering is staggered. The braces will be between the studs of the second inner wall. The inner frame is assembled around the braces and simply straddles them as it is being raised. Use a bar clamp across the tops of the upper plates to close any gap between the inner and outer plates. Put on the metal tie to hold the plates together at any point required. *Place each tie at a location that is not over a stud* in the outer wall frame. The roof trusses will be resting over these studs.

Installing an upper top plate of 2 × 8 girth removes the need for ties. Each 2 × 8 plate board must have one straight edge. Saw, plane, or joint it straight. Line up the straight edge of each plate board with the interior edge of the inner wall. This board will not completely cover the double wall. The 2 × 8 is 7¼″ wide. The wall is 7¾″ deep. The disparity is unimportant as long as the inside is made flush. The resulting ½″ inset on the exterior side will be up under the plancier, where it is of no significance. In fact, it can be made functional by nailing ½″ ply-sheath insulation stops to it.

Cutouts may be made in the 2 × 8 at each partition intersection (Fig. 4-24). The cutout will be 3½″ × 3½″ to accept the upper member of the interior partition top plate. The cross-lap tying function is thereby accommodated. To locate the partition

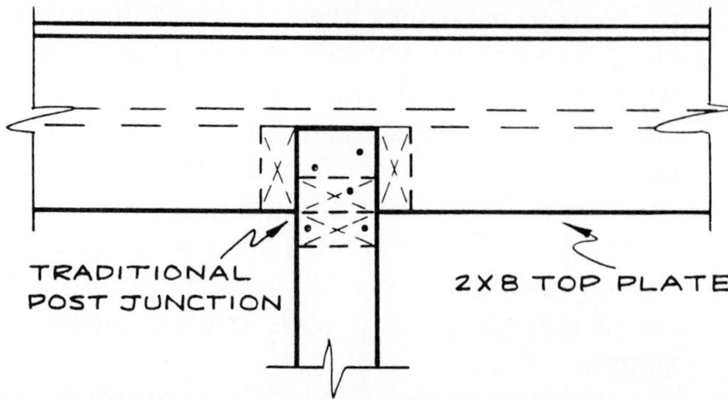

Figure 4-24 A 2 × 8 top plate may be notched as a means of tying the 2 × 4 top plate member of the intersecting partition.

cutout, the 2 × 8 plate is put in place and temporarily tacked with a couple of nails. The location of a cutout is marked by projecting lines up from the partition blocks found in the partition post below. Occasionally, these partition locking cutouts are overlooked until after the 2 × 8 plates are nailed down. This poses no serious problem. A small sheet metal tie is nailed over the intersection to substitute for the usual crosslap interlock joint (Fig. 4-25). The sheet metal tie may be used routinely. Some builders prefer the metal tie method. It takes less time, and there is no possibility of misaligning a notch.

Nail the 2 × 8 plate at 1′ intervals, staggering from the outer

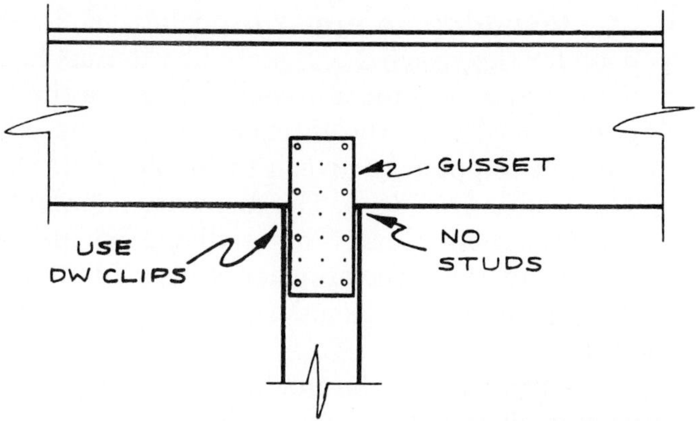

Figure 4-25 The partition plate may be butted against the wall and secured with a metal gusset.

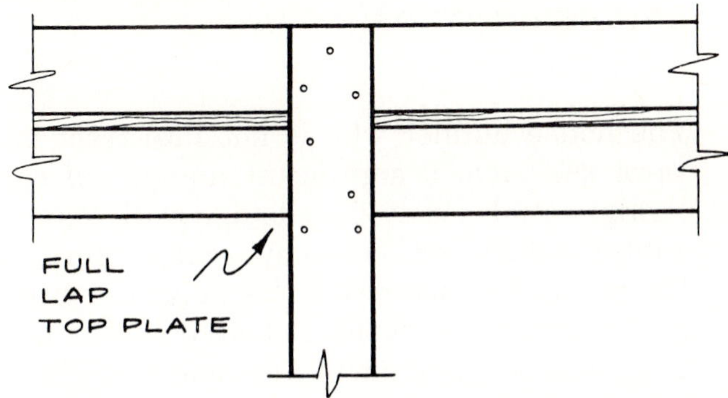

Figure 4-26 The top partition plate should run through and be fastened to both conventional 2 × 4 top plates of the double wall.

to inner plates below. 10d nails are adequate and will not penetrate through. Visualize the corner joints underneath the 2 × 8 so that nails are driven into effectual wood and not on top of other nails that are in the lower half of the double plate. The front and rear top plates may be allowed to extend beyond the end walls to support the birdbox cornice work.

Should the plate of preference be the traditional doubled 2 × 4 on both inner and outer frame, the top partition plate should run through to the outer wall (Fig. 4-26) or be metal strapped clear to the outer wall (Fig. 4-27), thereby sustaining the perpendicular brace of both frames.

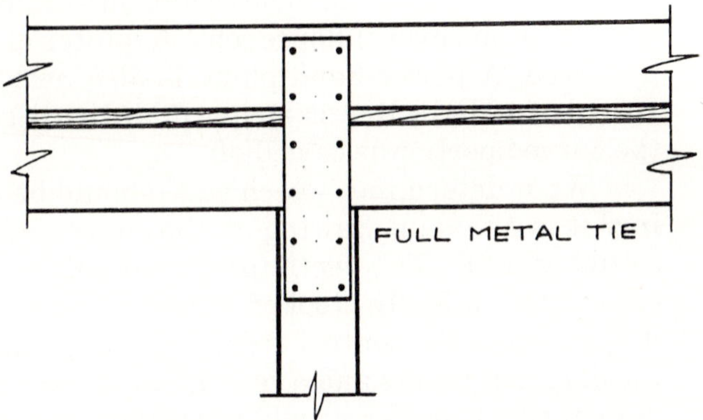

Figure 4-27 A butted partition should be tied to both inner and outer top plates of the double wall when conventional plates are used.

SALVAGING STUDS

The house builder who is not into tract building or production work can save a significant amount of cost by machining unstraight studs for use in a double wall. Many number three graded studs ("utility" or "economy") can be purchased at about one half the price of number two ("structural") studs. Most of the lower-grade studs are warped. A bowed stud is not a problem, as it can be pulled into alignment and held straight with the sheathing. A crooked stud is a problem. A crooked stud is curved on its edge. This characteristic will be found in the better studs to some extent, but is more prevalent in the lower-grade studs. When the curvature is greater than ⅛″, the stud should not be used in a wall frame. The soft sheathings currently being used (blackboard, Styrofoam, and the like) exert no straightening effect on a crooked stud as shiplap boards and five-ply plywood sheathing once did.

A crooked stud can be used in a double wall by straightening either the concave or the convex edge. Machine off an equal depth amount from each end of the concave edge, as shown in Fig. 4-28 C. The convex edge can be straightened, but more wood will usually be removed, as the taper cut cannot be controlled accurately. In the double wall, only one straight edge is required of each stud. The curved edge is faced toward the core. A brace is not nailed tight if it crosses a stud at a narrowed point.

Straightening a convex or concave edge can be done by sawing or jointing. The typical construction job is not likely to boast a long bed jointer. The cost of one could be justified with the savings from several house jobs. A jointer of ½″-depth capacity is preferred. A power hand plane is also usable. To saw the board straight, a chalk line is snapped on the edge of your choice and the curved portion is sawed off.

What determines which edge should be straightened by sawing? It is a toss-up. Sawing off the convex edge leaves the ends of a stud at a full 3½″ depth (preferred nailing-end surface). On the other hand, a badly crooked stud will be materially narrowed as it approaches the central area. This complicates the application of the diagonal braces and a central horizontal spacer band. The convex cut side is preferred where no band or diagonal brace is nailed to both inner and outer walls as with deeper wall cavities. Where a band is used and both wall frames are secured together, it is

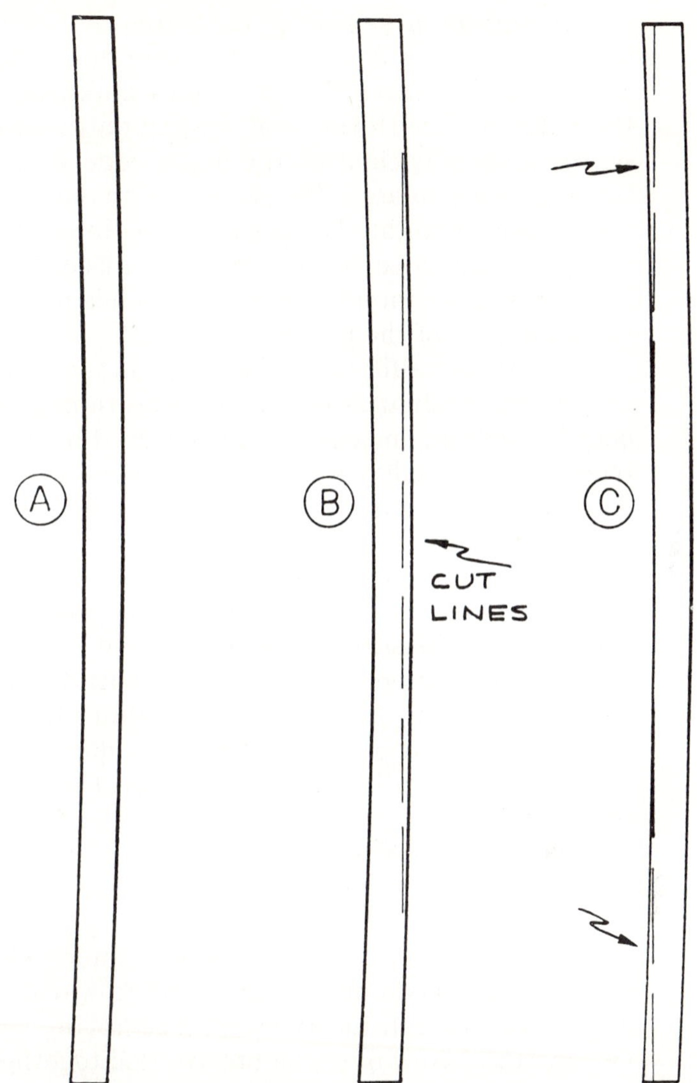

Figure 4-28 (a) A crooked stud may be straightened on one edge only and used in a double wall. (b) Crown-cut method. (c) Preferred concave edge. Trim equally from each end (exaggerated for graphic emphasis).

better to leave the central stud area at full depth by cutting the concave edge of the stud to form a straight edge. The latter will reduce the ends to less than $3\frac{1}{2}''$ in depth. This undersizing is of no consequence, as it will be on the inner core of the double frame.

Avoid misassembling the studs that are machined straight on one edge by indexing the straightened side with large coded crayon marks. Three Xs a foot apart make a good code. Assemble the outer wall with the studs placed on the floor *with the Xs up.* At the ends of each stud, the upper edge is nailed flush with the top edge of the plates. This produces an outer wall surface that is adequately straight. The studs for the inner wall are placed *with the marks down* so that when it is raised, the true surface will face toward the interior. These stud ends must line up flush with the underside of the plates.

Another malformed warp shape is the *twisted* stud. This propeller-type configuration can also be remedied by jointing. The board is started on edge on the jointer at a central point. The protruding angled edge is jointed off in a series of passes. The board is then reversed, end for end, and the same relative edge is leveled on the remaining end. One final pass on the newly planed edge produces a straight surface. All alignment pressure on the board with the hands is directed toward the jointer tables (infeed and outfeed). No pressure is exerted against the fence. The only true surface, the jointed edge, is marked with the code Xs. This rectified stud can only be used in the field of the frame wall. It will cause problems if placed adjacent to a door or window opening or on the end of a wall or partition corner. Its use is limited to standing alone with no attached parts.

The remedial stud system may sound like a time-consuming nuisance. In reality, several hundred dollars can be saved in a few hours. The author is not suggesting that wood of an inferior structural quality be used. However, much of the stud material available has been downgraded due to warpage alone. Since the double-wall design incorporates a centering system equal to 12″ OC and the two wall segments are tied together into a structural unit, the structural strength is far in excess of the usual minimum stud girth requirement.

In addition to economy, a much straighter frame wall is produced both inside and outside. The crooked edges that remain on the straightened studs are toward the cavity of the wall, where they have no effect on the lines of the wall.

Superior vertical rigidity is a fringe benefit of the double wall. This feature is compelling in cyclone-, tornado-, and earthquake-prone areas of the country.

An aesthetic feature of note is the deep window sill area

Figure 4-29 The deep window sill that is common to the double wall lends a feeling of grandeur and strength to the interior.

(Fig. 4-29). It provides a potential shelf for flowers and knick-knacks. With a small extension, it adapts well to an attractive cushioned window seat. For those interested in heat retention, the deeper window cavity provides an ideal setting for various forms of intermittent insulating (day and night), such as the blown bead wall or the roller insulation blanket.

OTHER DOUBLE-WALL DESIGNS

There are several other double-wall designs being used which are meeting with good results in the quest for heat and coolness retention. One such assembly of the exterior wall is a direct spin-off from the old balloon framing design. It is so close that it actually provides a viable retrofit option for the restorer of an old historical house. If lost square footage is no great drawback, the interior face of the exterior walls is gutted. The old walls are insulated and a new inside wall is erected. The cavity can be made as deep as desired and filled with insulation (Fig. 4-30).

DOUBLE-WALL COORDINATES

The effectiveness of the double wall is directly proportionate to an overall coordinated design. A ludicrous example of misapplication would be to have single-glass windows in abundance on the north side of a double-wall house. Similarly, a single-panel uninsulated exterior door with or without an accompanying storm door poses a weak link in the concept. The concept of superinsulation for the purpose of maximum heat or coolness retention must be an all-systems philosophy. Anything else is like toting water from a faraway well using a bucket with a hole in it.

A problem of concern has been observed with family building and small budget projects. It is repeated too often to be considered insignificant. Basically, the person(s) responsible for the budget is interested in heating, cooling, and maintenance economy and is also prone to be very cost conscious during the construction phase. This can lead to inconsistency in the long-range plan. As the building progresses, the harsh reality of large-size bills mounting up creates a poor psychological climate. The builder becomes more cautious, wary, and even stingy. Unfortunately, the timing is critical. One example of false economy that frequently strikes is in the selection of windows. Cheap single-pane windows in metal frames can be the undoing of the whole superinsulation objective. Many windows are represented to the market as thermal type simply because two panes of glass are set in butyl rubber surrounded by a thin metal channel. This type of "thermalizing" does not compare in resistance with genuine hermetically sealed glass such as Thermopane. Obviously, double-glazed windows, as the rubber-set panes are termed by accurate describers, are more efficient than a single-pane window. The cost-saving gain, however, does not rank it as an optimum coordinate to accompany the double-walled frame concept. Inexpensive windows are only cost saving initially. After five years or so, they become a perpetual expense to the owner. The expense could have been a savings had the budget for good windows been adequate and sustained.

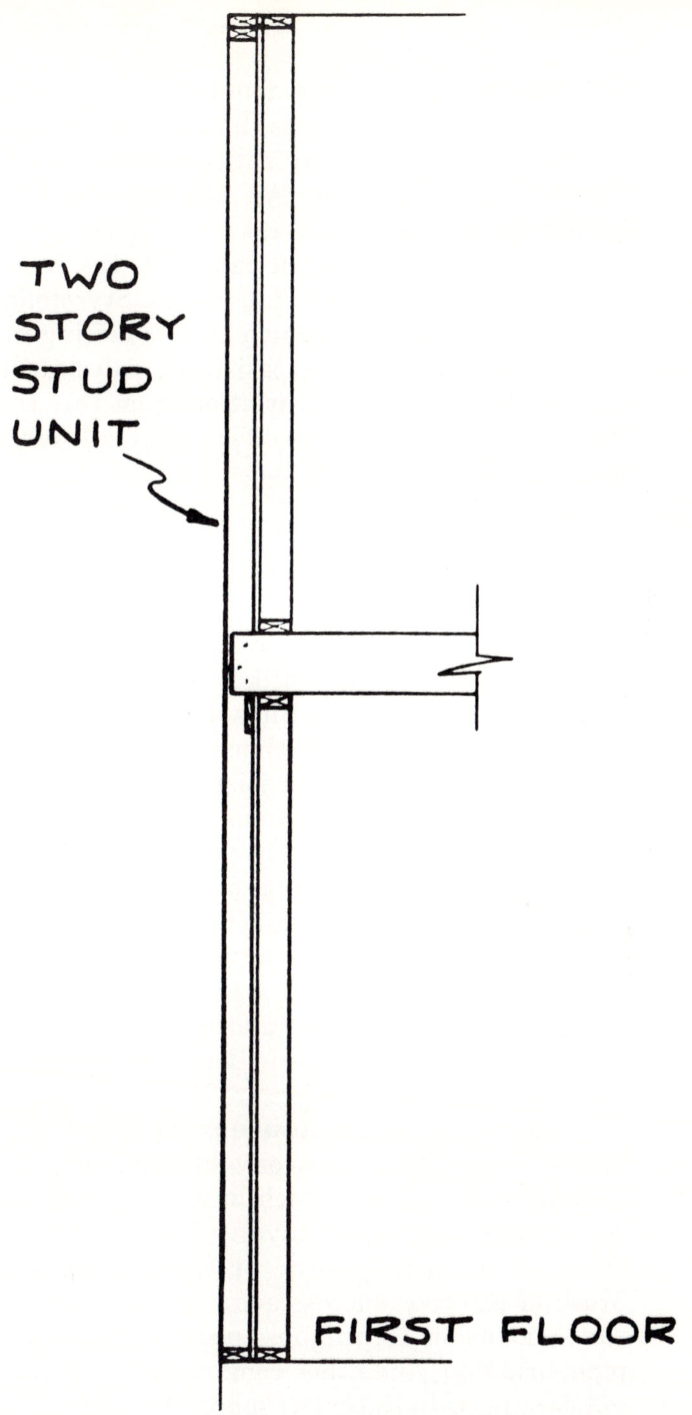

Figure 4-30 This two story, double-wall design is equally at home for new construction or for retrofitting an old balloon-framed house.

Whether a house is double- or single-walled, the heat- and coolness-retention features should be coordinated to form a logical balance. The insulation ratio between walls and ceiling, for example, is important. An old-style wall with noninsulating sheathing and 3½″ of blanket insulation (R-11) should have at least 6″ of insulation in the ceiling (R-18). A better-insulated wall, such as a blanketed 6″ frame with Styrofoam sheathing (about R-23), will profit significantly from a ceiling in the R-38 category. The ceiling should have a resistance value about 50% greater than that of the walls. Any variation from this theme will create an imbalance that is not cost effective. A rule of thumb proportion is: floor 1, wall 2, ceiling 3.

16 FLOOR INSULATION

Floor insulation seems to be a subject of little concern with builders and consumers alike. "Out of sight, out of mind" would seem to characterize feelings about this coordinate area of insulation philosophy. The author has been sandwiching 2″ of tightly fitted Styrofoam into floor-joist cavities for several years. On the first occasion, a utility company assessed the payback effectiveness on the first model at 18 years. The assessment was made on the utility cost of that date projected into the future. The next year the utility rate went up 25%. The following year it rose 25% again. In two years the payback figure had dropped dramatically. Present utility costs virtually warrant insulation in all crawl space homes and perimeter insulation for slab-floored homes. Homes with unheated basements will also benefit during the winter heating season.

The crawl space house is the type most needing insulation in the floor. There are conventional methods of insulating between the floor joists which have met with moderate to poor success. These techniques involve hanging blanket insulation with cross wires, chicken wire, or some other invention on the site. Much of the poor success achieved stems from the inadequacy of the suspension techniques; poor fitting of the blankets around pipe, bridging, and other construction obstructions; and to inherent dampness in the crawl space. Several jobs, supposedly done by reputable and knowledgeable contractors, have been seen where the insulation with a vapor backing was installed upside down (the vapor barrier should face up next to the floor). There is a natural inclination to place it with the paper down, as it can be stapled easily to joists from beneath. Some of these jobs were left with no other support but the staples. Naturally, there were many places where the paper had torn loose from the staples, allowing the roll batt to fall down.

Three elements are needed for successful insulating of a floor:

- The insulation must fit tightly throughout the entire floor space.
- The insulation should perform a vapor barrier function or have an integrated vapor barrier.
- The ground beneath the floor should be treated to maintain a dry air climate in the crawl space (ground cover barrier, adequate vents, and so on).

Treating the ground is done successfully in the following manner. Prepare the floor of the crawl space by removing all debris, rocks, and clods. Smooth the surface so that it is fairly flat and has no sharp protrusions or distinct cavities. Spread a thin layer (½″) of sand or crusher dust over the entire area. Lay a full-size sheet of plastic film over the entire area. Six mil is preferred, but 4 mil will suffice. At initial construction time the sheet is suspended over the piers until their location can be identified quite precisely. Cut an X over each pier and let the plastic slip snugly down around the pier. If more than one sheet is required to span the distance, lap over the edges at least 2 to 4′. Permit the sides and ends to rise up the foundation wall a few inches. Place a thin layer of sand all over the plastic to hold it in place and to cushion walking and crawling over it. Obviously, the plastic is vulnerable to punctures and tears. Construction crews will need to be made aware of the need for carefulness while it is exposed. Some more affluent contracts will specify a 2″ layer of concrete over the plastic to form a permanent shield.

Roll-type fiberglass is the least costly form of insulation per R unit of value. It becomes more costly by the coverage foot when a suspension system is added to the total cost. For this reason it is worthwhile to consider sheet forms of insulation.

Blackboard in 2′ × 8′ V-grooved edge form is a favorite sub-sheathing material in some localities. It is laid across the floor joists with end joints staggered and V-joined edges tightly compressed. Only four nails are needed on the ends of the sheets. Three nails are adequate in the field. The sheathing to come will hold the blackboard down. The sheathing installation should follow directly behind the blackboard. With this procedure the potential for breaking through the blackboard will be greatly lessened. Only 100% asphalt-impregnated fiberboard should be used. A single layer of ¾″ tongue-and-groove plywood completes the floor. The T&G ply serves as both subfloor and underlayment for wall-to-wall floor covering. Such a floor must be built upon and closed in against the weather as quickly as possible to avoid rain damage.

Styrofoam insulation in sheet form is installed between the floor joists. One or more layers may be used to accumulate as great an R value as desired. In relation to the proportion of insulation between floor, walls, and ceiling, the floor requires the least. In numerical form, the floor can be assigned one unit, the walls two units, and the ceiling four units. For example, in a superinsulated house with an R-40 insulation in the ceiling, and about R-25 in the walls, an R-11 or R-12 in the floor will meet the criterion. Two inches of Styrofoam is a little over R-11 in value.

Installing 2″ of Styrofoam is accomplished most effectively by double layering (Fig. 4-31). Two 1″ layers are installed. The end joints of the pieces in the top layer are staggered above the bottom layer (Fig. 4-32). This technique eliminates infiltration through joint cracks. No separate vapor barrier is required, as Styrofoam is impervious to moisture. To serve as its own vapor barrier, the Styrofoam must be tightly fitted.

Installation of the Styrofoam involves a press-fit technique and a conscientious philosophy. Ledger strips are installed first around the perimeter of each joist cavity. The least costly material for the ledgers is precut economy studs ripped into four equal strips. The strip will be about ¾″ thick by 1½″ wide. Where a budget is very limited, each of these can be ripped in half to net strips that are about ¹¹⁄₁₆″ × ¾″ in girth. The latter case will net about 60 linear feet of ledger material for the cost of one inexpensive stud.

The ledgers are power stapled or nailed in place. To control the exact location of the Styrofoam, a gauge is used to hold the ledger the correct distance down from the top surface of the joists. *A chalk line is of no value for this detail.* The ledger must be par-

Figure 4-31 Layered Styrofoam provides an effective floor insulation when installed tightly throughout.

allel to the top edge of the joist. Most of the joists will have a slight crown when installed correctly. Two short boards are nailed together as seen in Fig. 4-33. The gauge piece will be $\frac{1}{32}''$ narrower than the depth of insulation being installed. The gauge is held

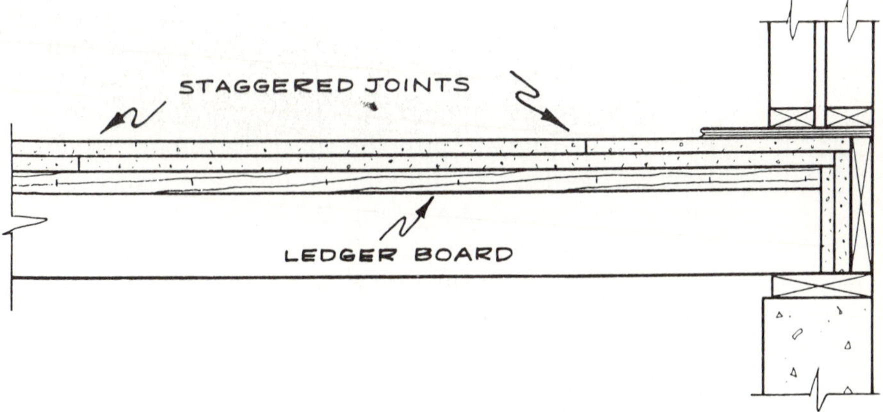

Figure 4-32 Stagger the end joints of layered Styrofoam to insure against infiltration.

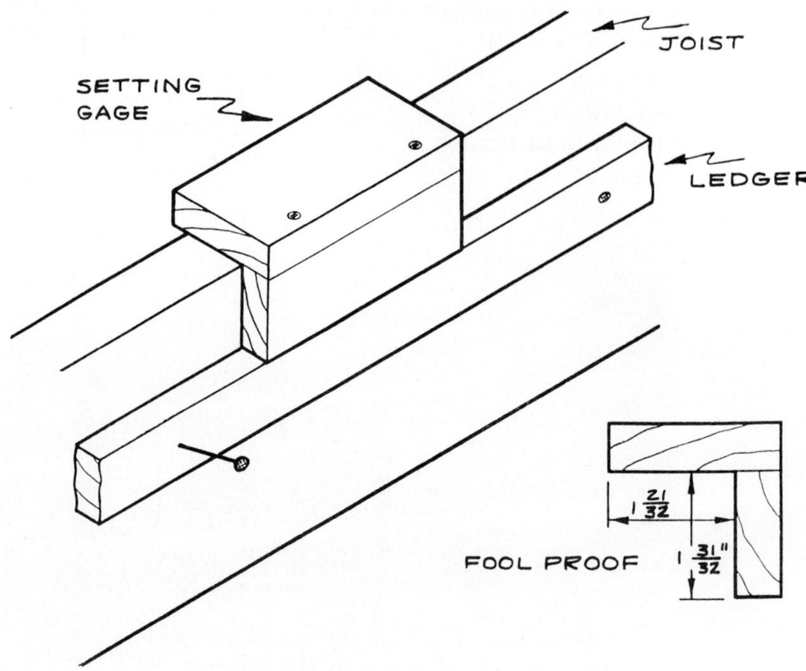

Figure 4-33 A simple, foolproof gauge is used to position the ledger boards accurately while nailing or stapling.

down over the edge of the joist. The ledger is held up firmly against the bottom edge of the gauge. The nail or staple is driven home opposite the gauge. Two men, one holding the gauge and ledger strip while the other operates the staple gun, can install the ledgers in a very short time.

The gauge is made to control the placement of the ledgers at a level 1/32″ higher than the total Styrofoam thickness. This position will cause the top surface of the Styrofoam to protrude 1/32″ above the top of the joists. When the subfloor is put on, it will compress the Styrofoam tightly, giving an excellent sealing effect.

The most economical Styrofoam unit to buy is the 4′ × 8′ large-bead type carried in stock by most suppliers. It is fabricated by ripping into slabs 14½″ × 8′. The 4½″ remaining scrap is saved to fill corner post and partition post cavities in exterior walls. Use a notched story pole or a temporary spacerboard to hold the joists in correct parallel spacing. Hump each 8′ slab a few inches in the middle while pressing the ends in. Leave it humped while putting in the next piece. After all pieces are in at their ends, go back and compress the middles down into position. This will cause the ends to compress tightly together. The last piece in a row will be custom cut to length. Cut it about ⅛″ long. A little experimentation with the first row will tell how high to hump each piece and how much excess to leave on the custom-cut piece. Reverse ends when starting the second layer. In most house depths this will stagger the joint adequately. The 24′-deep floor is the exception. With this floor one should start the second layer with a half-length (4′) slab and save the other half for the custom cut piece on the other side.

Leave the joist spaces at the ends of the floor until last. These spaces are less than 14½″ wide, since the POB is on the outer edge of the joist instead of the center. Other custom-cut widths may be required where double joists have been installed under partition locations or reinforced zones. These should be filled as they are reached, as the workers should not have to walk out over the Styrofoam on either side later to install these odd pieces.

Fitting around the ends of lapped joists is time-consuming but can be kept to a minimum by starting the coursing at the edge of the lap and working out. This requires custom cutting to length at each end of the run for the first layer. The second layer is started at either end. At the lapped joist point a piece is notched to fit precisely. A big-toothed wallboard saw is an efficient tool for this customizing. Assembly-line ripping of the duplicate slabs to go in the majority of the cavities is done on a table saw. At a little more expense, precut pieces are available in 14½ × 48″ size for floors.

DOUBLE-WALL INSULATION

A further savings can be realized with the double-wall concept because the blanket-type insulation is the least expensive form. The double wall's extra-deep cavity permits the installation of two layers of 3½″ blanket insulation. Both the outer and inner layers may be laid up with the nonpaper-backed type. It is called "friction fit" and comes in 48″ and stud lengths. These conveniently sized batts are handily worked into the outer wall cavities. The

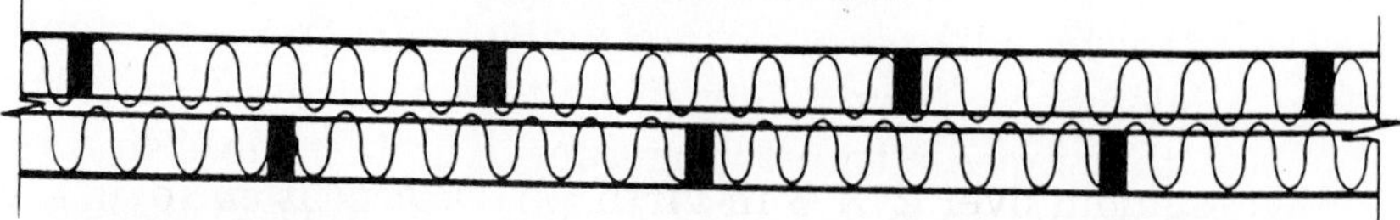

Figure 4-34 Double wall, two-stage insulating breaks up infiltration and stud "nosebleed" (heat conduction through the studs—also termed the wick effect). This staggered and layered insulating system prevents most of the conduction commonly found in single stud walls.

electric wiring is snaked between the studs after the first layer of insulation is in place. Any plumbing fixtures that are located adjacent to the exterior walls are rough plumbed. Vents and drains are installed. Freeze-ups of exterior wall plumbing are virtually nonexistent with the double wall because the outer layer of insulation is between the pipes and the exterior side of the wall.

The inner layer of insulation is installed next. It can be the friction-fit type covered with a continuous piece of plastic sheet or the vapor barrier paper-backed type in stud lengths. Because the studs are staggered from inner to outer frames, the insulation blankets are also staggered (Fig. 4-34). The effect is a tight infiltration-proof wall of R-22 value (just the insulation rating). By using the less costly blackboard for sheathing and any form of siding, the total wall value is about R-25 or more. In the final accounting, the double-wall cost of the design shown in this book falls somewhere between those of the conventional 2 × 4 stud wall and the 2 × 6 stud wall. It is cost effective in all respects when the plan is carefully devised (modular overall sizes and modular placement of openings and partitions) and the materials proportionately matched.

17 THERMAL ROOF DESIGNS

When considering heat and coolness retention, one must recognize the window of vulnerability that exists with conventional rafters. At the location of the birdsmouth (the seat cut), the distance from the surface of the top plate to the underside of the roof sheathing in some cases is smaller than the wall cavity depth. It is therefore virtually impossible to produce a 1½-to-1 ratio (ceiling to wall) of insulation value in this area. The largest conventional rafters are seldom over 2 × 8 in girth (7¼″). A seat cut over a conventional wall plate lowers the height for insulation to about 6″ or less. The conventional roof frame limits the area above the top plate from about 2″ for 2 × 4 rafters to about 6″ for 2 × 8 rafters (Fig. 4-35). Regardless of what depth of insulation exists over the rest of the ceiling, the area over the top plate is limited. A few attempts have been made to raise this area with cripple studs and an additional top plate. The design suffers from instability, labor-time consumption, and high cost. None has caught on seriously.

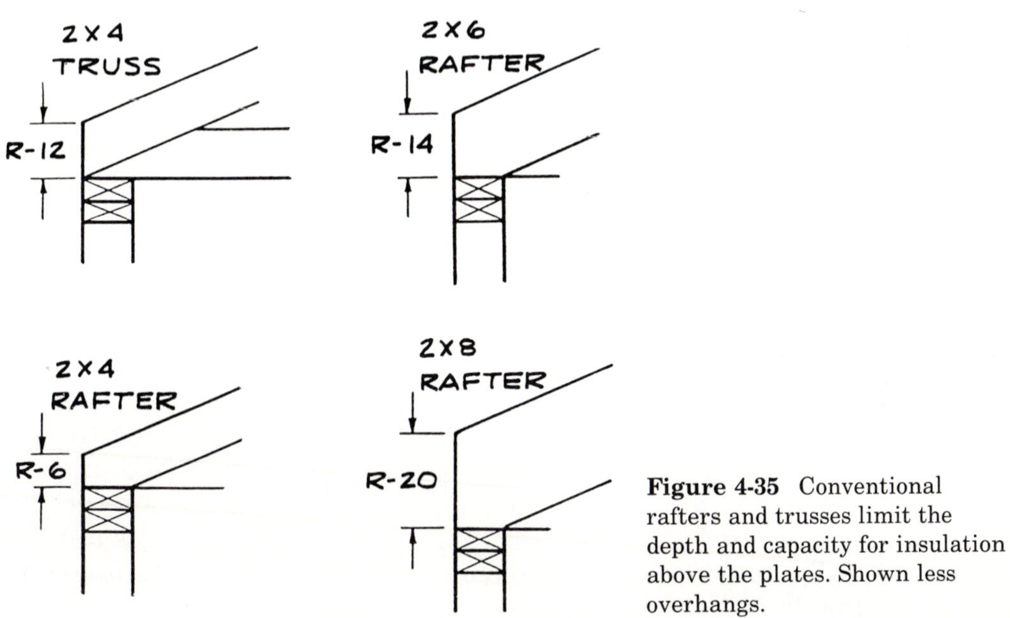

Figure 4-35 Conventional rafters and trusses limit the depth and capacity for insulation above the plates. Shown less overhangs.

THERMAL TRUSS

The thermal truss has become commonplace. Designs vary but most factory-made thermal trusses contain extra webs and cripple studs positioned to be above the wall Fig. 4-36. With this design,

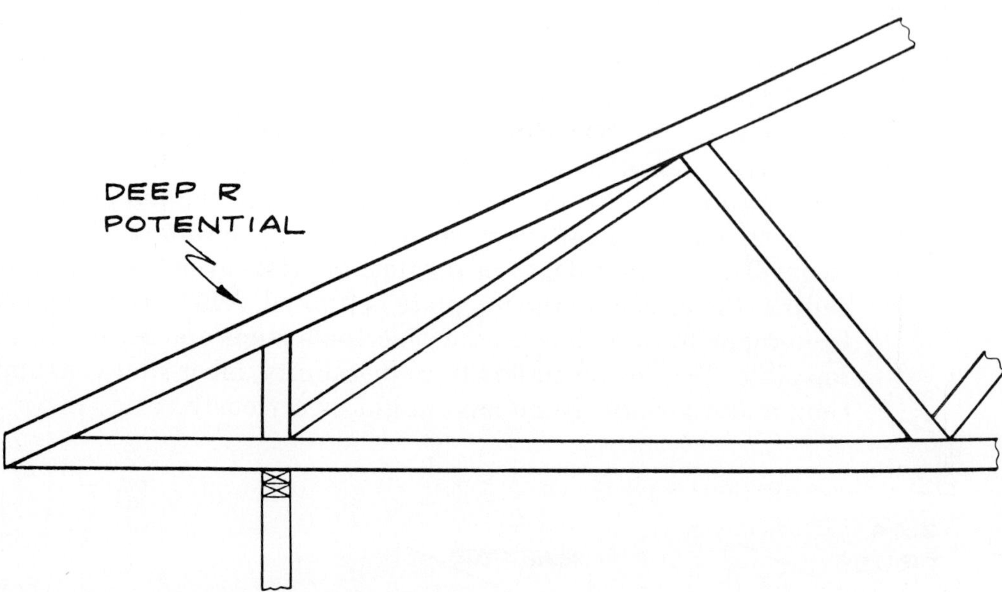

Figure 4-36 A thermal truss, where the upper chord is raised with vertical cripples and additional webs, can provide unlimited capacity for insulation over the top plates. This design is especially adaptable to the midrange such as 5 in 12 through 10 in 12.

any depth for insulation can be had. A drawback develops when the extended height becomes excessive. Unless enough overhang can be planned, a high frieze-board area develops over the windows. It is difficult to make this space look natural and intended. Americans are accustomed to seeing boxed eaves and possibly some frieze board just above the windows. Brick houses are especially vulnerable. An economy plan will not tolerate angle-iron lintels so that brick can be continued over the windows and doors. The finish carpenter is then burdened with the chore of filling in the void over the windows and doors with some nonmasonry material. It seldom looks anything but after-planned. An advantage of the high-thermal-truss design is that it works well with the intermediate pitches because the steeper angle contains the overhanging tail closer and lower on the wall.

A pitch wedge is another way to raise the upper chords (Fig. 4-37). The wedge is obtained from the end of the return piece or is custom cut from scrap stock. The lower chord is square cut.

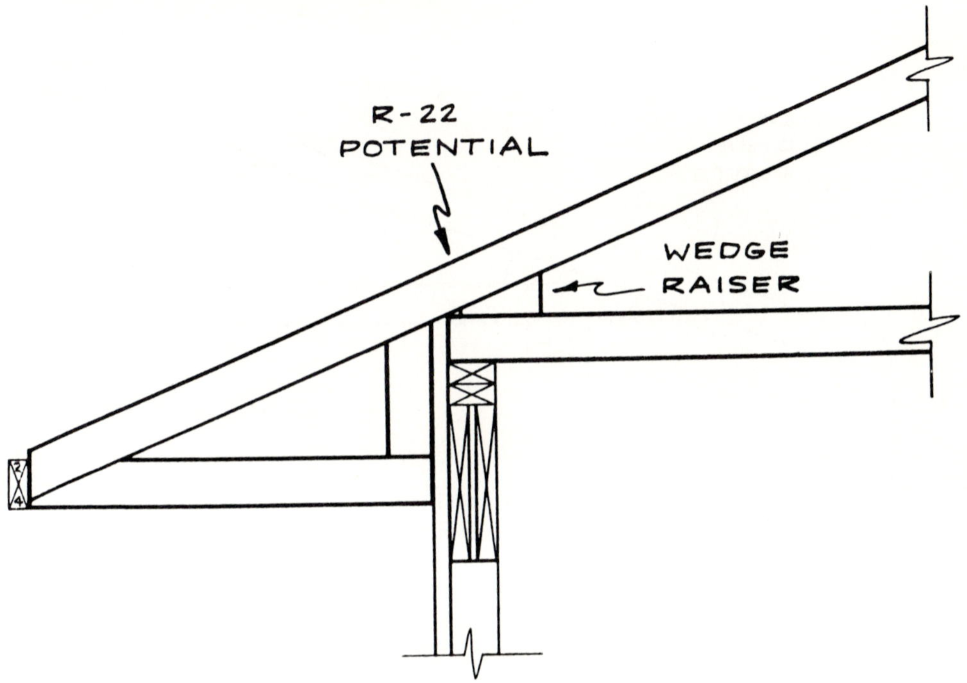

Figure 4-37 A plumb-cut lower chord (square cut at the building line) and a pitched wedge will effectively double the insulation capacity over the top plates.

EXTENDED SPAN TRUSS

The author has employed an extended span truss design with great success for many years. It is a simple, cost-conserving concept which closes the window of insular vulnerability. It works on all roofs with horizontal boxed soffit returns.

The design formula simply calls for a truss of a modular span one size larger than the house span. The builder who designs and builds his or her own trusses will find it easy to lay out the truss on paper and on the floor.

Observe some specific examples. For a 24' spanned house, a 26' spanned truss is laid out (Figs. 4-38 and 4-39). One foot of the lower chord overhangs the wall. The mitered cutoff piece from the end of the lower chord is retained and used as a chock-block wedge to reinforce the bearing characteristic of the chords above the top

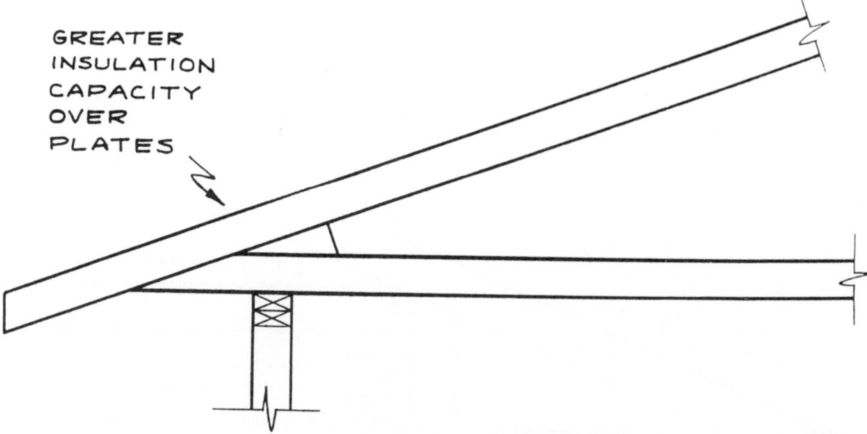

Figure 4-38 A truss, one nominal size larger (2′ greater span) with a wedge, provides a deeper insulation potential over the plates and strengthens the tails.

Figure 4-39 A standard truss that is 2′ wider (longer) than a modular span will about double the space for insulation over the plates.

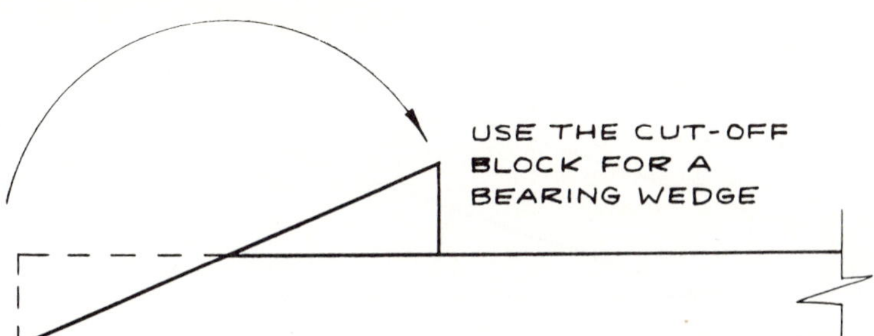

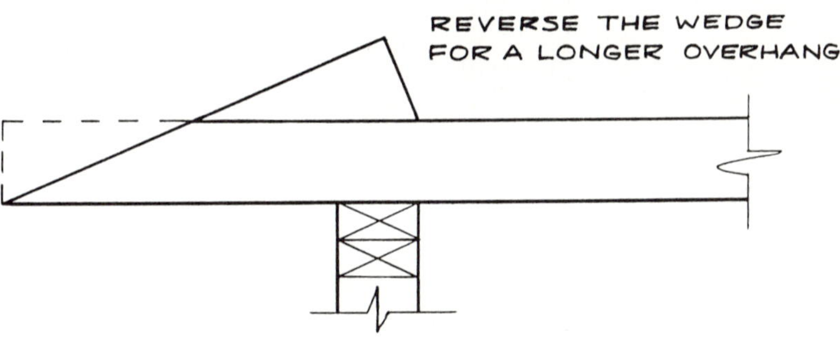

Figure 4-40   Use the cutoff, from the scarf at the end of a lower chord
or soffit return, as a wedge.

plate (Fig. 4-40). It also serves as a solid backing for the gusset.
The wedge is cost free, compared to a cripple, as it would normally
be discarded. Another feature of the overhanging lower chord is
that it provides a level under the edge to which brick pocket drops
can readily be fitted (Fig. 4-41). Square junctions are always less
critical to join than are mitered junctions on the rake.

A truss that is one size larger than the house span will
provide an insulation depth potential of about 10″ clear out to the
building line. This is right in line with present-day cost-effective
planning.

The depth potential for the insulation is variable with a nonmodular spanned house when a modular truss of greater span is
used. As the house span approaches closer to the span of the lower
chord, the space above the exterior wall will diminish. Stated a
different way, the space above a conventional truss of 2 × 4 components will be just slightly more than 3½″ at the building line

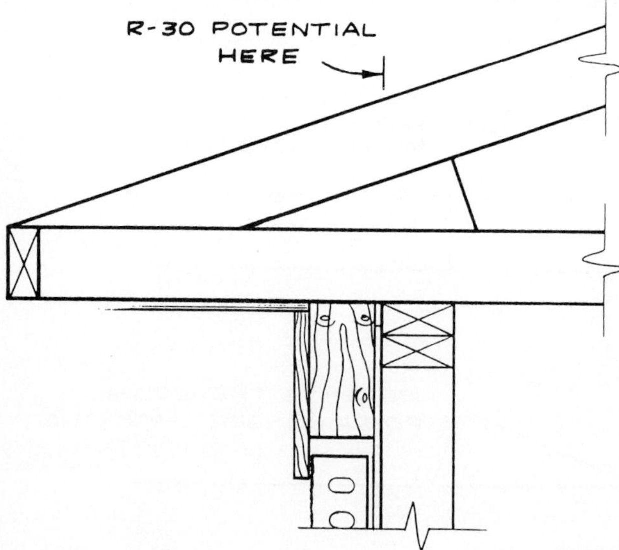

Figure 4-41 This truss design causes a higher frieze board area above windows—an advantage for solar exposure at the top of windows—and provides a ready-made soffit framework.

when the truss nominal span is equal to the house span. As the lower chord is extended out away from the wall, the roof line appears to rise. It will gain in height (the space for insulation) in proportion to the distance that the wall is from the end of the lower chord.

The principle is so simple that it has other applications. For example, a rule of thumb emerges. It is not necessary to have a custom-spanned truss built to fit a nonmodular span. An odd-sized span of 25′ (not uncommon) is simply roofed with 26′ trusses. The extra 6″ overhang of the lower chord on each side is an asset. A 26′ truss will usually cost no more to make than a 25′ custom-built truss. If purchased, it may cost less.

The same system works throughout the various spans. House spans in the range from 26 to 28′ will accept 28′ trusses, those above 28′ will accept 30′ and 32′ standard trusses.

WEB LOCATION ON EXTENDED TRUSSES

When a standard truss is purchased, the webs will be connected to the chords at standard third and quarter points of the truss span. These locations will not coincide with the actual quarter and third points on the house, which has a shorter span. This is not a problem, as the truss has been designed for its own span. For the builder who makes his or her own trusses, the opportunity is there to create equal spans on the lower chord and thereby rectify the disparity. For example, a 28′ W truss on top of a 2 × 4 plate conventional wall will have a clear-span factor of 27′-5″ (28′ minus two 3½″ plates). The third points of this span are about 9′-1⅝″. Placing this standard 28′ truss on a house span of 26′ (a clear span of 25′-5″) causes the central "third" to be much greater than the outer two actual clear spans. To overcome this discrepancy, the builder can lay out a truss jig to accommodate the third and quarter spacing according to the shorter span of the house by measuring from a centerline outward while the upper and lower chords are laid out on the profile of the next larger modular truss. In this way the best of two objectives is achieved.

The potential of greater disproportionate third or quarter spans in the lower chord exists with a deeper-walled house. On a double wall it is recommended that an extended truss have its webs at the actual clear span third points. This will guarantee equal spans, which in turn provide for the greatest inherent ceiling and roof support. When purchasing trusses, the buyer can furnish the factory with a simple drawing including dimensions to center lines (Fig. 4-42). This *should* assure the exact web locations desired. It does not, however, as workers are creatures of habit. Some will ignore the dimensions. Others will assume that the designer has misplaced the locations, especially if he or she is not a professional. It will help to avoid later confrontation if the designer is on hand to oversee that the jig is properly set up in accordance with the plan. And, of course, a simple contract agreement to follow the drawing specifications will help in case error occurs.

VENTILATION OF THERMAL STRUCTURES

Problems of condensation were experienced when insulation first came into widespread use. A pessimistic philosophy is still encountered from time to time which says, "Too much insulation can be as bad as too little." The philosophy is grounded in some truth and some fiction.

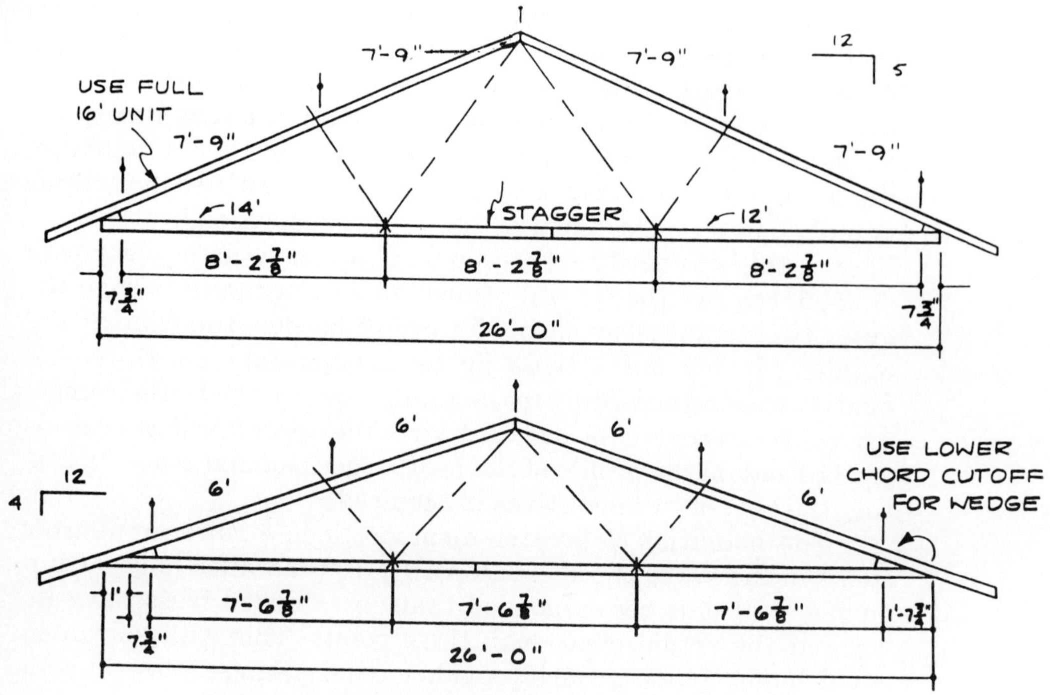

Figure 4-42 When constructing a thermal truss, be certain to place the third and/or quarter points according to the clear span (not the overall nominal span). Provide your builder with a clearly dimensioned plan.

A primary breakdown of early forms of fiberboard and blanket insulation came about because of the condensation that was created. Old-timers still have visions of windows with water dribbling down the inside of the panes and wood siding from which the paint peeled annually. The peeling paint was usually caused by fiberboard sheathing that did not have an asphaltum impregnation. Placed on uninsulated walls, the heat in the house would penetrate to the back side of the sheathing and cause condensation to form on the cold surface. The resulting condensation soaked the fiberboard, which in turn soaked the back side of the siding—usually cedar—which absorbed it like a sponge. This phase took place during the World War II period and on into the early 1950s. It was overcome by moisture-proofing of the various brands of fiberboard and by paper-backing the batt insulation with a moisture barrier. In these transition years, the theory was born that a house could be overinsulated. In reality, there is no such thing as overinsulating. But there is a point of diminishing return. Too much insulation is not harmful, it simply may not pay back its initial cost in fuel savings over the life of the house.

Ventilation, vapor blocking, and air exchange are the keys to the conservation of heat- and coolness-generating fuels. Obviously, the greatest economy is to use the free sources—the sun, the wind, and the earth—to as great an extent as possible for heating and cooling. When other costly fuels are used, the next-best system of conservation is to superinsulate. It will work best when it is accompanied by adequate ventilation and occasional exchange of interior air.

Figure 4-43 Attractive site-built ridge vents.

ROOF VENTILATORS

All the mechanical and powered roof ventilators are of moderate use for removing hot air from an attic. Static vents are too small. Nonpowered turbines don't suck out the air as they appear to. They turn on windless days from the impetus of the rising hot air. A turbine would be more effective as a simple screened chimney. Gable vents are directional. The most effective vent is the full eave and ridge vent combination. Full-length ridge and soffit vents do the best job (Figs. 4-43 and 4-44).

To clear an attic of all hot spots, the air must be moved out of all the spaces between the rafters. This is accomplished most effectively with a combination of full-length venting entrances in the eaves and a full-length ridge vent. The air will move freely and naturally up all of the channels between the rafters with this combination (Fig. 4-45). Care must be taken to provide a protected

Figure 4-44   A continuous soffit vent, teamed with a full-length ridge vent, provides optimum discharge of hot air.

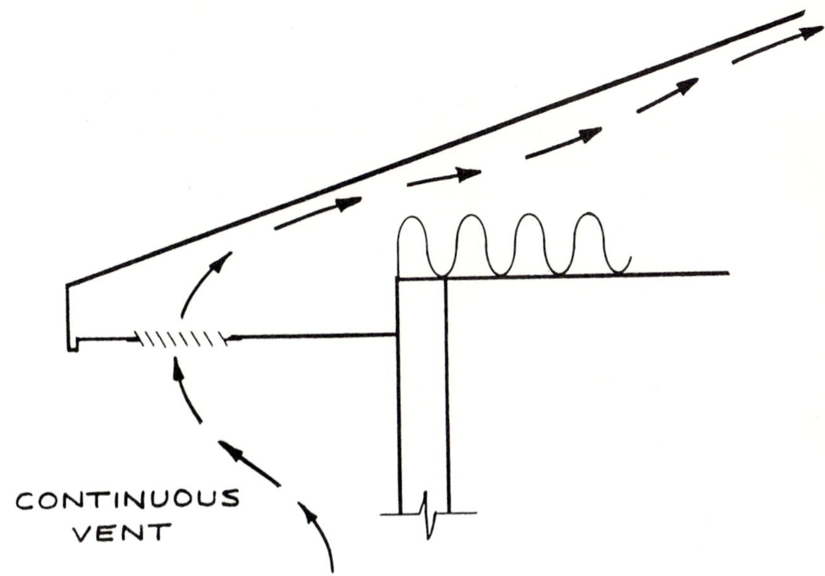

Figure 4-45   A full-length eave-venting system will permit the hot air to move out of all rafter corridors.

corridor above the insulation over the plate area (Figs. 4-46, 4-47, and 4-48). Manufactured ridge vents are obtainable in some areas. A simple and attractive vent can be built on site (Figs. 4-49, 4-50, and 4-51).

Air exchange inside the house is another important factor in controlling condensation during the heating season. Condensation is a heating season problem. Occasionally, the statement is heard, "The house has to breathe to be free of condensation." The breathing need not be accomplished via skimpy insulation and certainly not by tolerated infiltration. The theory that a house can be too tight is not logical if it implies that built-in leaks are good. The practical situation is for the tenant to be in control of conditions and still sustain and contain the heat that is being introduced as long as possible. Such control is maintained by periodic air exchange when humidity becomes excessive.

Partial air exchange occurs every time an exterior door is opened. Vent fans over the kitchen range will remove air on command. Vent fans in the bathrooms take care of steamy air.

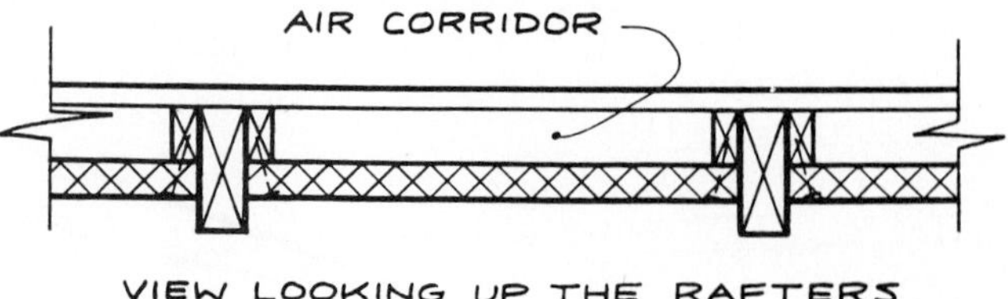

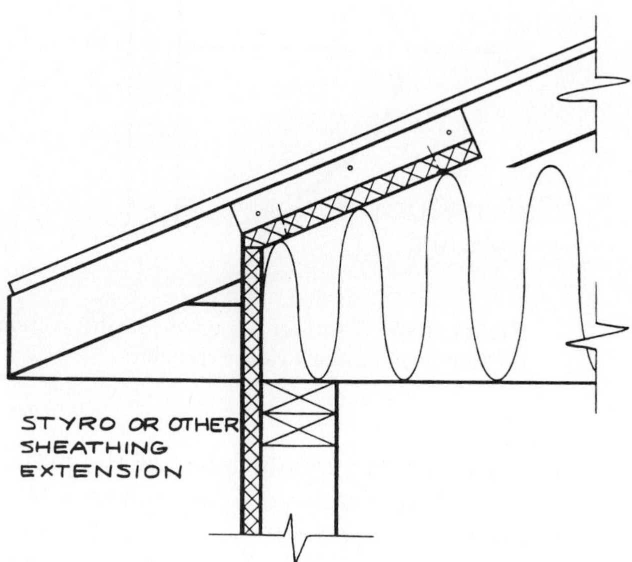

Figure 4-46 The air corridor must be kept open with an insulation stop.

Full air exchange is achieved by opening doors and windows on opposite sides or ends of the house for a few minutes. One might think such a practice was in direct conflict with the heat-saving objective. Not so. The heat loss is only momentary and quickly recouped. The dumping of stale, moisture-laden air will take only a few minutes, not long enough to cool down all the heat-holding objects and materials in the house.

The chimney flue in a fireplace is another excellent venting source. Once the air seems fresh and crisp, all the openings are closed. A hot-air furnace should be turned off during the air

Figure 4-47   An exterior view of a full stop and a corridor stop. Corridor stops are used between all rafters with the optimum system.

Figure 4-48   Interior view showing vent corridors at locations above unit soffit vents.

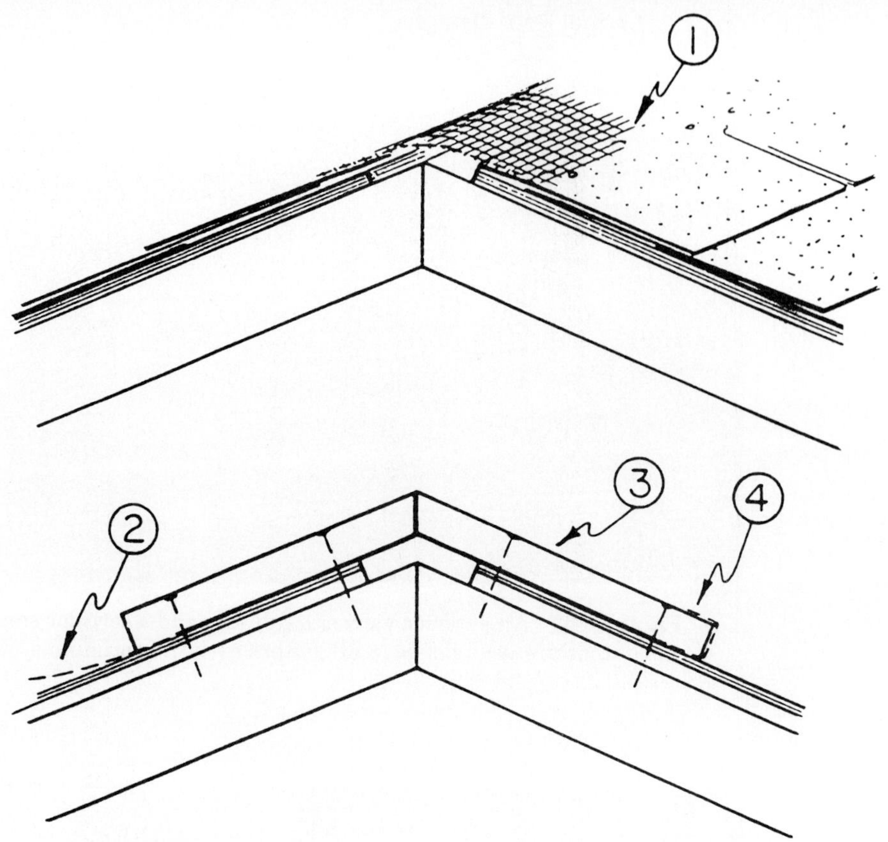

Figure 4-49 The first four steps in making a functional and attractive ridge vent on site. (1) Lay out the hardware cloth. (2) Lay out and staple the outer screen. (3) Install the 2 × 4 × 12″ blocks. (4) Fold up and fasten the outer screens.

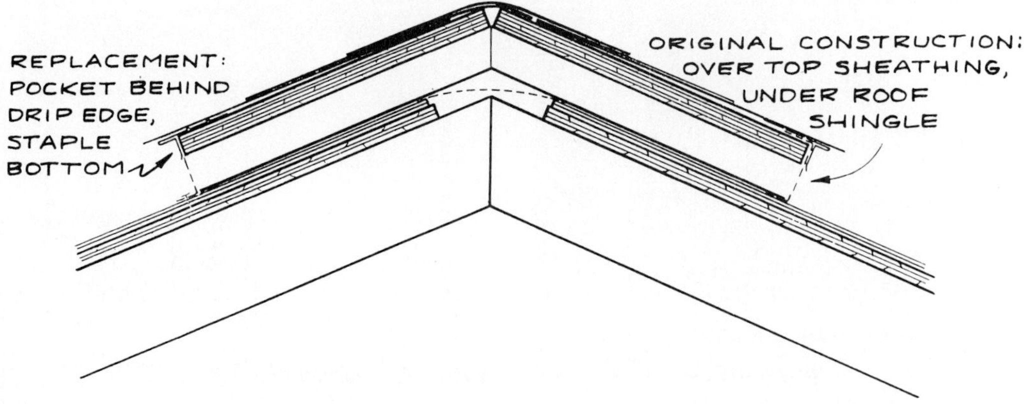

Figure 4-50 A section view of a site-built ridge vent.

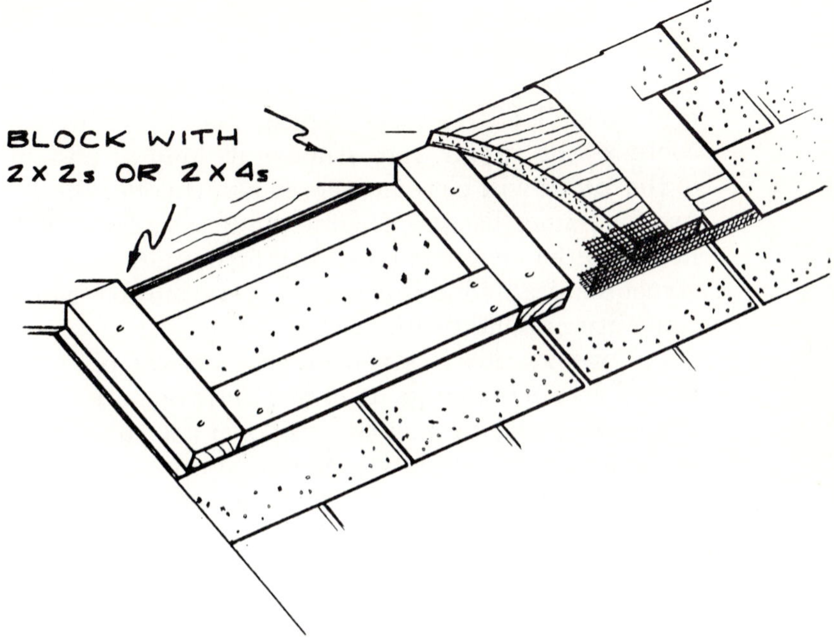

Figure 4-51   Extend the vent roof to the end of the regular roof. Close those sections that are over a boxed-gable overhang if the channel is compartmented by lookouts or blocks.

exchange; however, the blower may be operated manually to circulate new air rapidly, after which the thermostat may be returned to the desired operational settings. In a matter of minutes, the condensation is eliminated.

18 COST EFFECTIVENESS OF THERMAL CONSTRUCTION

The term *cost effective* relates to a comparison of the initial cost to construct or install something compared to the long-range saving it will generate. Scientists tell us that the world's fossil fuel sources are diminishing at an alarming rate. Costs go up as supply dwindles. Obviously a home requiring no consumable fuels will be the most cost effective if construction cost is reasonable.

Two doors are open to the designer-builder to approach this ultimate objective. One door leads to the use of the sun and the earth as the only truly free sources of heating and cooling. The other door leads to ways and means of holding onto the heat or coolness that is put into a house as long as possible. The decade of the 1980s will be remembered as the time when solar and earth use for homes became feasible and cost effective. The reader and homebuilder now has enough information from this book to construct a suitable habitat within the same cost range as a house of conventional (old fashioned?) utilities.

Consistency is stressed when developing the cost-effective plan. Certain things go together. The mismatching of philosophies will nullify or diminish the effects of the super features. The conservation and retention theme must prevail with all systems and materials in a particular structure. Cost must not dominate a selection of materials. The quality coefficient is the criterion of importance.

Build a house to fit the land. If a plan is admired and selected first, a suitable lot must be found to fit the plan. Orient and size windows according to solar gain or loss. Extend eaves in accord with the sun's angle in summer and winter. Orient exterior doors in accord with the effects of prevailing winds. Include compartmented entrances. Use a 1-to-2-to-3 insulation proportion for the floor, the exterior wall, and the ceiling. A cost-effective example for a crawl space structure is 4" of fiberglass blanket in the floor, 8" in a double wall, and 12" over the ceiling. Increase these figures in colder climates. Windows to match will be Thermopane with a combination storm sash. Insulated doors are a must with a combination storm door in front. Use of light roof shingles in predominantly hot climates, and dark shingles in predominantly cold areas of the country is desirable.

Long-range planning is a moral responsibility. This concept is worthy of exploring, although usually is avoided by authors. The cost effectiveness of materials should take into account the fact that someone will be paying utility bills for many years. Fifty years might be considered a minimum expectation.

The most flagrant and obvious example of short-range planning, visible in most housing developments, is witnessed in the quality of windows. It can only be accounted for by the naiveté of the average purchaser, who does not recognize window quality by sight. The typical buyer is likely to be impressed by the appearance of a house rather than by the quality of the components. It is a rare buyer who is brand conscious of such things as windows, doors, air conditioners, and furnaces. The average buyer is usually under some degree of pressure to acquire and establish a home without delay. In this atmosphere of anxiety (it is the biggest purchase of a lifetime for most), it is almost axiomatic that the buyer takes the word of the seller for about everything that is not obvious.

There is a broad degree of latitude between pure fiction and whole truth when it comes to describing the assets or liabilities of a house. Many of the features affecting long-range utility costs are not visible on a cursory inspection. For example, the buyer has picked up a few terms in his or her quest. The question is asked, "Is this a thermally constructed type of house?" The "yes" response puts the issue to bed, and the wife goes about admiring the fancy kitchen while the husband fantasizes at the workbench counter in the garage. What a heavenly change from the cramped apartment or living with in-laws. The trap in which they may be snared lies in the term "thermal." The word "thermal" can be used to describe a house with any type of insulating material in it that does not classify as a structural component.

One time in his legal expert witness role, the author uncovered an entire subdivision of houses with only a sheet of 4 mil plastic under the plastered walls. No insulation was present in the cavities. The houses were advertised as "fully insulated." This was an extreme case of misrepresentation in the moral sense. It would never have come to light had heat bills not been compared with those of neighbors in homes built by more scrupulous contractors.

INSPECTION BY THE BUYER

The prospective buyer can inspect some places in a house to judge its thermal efficiency. There will be an access port into the attic somewhere. Armed with a flashlight and a tape measure, get up there and check the depth of insulation. Check for full coverage throughout. If it is blown insulation, is it evenly spread? If it is blanket type, has it been fitted around rafters, webs, and strongbacks, or has it simply been rolled up around them? Are the furnace ducts in the attic (the poorest location for conservation)? If so, are they wrapped to a depth equal to the ceiling insulation? The customary system is to wrap them with 1½ or 2″ of vinyl-backed, fiberglass blanketing.

Inspect the basement. Is the foundation insulated where it is exposed to the outdoors? Adhesive-bonded Styrofoam is cost effective. Is there insulation behind the wood header (above the foundation) between each joist? Is there insulation the full length of the band headers at the ends of the house? Are the basement windows of thermal type (double glass, Thermopane, or with storms)? If these thermal characteristics do not exist around the exposed part of the foundation, the heat loss can be as great from this seemingly insignificant area as it is from the whole first-floor exterior wall.

Check the crawl space. Plan to don some old clothes and crawl under there with a flashlight. Can you smell any evidence of termite treatment (chlordane odor)? Is there insulation between the joists? If not, is there Styrofoam sheathing glued to the foundation? Are there enough foundation vents to let the stale air out of the corners? Is there a vapor barrier, and a layer of sand and plastic over the dirt?

Inspecting a slab floor for thermal characteristics is more difficult but not completely impossible. To be considered thermal, a slab must have a barrier between the exposed foundation and the interior floor (Fig. 4-52). Styrofoam is the usual material. Somewhere in the house it may be exposed. If there is plumbing access behind a tub adjacent to an outer wall, it could reveal a Styrofoam strip between the foundation and the floor slab. Behind a washer and dryer, the baseboard may have been omitted, exposing the Styrofoam barrier. The junction between the floor slab and an attached garage slab may furnish a clue. Sometimes taking up an aluminum door sill from this junction will reveal the needed barrier. All these techniques failing, there is still hope. On a cold winter day or hot summer day, feel the surface of a tiled part of the floor that is next to the exterior wall. It should feel comparable to the temperature inside the house if a thermal barrier exists. Where all these clues are absent and the house is one of several in a tract-built addition, there is one last possibility. Locate a new house-start at the end of the tract where the foundation is in but the floor is not yet poured. If it is the same builder, the construc-

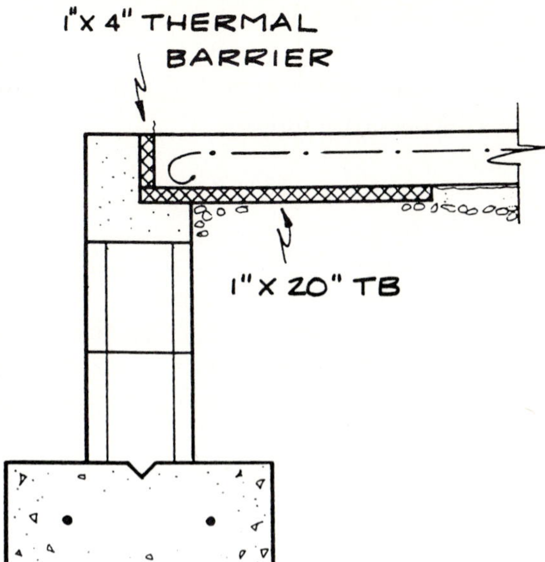

Figure 4-52 A slab floor does not qualify as a thermal coordinate unless there is a tight thermal barrier between it and the foundation to prevent conduction.

tion will probably be the same. Try to be on hand just before the slab is poured. The presence or absence of the thermal barrier, the reinforcing mesh, and the vapor barrier will be exposed.

19 ENERGY-SAVING HEATING SYSTEMS

SOLAR SYSTEMS

Solar heat, teamed with superinsulation, spells freedom from excessive fuel costs. No discussion of fuel conservation would be complete without some reference to the potential of solar gain in the superinsulated house. The double-wall design presents an ideal opportunity to incorporate built-in solar panels. Sandwiched into the outer walls, these panels will not give the appearance of retrofitted boxes. Panels of 2 or 4' width are attractively coordinated alongside windows or doors to give an appearance of unity. For example, 2'-wide collectors can be placed on both sides of a patio door. With the tops and bottoms coordinated on the same level, all the casings are trimmed as a single unit. It gives off the same aesthetic sense of beauty as is achieved with a broad expanse of glass doors or full-length windows.

ORIENTING THE COLLECTOR

A solar collector's efficiency is in direct proportion to two factors. One is the length of time the collector surface is exposed to the sun's rays. The second is the angle of the sun's rays against the collector.

The time-exposure factor will be at its optimum when the collector is facing directly south. The sun will contact a stationary south-facing collector for a longer period than if it were placed facing any other direction. A rotating collector that begins its day facing east and follows the sun's path toward the west is the ultimate concept. This concept can be followed in a limited way by having several collectors facing in different directions. An east-to-southeast exposure will accommodate the morning sun. The southeast-to-south-to-southwest span on the compass will be exposed to the late morning, noon, and early afternoon period. The southwest-exposed collector takes over late in the afternoon. A direct-west exposure is least efficient, as the sun is too far away and its effect is beginnging to be felt less.

The fixed or built-in collector, according to these principles, is most beneficially placed on the south side of a house. Those consumers and builders who are interested in free heat via the solar collector will consider the house design and the building site orientation as critical elements of the planning phase. For example, a floor plan may have a limited number of places along the exterior walls where one or several collectors can fit in both aesthetically and functionally. Usually the longer side of a basically rectangular house will present more expanse for collector location. Once it is determined into which wall of the house the collector(s) will be built, it is possible to specify the required orientation of the lot and its size. When you own a lot before planning a house, it will be necessary to design the house around the fixed orientation of the lot. Urban lots will not present the flexibility found in most rural plots, where a house is not confined by setback regulations and parallelism requirements. A house in the country can usually be rotated to face the sun to advantage and still blend in with its surroundings.

COLLECTOR ANGLE

The most efficient angle of the collector to the ground is when the sun's rays strike the collector surface at 90°. The sun arcs across the sky such that the rays never strike on the same degree line as time passes. The optimum angle for a collector surface is that which matches or is close to the latitude in a specific locality. Many early wall collector designs featured sloping glass walls. The track record of a few years proved the effects of this design to be uncontrollable (*Popular Science,* August 1983, p. 70). The summer heat gain is too great to be turned away with blinds, ventilators, or any other internal mechanism. One such award-winning collector two stories high has been converted to a vertical posture and is working successfully. The principle defies theory but proves out in practice.

The boxed collector does not suffer from the same problem, as it heats through the movement of hot air. In the summer the hot air is vented outdoors. Unlike the direct-gain principle of the glass wall, the boxed collector's registers are shut during nonheating times.

Coordinating the eave overhang will virtually eliminate overheating of the collector itself. The eaves are designed to be long enough to shade the collector completely during the nonheating season. This eave length can be found nontechnically on the longest day of the year, June 20 or 21. Hold a 7' board in a vertical posture. Hold another board horizontally on top of the vertical board. Extend the end of the horizontal board toward due south until its shadow touches the bottom of the vertical board (Fig. 4-53). The horizontal distance that the board extends beyond the upright post will be the required amount of soffit depth above the windows in order to cast shade to the level of the floor. Take the reading at noon when the sun is at its highest point.

This test shows how much eave is needed to eliminate all sun from a collector surface on the longest day of the year. That is part of the analysis. The object of the collector is to supply heat in the

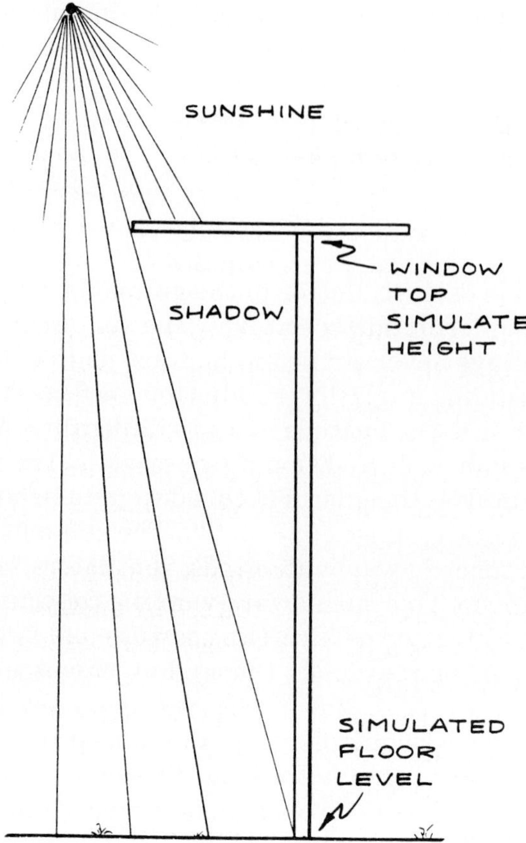

Figure 4-53 An on-site technique for determining shadow patterns can be performed with a T-pole. At the drawing board, the chart in Fig. 3-2 will tell you how much overhang is needed to produce a certain shadow level on the wall. Shadow level should be below all windows unless exterior shade is planned.

winter. In some latitudes an eave long enough to completely shade a collector to floor level would also shade the top part of it on short winter days.

The problem of determining the collector size of a built-in box-type collector can be approached from several different objectives. Following are two approaches.

1. The eave method starts with a predetermined eave depth. The shadow line boundaries on the wall are established. The effective collector surface zone will start from the top line (the winter line) and extend to ground level. The effective shade line in summer will be the lower line. The height between these two lines is the optimum height for both collector panels and windows in

terms of efficient heat collection in winter and rejection in summer. Where this height does not provide enough square-foot area, the difference may be made up by broadening the collector width. The box is expanded into another stud cavity to make up the loss in height.

2. Another systematic design approach is to design collector sizes and shapes to fit the wall elevation design. Then the eave length is custom coordinated.

Some compromise is mandated, as it is rarely possible to have a full-height panel that will be fully exposed in winter and fully shaded in summer. Each day presents a different exposure situation. This is the basic problem to be compromised with all forms of fixed-mount collectors. The most efficient fixed collectors will be those placed in locations not affected by eaves, such as ends of a gable-roofed house or on the roof.

Where the collector is built into the wall in a vertical position (Fig. 4-54), the exposure angle is attained by another means. The vertical collector suffers a little efficiency loss due to the vertical angle discrepancy. It is regained by the use of corrugated aluminum sheet metal for the absorber. The corrugations are arranged horizontally so that, regardless of the angle of the sun, it will play on some part of the curved surface.

SIZING AN INTEGRAL COLLECTOR

The size of the collector relates to the quantity of heat desired. A basic formula for the type being described and illustrated herein will produce enough heat for homes in central and southern belt climates at a rate of 1 square foot of collector surface for 10 square feet of floor area. A 4′ × 8′ collector heats about 300′. There are so many variables, such as R values in walls and ceiling, that it is a difficult task to quote a reliable formula that will meet more than an isolated situation. It is logical, however, that any substantial quantity of heat that can be transferred into a home by the free use of the sun will net a savings over the cost of fossil fuels *if* the initial cost of the collector system is reasonable. Herein lies the feasibility of the collector design being described.

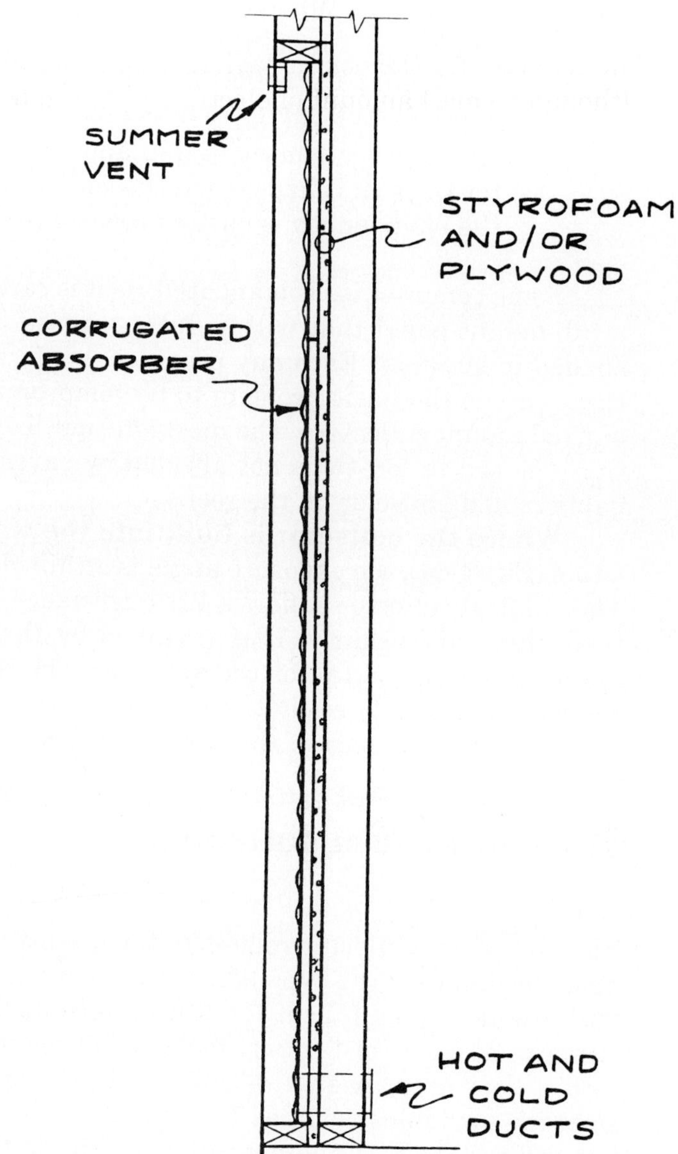

Figure 4-54 An integrated solar collector fits conveniently into the outer cavities of a double-wall frame. The black-painted, corrugated-sheetmetal collector plate catches the sun's rays from all seasonal angles.

CONSTRUCTING AN INTEGRAL COLLECTOR

The collector for the double-wall house is basically a passive type, although a small amount of electricity is used to power a minifan. Each 2′ cavity between the studs of the outer wall of the double-wall house can be used to form the shell of a collector. From test results, it has been found that the use of two cavities side by side provides the most effective module.

The back of the collector is a single sheet or combination of material sheets, 4′ × 8′ in size. The thickness fills the ¾″ space between the inner and outer walls. A single sheet of ¾″ CD grade plywood works well. In addition to its collector function, it provides an ideal bracing feature to the wall in the same manner as corner-bracing plywood. Another combination of materials is to place a ¼″ sheet of plywood to form the back of the collector, followed by a ½″-thick sheet of Styrofoam. A ¾″ sheet of foil-backed Styrofoam provides the highest R rating against heat loss when the collector is not functioning.

DETAILS OF CONSTRUCTION

Following are the sequential steps for constructing a built-in collector.

1. The first step is to block off an area at the top of the two stud cavities. Two blocks of 2 × 4 stock exactly 22½″ long are required. The blocks are placed at a height that is ¾″ above the underside of the door and window jambs (not the rough opening but the finish casement jambs). This location permits trimming of the collector to coincide exactly with doors and windows. The blocks should be glued or caulked, or both, so that the joints are airtight.

2. Next, a long notch is cut in the upper part of the center stud. This notch provides a crossover opening under the absorber through which the warm air moves from one side to the other. The notch is ¾″ deep by 21″ long. As

shown in Fig. 4-55, it starts under the top blocks and goes down the interior side of the center stud.

3. Center and nail an aluminum strip 4″ × 21″ on the interior face of the notch. The aluminum can be 22 gauge or heavier. This strip forms a ledger on which the absorber metal will rest.

4. Nail the plywood back to the collector opening before raising the inner wall. A bead of adhesive is spread around the perimeter of the collector into which the plywood is pressed and then nailed. Give attention to perfect centering of the middle stud throughout its length. Also, the side studs should be exactly half-covered by the plywood backboard. If the floor is level, the plywood sheet acts as a squaring device to plumb the wall.

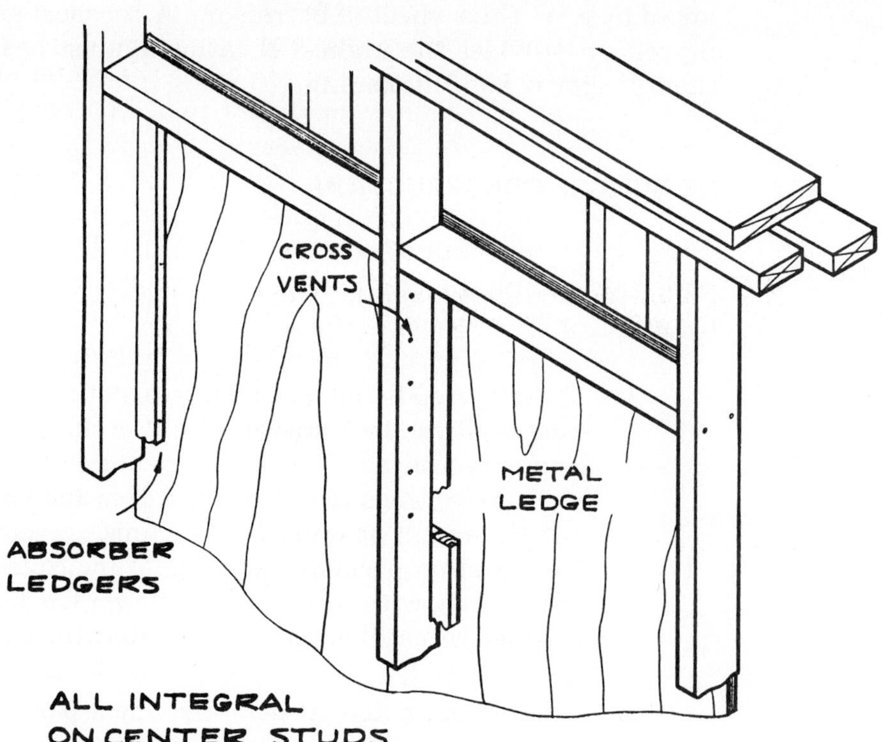

Figure 4-55 Notch the center stud, nail on the 4″ × 21″ metal ledger, and glue and nail the back panel on before raising the inner wall.

At this stage, work on the collector is discontinued until the house framing is completed and the house is closed in. It is prudent to cover the entire opening with a plastic sheet lapped over the top edge of the plywood to protect it from the weather.

5. Surround the perimeter of both cavities with a 1×2 board laid flat against the plywood back. These pieces can be ripped from stud material at minimum cost. The strips form a ledger for the absorber.

6. Cut the rectangular openings in the plywood back for the intake and outlet ducts (Fig. 4-56). Make the ducts of wood or metal to fit your register and fan sizes. Install them glue tight.

7. Cut the corrugated roofing aluminum absorber pieces to the exact distance across each stud cavity (should be $22\frac{1}{2}''$). Clean the metal surface with vinegar or cleaning acid. Nail each piece on the ledger strips (omit nails over the metal ledger at the top of the center stud). Use only enough nails to hold the panels in place until the casing jambs are put in. Start the absorber plates at the bottom, lapping one or two corrugations. Place a heavy bead of latex or silicone on the crest of the lapped corrugation at each joint. After all absorbers are permanently in place, caulk along all the edges around the perimeter of the absorbers to form an airtight seal.

8. Drill several $\frac{3}{8}$- to $\frac{1}{2}''$-diameter crossover holes through the upper and lower $16''$ of the center stud. Center each hole in the area adjacent to the concave corrugation of the absorber.

9. Bore a $2''$ vent hole through one or both side studs near the top of the collector. Construct a small box channel for the hot air to escape in the summer or other non-use times (Fig. 4-57). An automatic control may be installed in this hole, or a simple manually operated wood or metal closer can be placed over it with one screw to pivot on.

10. Install jamb strips around the inside perimeter of both absorber compartments (Fig. 4-58). These will be $\frac{3}{4}''$ thick wood as deep as the distance from the surface of the absorber plates to the sheathing or siding level. These jambs are the nail backing for the exterior trim

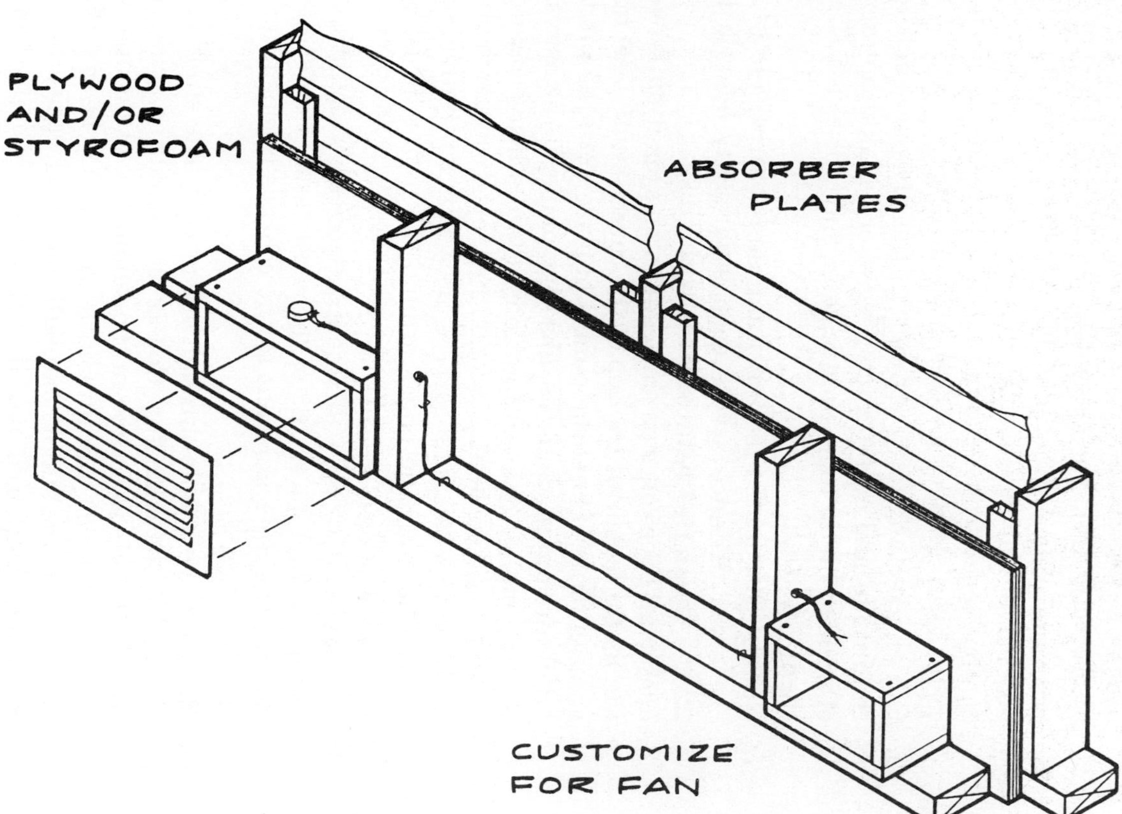

Figure 4-56 The inner wall contains the inlet and outlet ducts. The return air is drawn in one side by a 200 CFM fan. It moves up the backside of the absorber plate, crosses over and moves down to the heat discharge register. Locate the thermostat to touch some part of the absorber plate.

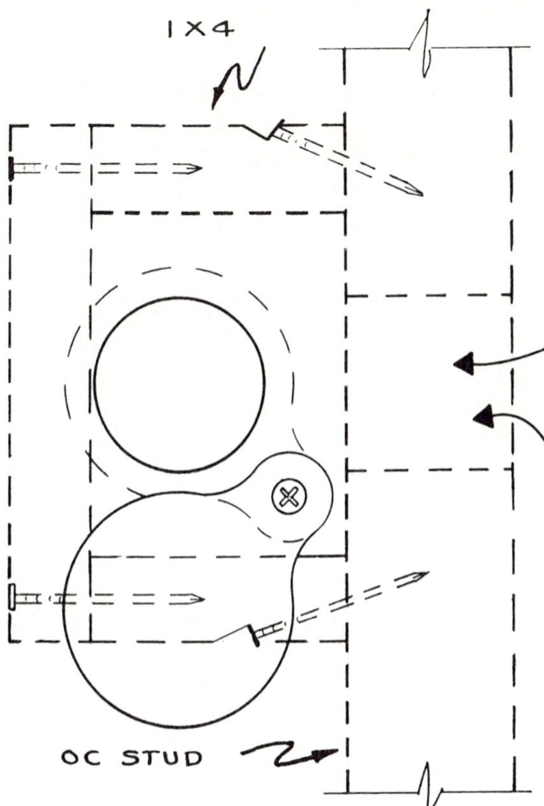

Figure 4-57 A 2″ vent may be placed in the corner of the collector box by cutting off a corner of the glass and adding a wood block to hold the vent. A method that avoids glass cutting is to place the vent in a facia board above the glass, or tunnel it through a side stud or the top 2 × 4 block and direct it out the face.

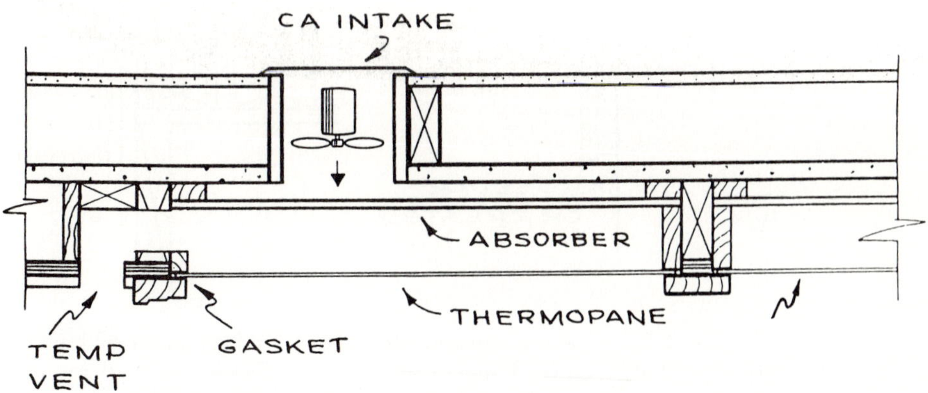

Figure 4-58 A top section view showing how the jambs and casing blend the collector into the architecture of the wall like any other window.

casing. On a brick- or stone-veneered house, match the depth to that of the windows and doors. A filler strip is required on the center stud to bring its surface to the same plane as the vertical face of the jambs. Reduce the jamb by as much as the thickness of the glass or film.

11. Paint all the internal surfaces of the collector with a flat black heat-resistant paint such as Krylon or Rustoleum. Engine manifold or cast iron stove paint is also suitable.

12. Install the window cover and casing simultaneously (see A, Fig. 4-59). Have the glass cut to allow a clearance of about $\frac{3}{16}''$ of an inch on all four sides. Block the glass up in the bottom rabbet so that it is centered. Center it horizontally. Hold it in place with triangular putty darts or small nails. Run a continuous bead of butyl or silicone caulk all around the glass in the gap. The junctions should be airtight but made in such a way that the glass can be removed without damage. With real glass, care

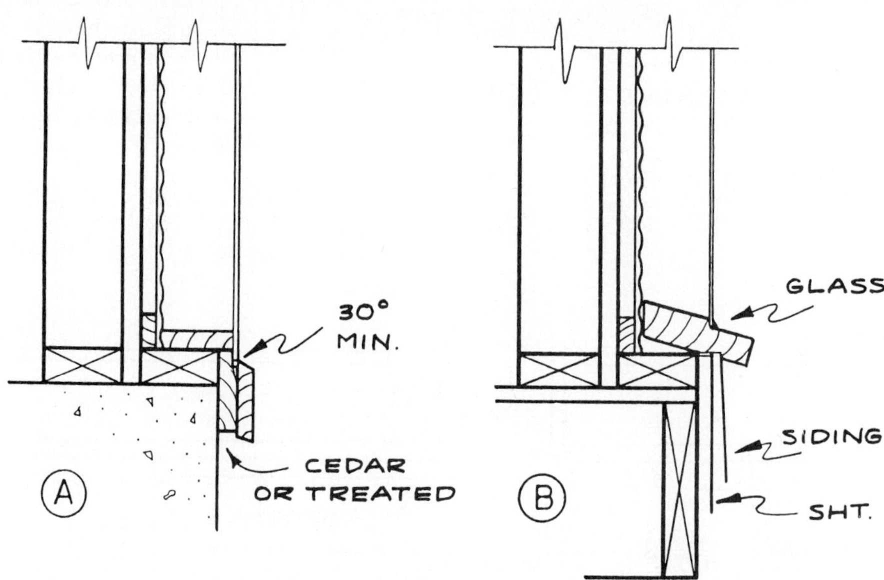

Figure 4-59 (a) A built-in collector sill will deflect water as long as the seal holds up. (b) This better-quality rabbeted seal will require less maintenance and will last longer. Both custom sills can be fabricated with a table saw.

must be taken not to hit the glass under the trim with a screw. Galvanized or brass screws are a better choice than rustable iron. Although many trouble-free years are possible, there may come a time when it is desirable to remove the glass to repaint the absorber, to clean the glass or to reseal the glass edges, or to replace damaged Filon. Pilot holes are drilled for screws to avoid splitting and to assure that no contact with the glass is made by the screw. An alternative method is to rabbet the casing instead of undercutting the jamb.

The bottom filler board will be rabbeted on its top edge to shed rain. A thin bead of latex is placed along the upper edge of the rabbet to seal the joint against the glass. A noticeable squeeze-out should exist to assure a seal that is free of voids. In very wet areas, a genuine rabbeted sill board is advisable (see B, Fig. 4-59). The rabbeted shoulder rises behind the glass about ½″. All the trim boards will be set in butyl or window caulk where they contact the glass.

13. Interior completion of the blower and the hot-air register is all that remains to complete the collector. A low-cost adjustable thermostat is installed in the heat duct. A squirrel cage blower or fan, delivering approximately 200 cubic feet per minute or more, is installed in the cold air return opening. A thermostat and blower may be wired to plug into a duplex externally, or they can be wired internally as for any other permanent electrical fixture in the house.

Full-house heat assisting is possible by running the heat duct from the collector into the furnace main duct or plenum. The added heat will be a direct subtraction from what the furnace would be called upon to produce. During mild demand times the central service fan can be switched manually to distribute the solar collected heat throughout the whole house.

Solar heat is a genuine "freebie" in our age of high-cost fuels. Solar harnessing is something to be considered by anyone wishing to reduce home heating costs and dependence on utility companies.

HEAT PUMP

No discussion of heating and cooling a residence would be complete without consideration of the heat pump. Unlike furnaces, which derive their energy directly from gas, oil, or electricity, the heat pump takes advantage of nature's elements (at no cost) to assist in cooling or heating. It uses the most constant source that exists: earth temperature. Windmills work only when the wind blows. Solar devices work only marginally on sunless days and not at all after dark. In winter, when needed most, the nights are longest. The temperature of the earth below a certain surface level maintains a fairly constant temperature. The heat pump extracts this temperature and uses it to temper the air in a home night and day, summer and winter.

The water-to-air type of heat pump is the most efficient due to the constancy of the temperature of groundwater. Air-to-air heat pumps, although more efficient than fossil fuel air exchangers, suffer from outside temperature variation. As temperatures progressively drop below freezing, the ability of the heat pump to draw warmth from the air diminishes to a point of little use. In the cooling cycle, a parallel effect takes place. As temperatures outdoors increase, the ability of the heat pump to convert hot air to cool air decreases. By contrast, the water-to-air heat pump deals with a temperature variable in the water from about 50° in the north to about 65° in the south. The variation of the earth's temperature, transmitted to earth water below the frost line, is very small from season to season. Therefore, the water-to-air heat pump ranks at the top of the efficiency and consistency scale as a means of both heating and cooling.

COP

The degree of efficiency is ranked on the basis of 1 kilowatt-hour of electricity. This is called the coefficient of performance and referred to as "COP." A high COP rating is desirable. A low COP translates to high fuel bills. A dollar's worth of electricity may furnish 3.5 to 4 COP with a water-to-air heat pump, compared to about 2 COP for oil or gas or 1 COP for direct electric heat furnaces. These figures, though general, represent a great savings over a period of years.

The initial cost of a heat pump exceeds conventional fossil fuel systems by about one-and-a-half to two times. The difference is usually recouped in three to five years. From then on it is pure gain through savings to the homeowner. Should the buyer need additional rationale or motivation, it may also be considered patriotic to use the free sources of energy, thus saving our country's fossil fuel reserves.

TWO WATER-TO-AIR SYSTEMS

Closed loop is the name of one design for supplying ground-temperature water to the heat pump. In this system, several hundred feet of plastic pipe are buried below the ground in a looped formation. The loop is placed far enough below the grade line and frost line to be virtually isolated from above-ground temperature extremes. The same clean water is circulated through the loop whenever the heat pump places a demand on it. It is a dependable and constant source of heat and cooling transmission.

The open system takes its water directly from a well, a spring-fed pond, or sometimes from a river (river sources are frequently too polluted to use). The water is circulated directly through the pump to cool or warm its coils and is then discharged. It may be dumped into a discharge well at a distance from the drawing well, into a stream or a pond, or may be used to water the yard or the garden. A combination of these discharge means can be set up with diverting gate valves so that watering potential exists during the growing season and unattended dumping during the winter season.

The water supply must be adequate for the open-loop system. A pond must be deep enough year round to furnish constant-temperature water. A well must have an adequate recovery table rate to supply both domestic and heat pump demands. An artesian well provides an ideal water source.

Comparison of open- and closed-loop systems must take the foregoing characteristics into consideration as well as the initial cost. As a rule, a closed-loop system involves much more pipe burying. The cost of pipe and the labor to bury it will be substantial. On the other hand, the constant nature of the permanent water source trapped in the loop removes all concerns about water supply.

WATER-HEATING ASSISTANCE

An auxiliary benefit of the heat pump is its ability to effect a substantial savings in domestic water heating. Heated water, which normally would be discharged, is used to add to the temperature requirements of the water heater, thereby lessening the demands on the conventional water heating source.

CONCLUSIONS

Any attempt to make a house more successful at retaining heat or cooling will net dividends. In the long run, the greatest success will be achieved by balancing the systems and approaches and keeping it simple. In a new house, cost effectiveness will result from a concept of total adaptation, as compared to fragmented schemes. Go with a complete plan of procedure from the outset. Do not be dissuaded by costs or by undocumented gossip. The end result for those who hang tight will be a house good to live in throughout the ages.

For those whose motivation is to gain money by selling, it is a proven fact that good quality houses—those with documented utility bills—sell more easily and quickly than the house where a track record is obvious by its absence.

REVIEW TOPICS

1. Discuss the pros and cons of each of the three basic conservation types of houses.
2. Explain and discuss the meaning of Btu as applied to housing.

3. Explain the difference and significance between single-pane, double-glazed, and Thermopane glass windows.

4. Explain in detail why a solid wood door with molded and carved panels has such poor insulating characteristics.

5. Describe a compartmented entry, and explain how it saves energy.

6. Explain how each of the following elements is harnessed to provide temperature control in a house: wind, sun, earth, and groundwater.

7. Describe the general characteristics of the double-wall house described in detail in this book.

8. Describe the fabricated I-beam window header that evolves during double-wall erection when a single piece of plywood forms the header.

9. Describe the designs for a boxed header that may be used for openings from 8 to 12' and from 12 to 16'.

10. Recite the sequence (the order) of raising the walls of the double-wall design described and illustrated in this book.

11. Describe a K brace and explain its use.

12. Explain the reason for staggering nails where a diagonal brace is fastened to a stud or plate.

13. Fully explain a procedure that may make it possible to cut the cost of the stud inventory by 50%.

14. Explain what is meant by layering Styrofoam insulation in the floor joist cavities and how to go about placing all the components.

15. Explain how a stick-built roof will suffer from insulation starvation above the top plates of the exterior wall. Describe the effect of a 100% seat-cut birdsmouth.

16. Describe graphically on paper or a chalkboard how a cripple-raised truss is built. Describe the effects of this design on the frieze-board area as related to roof pitch.

17. Describe graphically the method of gaining insulation capacity above the top plates by the extended lower-chord technique.

18. Describe the plumb-cut chord and wedge block technique of increasing the insulation area.

19. Explain precisely where the webs should be located in a W truss that has an extended lower chord *and* double walls. Use a specific set of dimensions for your example.

20. Explain in detail how to construct an integral solar collector of a two-stud cavity size into a double-walled building.

21. Describe the different types of heat pumps: air-to-air, closed-loop water, open water. Tell what COP means.

Glossary

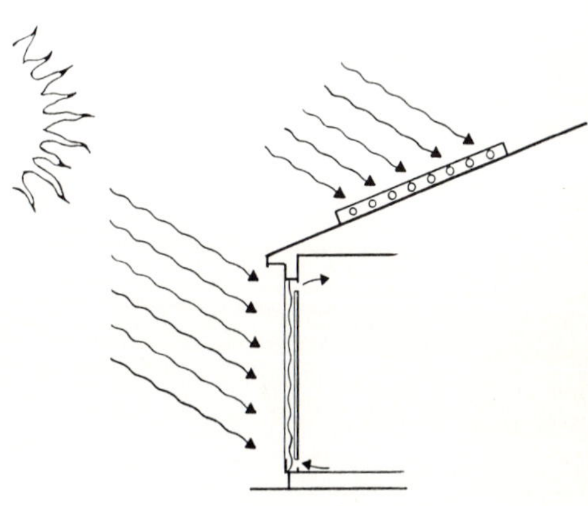

Note: Many of the terms in this glossary are defined in the context of utility fuel conservation and may or may not have other meanings relating to conventional construction.

A

Absorber: The part of a solar collector that absorbs the heat rays from the sun.

Absorber plates: Plates of sheet metal used as an absorber media for solar collection.

Active solar heaters: Solar heaters of air or water that use electrical controls and sensors as the primary means of control.

Active solar systems: Solar collection and distribution systems that are dependent on mechanical controls or electrical sensors, or both, for operation.

Aesthetics: The outward beauty of things as contrasted to sole functionality. Things that are stylish, classic, or attractive as well as useful.

Air exchange: Moving stale, moisture-laden, or overheated air out of a house (crawl space, living quarters, or attic) and replenishing it with fresh air.

Alcove: A small area of a floor plan that is out of the traffic pattern and secluded. A recess off a larger room.

Anteroom: A waiting room. A compartmented entrance.

APA: American Plywood Association.

Arch: A passageway through a partition having no door. Historically curved at the top. A contemporary arch may be straight headed (square at the top).

Artesian well: A well that flows out above ground due to its water supply originating at a higher level.

Auxiliary heat backup: A heating system for use when the primary natural source is inadequate.

AWPB: American Wood Preservative Bureau.

AWPB FDN: Foundation grade of pressure-treated wood.

AWPB grade: Lumber treated to the standard prescribed by the AWPB.

AWWF wall design: A foundation made to all weather-wood design principles.

$$\boxed{\text{B}}$$

Back filling: Filling in the gravel, sand, and earth around a foundation wall.

Balloon frame: An historical two-story framing system where single-piece studs reach from the sill plate to the top of the second story and ribbons support the second-story floor.

Bermed house: A house with some or all sides banked up with earth to provide insulation benefits.

Birdbox cornice: The trim portion of a boxed, overhanging corner where a roof overhangs both the gable end and the eave.

Blackboard: A nickname for asphalt-impregnated, fiberboard sheathing.

Bleed-out: Heat that escapes through solid materials (steel rods, concrete, and wood) that connect the interior atmosphere with the exterior environment. Conduction. Also nicknamed "nosebleed."

Blown-in cellulose: A fluffy, cotton-like form of insulation. Commonly used in attics between and over the ceiling joists.

Bore test: The removal of a core sample from the earth to determine the suitability for foundation support and the subsurface character that affects the long-term life of a structure.

Boxed soffit return: The structural, horizontal framing member that spans from the end of a rafter tail back to the wall. The framework that receives the soffit skin.

British thermal unit (Btu): The quantity of heat required to raise the temperature of one pound of water one degree Fahrenheit. In construction, a measure of resistance to heat loss, the R factor.

Brownboard: A form of fiberboard that is not moisture proof.

Building board: A 4 × 8′ sheet of sheathing with some recognized insulation value.

Buttress: A permanent, structural wall brace usually at right angles to the wall being supported.

Buttress effect: The bracing function that is planned or incidental to a partition that is perpendicular to an exterior wall.

Buttress-mode partition: A partition specifically braced with diagonals or plywood to function as a buttress to an exterior wall.

Bypass valves: In a solar water heater system, valves that can isolate the heater and direct the water supply around it.

C

Celotex: The brand name of early and current forms of building boards and other building products.

Chalk box: A string on a spool in a self-dispersing box of chalk. An important tool in a carpenter's kit for maintaining straight lines.

Chalk line: A line struck by snapping a length of string imbedded with blue or red chalk.

Chock-block wedge: The wedge, cut from the end of a truss lower chord or a soffit return, used to extend the bearing point of a bearing truss.

Circulation: An in-, around-, and out-movement of air caused by any combination of vents, open windows, blowers, or fans. Also, the round-robin traffic of air in a forced-air heating system. Also, water progressing through pipe under pressure.

Classic traditional: A broad description of house designs, which, from an early period in time, have sustained their nostalgic and functional attractiveness to a point of being copied.

Climate control: Having the facilities to control indoor climate to desired temperature and humidity levels during both hot and cold seasons.

Collar braces: Horizontal ties between opposite rafters to help prevent the bottoms of the rafters from spreading outward. Placed in the upper third of the rise.

Collectors: Various contrivances to gather and concentrate the heat from the sun for utility use.

Compartmented entry: An anteroom with doors to close it off from living areas. An air chamber between the outdoors and the adjacent functional rooms.

Concave: An inward curved surface. The opposite edge to a crown on lumber.

Concrete joist-and-plank: A precast concrete unit serving as both floor joist and rough surface for industrial buildings and masonry earth homes. Slabs are poured on the surface.

Condensation: The moisture formed on the warmer side by the meeting of widely different temperatures on opposite surfaces.

Conduction: The movement of heat through matter to the colder side. In construction, the heat loss occurs through concrete, steel, and wood. In summer, the outside heat conducts toward the cooler indoor temperature.

Conductive bridge: A solid-material link from a warm atmosphere to a cooler side. Examples are studs, reinforcing rods, and concrete.

Conductors: Solid material. Wood, metal, masonry, and so on.

Constant temperature: An atmosphere where the temperature varies only minimally. The earth temperature below the frost line. The water temperature at the bottom of a deep lake.

Contoured panels: Inserts in a solid door whose molded shapes present nonuniform thickness of the material.

COP (coefficient of performance): A measurement proportion for the heating efficiency of natural gas, oil, coal, water, and air. Based on one kilowatt of electricity. Example, a water-to-air heat pump system rates about 4 COP (four times as efficient as direct coil electrical heating elements).

Corridor hub: A hallway designed to lead into various rooms from a central location. A minimum square-foot area, a maximum-effective traffic concept.

Cost effective: Use of building materials and components in a price range that will pay back the difference over less costly components in utility savings within a reasonable length of time (about five to ten years).

Cost effectiveness: A consumer philosophy of building with high-rated thermal components to save operational costs for long-term survival. A corporate and build-for-sale philosophy of using minimum material and labor quality for the structural and hidden features of a building and covering with attractive features (sale profit motive through minimum material and labor cost). Steady companies—those who shut down infrequently—find a compromise position between these two philosophies.

Crawl space: The space beneath a wood floor where a foundation rises above the ground and no basement exists. About a 24"-deep minimum.

Crown: The convex edge of a joist or rafter placed with the crown up.

DHW (domestic hot water): Hot water for personal use in the home.

Diagonal corner brace: A brace on the corner of a structural frame wall placed diagonally within a range of 45 to 60° from the floor. Often called a wind brace.

Distribution: Reference to spreading warm solar-generated air throughout the environment of a house.

Double glazing: Two panes of glass, spaced apart, in the same sash.

Double-wall framing: Constructing an exterior wall by joining two walls together to improve the insulation capacity and the structural strength.

Double-wall headers: Unique plywood headers with an I-beam sectional appearance. Glued, nailed, and sandwiched between the outer and inner wall frames over window and door openings.

Drainage: A water removal system by contouring a surface, ditching, and tiling below ground.

Drainage envelope: An encasement of carefully placed crushed stone that surrounds the top and sides of an earth shelter so that all subsurface water will reach the foundation drain and be carried away.

Drain bed: A bed of crushed stone to collect water seepage and conduct it away through drain tiles or perforated pipe.

Draindown valves: A primary valve (or plug) at the bottom of a solar water heater to permit emptying the collector. A combined gate valve with an air release valve is usually required at the top when a bypass setup is operating; otherwise, a vacuum will stop the water from emptying out.

Duct: A fabricated passageway for directing and carrying hot or cool air to outlet and return registers.

Earth-sheltered: A description of a building that is warmed, cooled, and protected from the elements by earth that surrounds a major part of the structure.

Eave overhang: The lower portion of a roof or gable end that extends beyond the wall.

Electric outlets: Electric service receptacles and fixtures at the points where they emerge into the living area—that is, duplexes, lights, switches, and so on. Narrowly used for just plug-ins (duplex outlet).

Encroachment: A neighboring property that creates some negative or devaluating influence on an established property.

Exposure area: The exposed portion of a foundation from grade line to siding.

F

Facade: The front or false front of a building. On an earth-sheltered house, the earth retainer wall above the exposed southern front.

False economy: False economy in house construction is when a consumer permits the use of inexpensive, bargain components to save a few initial dollars followed by many years of high-cost fuel consumption. Immediate economy, future burden.

Fiberboard: A building board (usually 4 × 8′) made of fibrous plant residue. Primarily used as sheathing on wall frames.

Flow regulator: A restricting shower head or sink tap attachment to change the flow rate or pattern of water spray.

Fluid media collector: A solar collector that uses water to collect the heat for storage and distribution.

Fossil fuels: Fuels derived from organic changes that took place in the earth. Coal, oil, gas, and so on.

Foundation bed: The supporting surface directly below a foundation footing.

Foyer: A separate and definable entrance room that provides privacy from living quarters.

Free heat sources: Natural sources that can be had for nothing after harnessing—that is, wind, water, sunshine, and earth temperature.

French drain: A system of drainage composed of a perimeter bed of crushed stone with a perforated tile that empties at a lower level.

Friction fit insulation: Fiberglass insulation with no vapor barrier backing. Holds its position by simply pressing into place between studs.

Frost line: The deepest level to which the earth freezes in wintertime in a particular area.

Gable facade: A gable-shaped front on an earth-sheltered house.

Gauge blocks: Small, temporary 1″-nominal spacing blocks (¾″ thick) used to hold an inside wall apart from the outer wall (double-wall construction) while permanently nailing the sole plate in position.

Glazing: The practice of installing window and door glass in a sash. Any type of light-emitting material used in a window sash, door, or solar collector.

Green belt: A ribbon of grass or floral adornment between a patio slab and the front window wall of a solar-heated earth shelter. Acts as a barrier to conduction and reflection.

Greenhouse collector: A solar collection room with a sloping glass roof and glassed front and sides.

Ground cover barrier: A moisture barrier spread over the ground surface in a crawl space. Usually of plastic film covered with a little sand.

Ground water: Water found in earth stratas of gravel.

Gusset: Small sheet-metal plates or plywood used on the surfaces of joints on roof trusses. May also be used as small tension straps (ties).

Hardwood shade trees: Trees that give shade in summer and that will lose their leaves in winter to permit sun rays to enter and warm a house.

Heater elements: Submergible electric heating elements used in hot water tanks.

Heat pump: A heating and cooling house conditioner that draws on air or water to lessen the temperature difference by reversing cycles in winter and summer.

Heat-rise principle: A passive way to cause water to rise in a solar water heater.

Heat storage: Sustaining heat in a sump, a solid masonry material, or water. Water has the greatest ability.

Heat storage bin: A heat sump in a large area such as a crawl space.

Heat storage media: Water and masonry are the most common materials. All solid objects in a room will store heat to varying degrees.

Heat tape: An electrical cord with heating wires and a simple thermostatic control.

Heat transfer: Heat that moves from its origin to another place by conduction, convection, or radiation.

Hermetically sealed: Double or triple glass with a space between each pane. Air is drawn out and the space is sealed airtight.

$\boxed{\text{I}}$

Infiltration: The entrance of cold air through voids and cracks around doors, windows, junctions between masonry and wood, and other joinery.

Initial cost: Total cost of building a house to completion in accordance with the contract. "Turnkey job" is a term used to describe complete readiness for occupancy.

Inletted brace: Usually a 1 × 4 or 1 × 6 placed diagonally across notched studs so that the surface of the brace is flush or slightly below the surrounding surface.

Inletted ribbons: Boards that are notched into two-story studs and that support the second-story floor joists in the balloon framing system.

Insulated doors: Exterior doors with cores filled with a type of foam insulation.

Insulation barrier: Some form of nonconductive material or space that separates solid materials in a house from contacting conductive materials outside, thereby preventing bleeding.

Integral collector: A solar collector panel that is built into the wall of a house and appears as a normal, integrated feature of the house design.

Integrally reinforced: All parts tied together with reinforcing steel to function as a unit. For example, interior footing reinforcement carries around corners into the perimeter footing.

Inverted knee brace: A knee brace that runs upward instead of downward from horizontal.

$$\boxed{\text{J}}$$

Joint: A fixed junction of two pieces of material.

Joists: Horizontal boards placed on edge that form the framework for floors and ceilings.

$$\boxed{\text{K}}$$

K brace: A modified wind brace at the corner of a building frame occupying a space too narrow for a full diagonal brace at the proper angle. Shaped like the letter K.

Knee brace: A brace, usually at a 45° angle, that reaches from a vertical support upward to a horizontal member.

$$\boxed{\text{L}}$$

Lateral pressure: Pressure exerted horizontally (compressive or tensile).

Lateral span: The unsupported distance between two bearing points or pressure points (vertically or horizontally as well). For example, the distance between pilasters along a basement wall or earth shelter wall.

Layered insulation: Two or more layers of roll-batt insulation either cross-laid or lap-laid, with ends staggered, so that no joints are over each other. Breaks up exfiltration (heat loss).

Ledger strips: Small strips of wood (1 × 2 or 1 × 1) fastened near the top edge of joists to support Styrofoam under a floor.

Masonry storage wall: A wall of brick, block, or concrete designed to serve as a heat sump.

Metal tie: A sheet-metal strap or gusset holding an inner wall to an outer wall when conventional 2 × 4 plates are used. Also a strap or gusset holding a partition to a 2 × 8 top piece on a double-wall plate.

Modular span: A span that receives full-length framing materials or sheet materials in full or half-sheet sizes. Spans of 20, 22, 24, 26, and so on are modular. Figures between these are not.

Nosebleed: A nickname for heat loss (winter) or penetration (summer) by conduction through materials that join the interior with the exterior atmosphere.

O

One-piece joist: A long joist that spans from the front to the rear walls of an earth shelter without a joint over a partition or beam.

Optimum insulation: Insulation in quantity and depth sufficient to pay back in fuel-saving cost well before the demise of the property. Payback within 5 to 10 years is reasonable in the con-

servation philosophy, as it leaves many years of savings ahead for
the consumer.

Overinsulating: Excessive quantity of insulation is only a reality in the payback sense. Too much is never harmful. It simply
might cost more than it may save over the long haul.

$$\boxed{\text{P}}$$

Partial berm: Earth, banked part way up a wall.

Partition blocks: Concrete blocks of $4 \times 8 \times 16''$ size used in
conjunction with a slab floor for partition walls.

Passive solar system: A method of collecting and dispersing solar heat naturally (without automated controls).

Passive solar windows: Strategically placed windows to bring
in solar heat without electric controls.

Passive space heating: Heat that results from windows in
south-facing windows. Planned or incidental.

Payback: The quantity of time it takes to recoup the extra initial expense of some sort of conservation utility derived from re-
sultant fuel savings.

Plenum: A distribution box, or trunk line, for hot or cool air;
attached to the discharge opening on an exchanger (furnace or air
conditioner).

Plywood header: A sandwiched board over an opening, positioned between the inner and outer wall of a double-wall design.

POB (point of beginning): Initially, the building line is where
measurements originate. Other perfected reference points may be
used as POBs later on.

Precut studs: Studs of 2×4 girth, cut to a modularized uniform
length of $92\frac{5}{8}''$. Coordinated with wall-height covering materials
such as gypsum board (dry wall) and paneling.

Pressure treated: A preserved state of lumber that has been
treated by forcing chemical preservatives into all the cores.

Quonset hut: A half-round, steel tunnel with large corrugations running over the circumference. Some earth homes were built by assembling the erector-style components and covering the structure with a layer of concrete followed by earth.

Quonset shaped: A building shape that resembles the World War II semi-circular shaped metal structures used by the military.

R-factor: A quantity number denoting resistence to passage of heat through a particular material or combination of materials. The higher the number, the more resistance.

Reflected heat gain: Heat gained from sun rays that reflect off an adjacent surface onto a collecting surface.

Reflective heat: Heat from sun rays that bounce off one surface onto another.

Reinforcing bars (rebars): Steel bars imbedded in concrete to resist tensile and compressive stresses thereby preventing the breaking up or shifting, or both, of segments of the concrete structure.

Reinforcing mesh: A welded-wire grid mesh imbedded in concrete slabs to prevent cracking and separation. In residential work, the squares in the mesh are usually 6″ and the wire gauge is number 10.

Resale feasibility: A design consideration that rejects unusual features in a house plan that will make the property hard to sell.

Retrofit: A feature of a house that is constructed after the original design is completed. Not a part of the original plan. A coordinated add-on.

Reverse-flow valve: A valve that closes when liquid attempts to reverse its intended flow direction. Used primarily in drains.

Revetment window: A window in an earth shelter house. Earth is bermed on both sides of the window, causing an open-topped tunnel appearance.

Roll-type fiberglass: Glasswool insulation that comes in rolls containing so many square feet per thickness. Stud-cut lengths are modular coordinates for precut stud walls.

Rough window sill: The structural member at the bottom of an opening in a frame wall where a window jamb will be installed.

$$\boxed{\text{S}}$$

Safety valve: A valve on a water heater that pops open, permitting discharge should the water temperature approach a steam blowout. Also, a temp valve on a box-type solar collector that opens in summertime, or excessive heat times, to prevent combustion of the wooden materials and deterioration of sythetic glazing.

Seasonal lag: The temperature of the earth below the frost line that cycles from warm to cool and cool back to warm about six months behind the atmosphere above ground. This is the characteristic that makes an earth-sheltered house environment so constant.

Sediment accumulation: The forming of solid mineral in water that settles to the bottom of a water heater tank.

Serpentine pattern: A back-and-forth pattern of piping in a solar water heater.

Site factors: Building site characteristics that encourage, discourage, or forbid construction at a specific locality.

Skylight: A window in the ceiling or roof that brings natural light into a house.

Sod house: An early American form of shelter built by stacking rectangles of sod cut from the prairie ground. A pioneer concept to "winter over" on a new claim where wood was scarce. A "soddie."

Solar coordinates: Special methods and conservation materials that go together to sustain and compliment solar-heated dwellings.

Solar-heated house: Solar-generated heat is the principal provider. Other heat is considered backup.

Solar storage: An attempt to hold heat within media to be dispensed during sunless hours.

Solar storage system: A calculated and designed means of storing heat from the sun as efficiently as possible.

Solar storage wall: A masonry wall designed and located to absorb and hold heat until needed.

Solar water heating: Heating domestic water with the energy from the sun.

Solar wick: A construction material that bleeds heat or coolness to the wrong side of a wall by conduction. "Nosebleed."

Spillway: A small concrete apron where an underground drain pipe empties out onto a lower ground surface.

Sound deadener: The earth surrounding an earth shelter home is an effective barrier against the invasion of sound.

Storm door: A door on the outside of an entrance jamb that is the first line of defense against inclement weather. The main door is hung on the inside of the jamb and serves as the primary security door.

Stud, bowed: A stud that is curved on the wide faces.

Stud, crooked: A stud that is curved on its edges (pronounced "crookt").

Stud, twisted: A warped stud in the shape of a propeller. A wind (pronounced as in "winding road").

Styrofoam: A rigid, lightweight form of insulation. The most common size is 4 × 8', which comes in sheets of various thicknesses.

Sun angle: The angle of sunshine to a vertical line on the earth.

Superinsulate: To use more insulation in all areas of a house than a recomended minimum.

Superinsulated house: A house with balanced proportions of insulation between floor, walls, and ceiling and in quantity that exceeds recommended minimums.

Surface drainage: Planned and executed contouring of a lot so that water drains away naturally.

Swedish drain: *See* French drain. It is the same.

T

Temperature differential: The difference between outdoor temperature and what a person wants the indoor temperature to be (the setting on the thermostat).

Thermal: Having to do with heat.

Thermal break: A separation or a non-thermal material, or both, between conductive components in a house. For example, a greenbelt between an indoor floor slab and an outdoor patio of concrete.

Thermal bridge: Integral material that connects conductive components. For example, steel reinforcing bars that continue out of an earth-sheltered concrete wall into an exposed concrete outdoor retainer wall.

Thermal conserving: A descriptive term for any material, or media, that saves fuel.

Thermal cripple stud: A short stud located above a wall plate that raises a truss to provide adequate space for insulation. An integral part of a conventional thermal truss.

Thermal gifts: Thermal sources that are available free for the harnessing from Mother Nature.

Thermal insulation: Insulation designed to resist heat loss in cold weather and stand off heat penetration from outdoors in hot weather.

Thermal truss: A raised roof truss that provides greater insulation above the top wall plates (a constricted area with regular trusses and small-girth rafters).

Thermal wicks: Materials in a structure that are conductors from the inside atmosphere to the outdoors and vice versa.

Thermal windows: Windows that have two or three panes side by side with an airtight space between.

Thermostat: An electrical heat sensor and switch for regulating heating devices and maintaining constant temperature.

Timer: A clock and switch that permits automatic turning on and turning off of electrical current. A cost saving device for an electric water heater.

Topography: The lay of the land. The ups and downs as shown by elevation lines on a contour map.

Traffic pattern: The potential walking paths in a floor plan after the furniture is in place.

Transom: An opening and closing window above a door. Helps to ventilate warm air that gathers at the top of a room.

Treated plywood: Plywood that is chemically treated to survive underground for an estimated 100 years or more.

Trombe wall: An exterior, south-facing wall that is fitted with protruding solar glazing to serve as a large, passive solar collector.

Underground: Below the ground surface. Below grade.

Unstable bed: A foundation location that is not adequate to support a planned structure. A changeable earth character (clay, sand).

Ventilation: Moving air that replenishes stale or hot air with fresh or cool air.

Wagonwheel arrangement: An efficient corridor design where other rooms can be reached with minimum travel. *See* Corridor hub.

Water table: A strata or level in the earth where water is more or less constant.

Wedge: A triangular-shaped block used to improve the joint and to advance the span-bearing capacity of a truss. Placed at the bottom junction of an upper and lower chord.

Window of vulnerability: Any spot in a thermal house plan that represents inconsistency with the conservation objective. For example, an uninsulated exterior door in a double-wall house; single-pane windows; fireplace masonry through an exterior wall.

INDEX

Absorber, 195
Absorber plates, 184, 195
Active solar heaters, 195
Active solar systems, 195
Air-exchange, 32, 195
Alcove, 196
All-weather wood
    foundation, 56–57, 61,
    124
Ante room, 9, 196
APA, 57, 196
Archway, 9
AWPB, 196
AWPB FDN, 196
AWPB grade, 196
AWWF, 56–57, 124
  ceiling-bearing ribbon, 61
  pressure-treated
    materials, 61
  wall designs, (Fig. 2–24)
    57, (Fig. 2–25) 58, 196
Auxillary heat, 94

Back filling, 37, 64, 196
Balloon frame, 58, 147, (Fig.
    4–30) 149, 196
Bearing partitions, 37
Beaverboard, 4
Bermed house, 52–62, 196
  ceiling framework, 59
  direction of force on, 62
  full, 56
  insulation barriers, 52, 55
  joists, 59
    adjacent to end wall, 59
    notching, 59
    one-piece, 59
  minimum berm width, 52
  nails, 65
  one-piece tying, 62
  partial, 52
  partial, roof for, 33
  placement, 52
  pressure-treated, 52
  PWF, (Fig. 2–25) 58
  rafter anchoring, 62
  rafters, 62
  rafters, stick-built, 60
Birdbox cornice, 196
Blackboard, 4, 196
Bleed-out, 5, 196
Blown-in cellulose, 55, 197
Bore test, 24, 197
Boxed soffit return, 159, 197
Breadbox collector, 109
  glazing, 113
  tank arrangement, 112
British thermal unit (Btu),
    197
Brownboard, 4, 197
Btu rating, 5, (Fig. 3–3) 82
Building board, 4, 197
Buttress, 197
Buttress effect, 197
Buttressing, 69
Buttressing, long walls, 69
Buttress mode, 69
  partition, 70–71, 197
Bypass valves, 114, 197

Celotex, 4, 197
Central heat backup, 94
Chalk box, 197
Chalk line, 197
Chock-block wedge, 159, 197
Circulation, 29, 83–84, 198
Classic traditional, 47, 198
Climate control, 20, 83–84,
    198
Coefficient of performance
    (COP), 31
Collar braces (ties), 63, 198
Collector, 21
Collector, venting, 184
Collectors, 77
  breadbox, 109
    overheating protection,
      111–12
  flat plate, 102
  greenhouse, 83, 197
Compartmented entry, 9–
    10, 198
  modified, 10
  retrofit, (Fig. 1–3) 10
Concave, 198
Concrete joist and plank,
    (Fig. 2–15) 42, 198
Condensation, 164, 198
Conduction, 5, (Fig. 4–34)
    156, 198
Conductive bridge, 6, 12, 198
Conductors, 39, (Fig. 4–20)
    138, 198
Constant temperature, 20,
    198
Contoured panels, 8, 199
COP, 31, 188, 199
Corridor hub, 48, 209
Cost effective, 14, 171, 199
Crawl space, 89, 199

**DHW (domestic hot
    water), 94, 199**
  flow regulator, 99
  heater elements, 97
  heat pump assistance, 190
  pipe insulation, 97
  replacing an element, 98
  sediment accumulation,
    98
  thermostatic control, 95
Diagonal corner brace, 132–
    34, 199
Distributing heat, 90
Domestic hot water. *See*
    DHW

Door types:
  insulated, 8, 80
  solid molded, 7
Double glazing, 6, 7, 32, 80,
  200
Double-wall, 121
  framing procedure, 132
  section view, (Fig. 4–2) 123
Double-walled house, 14
Double wall frame:
  braces (sanwiched), 131
  bracing, 128
  door headers, 125
  double top plate, 128
  firestop plate, 122
  headers, 121, 134
  headers over 8′ span, 126
  K-brace, 133
  rough window sills, 125
  section view, 121, (Fig. 4–
    1) 122
  sole nailing, 139
  spacer strip, 128
  studs:
    crooked, 144
    salvaging, 144
    straightening, 145
  surrounds (window and
    door), 137
  top plate (one piece), 127
  top plate and ties, 141
  window headers, 125
  windows, 137
Double-wall framing, 132–47
  partition studs, 138
  procedure, 132
Double-wall headers, 125–
  27, 134–37, 200
Double-wall insulation,
  155–56
Drainage, earth shelter, 67
  bed, 24, 200
  entrance, 68
  envelope, 41, 200
  reverse flow valve, 68
  shower drain, 68
  surface, 41
Draindown valves, (Fig. 3–
  23) 115, 200
Duct, 89, 200

Earth house, structural:
  drainage, 24, 39
  footing drainage, 56

full-bermed wood, 56
  partial-bermed, 53
  partitions, 71
  reflective heat, 25
  sole plate nailing, 71
  suitable soil, 34
  ventilation, 29, 49
  wall framing, 56
  waterproofing, 39
Earth-shelter aesthetics:
  appearance, 44
  facade styles, 46
  floor planning, 48
  light, 49
  optimum exposure, 23
  orientation, 25
    sunlight, 26
    wind direction, 26
  site factors, 23
Earth-sheltering:
  advantages, 21
    cost effectiveness, 22
    low maintenance, 22
    payback, 22
    quietness, 21
    storm protection, 21
  seasonal lag, 19
Eave overhang, (Fig. 3–2)
  81, 200
Electric outlets, 156, 200
Electric water heater:
  elements, 97
  sediment, 98
  thermostat, 95
  timer, 95
Encroachment, 43, 200
Energy-saving systems, 4
Entrance drain, 68
Extended span truss, 159
Extended trusses, web
  location on, 162

Facade styles, 46
  French mansard, (Fig. 2–
    17) 46
  gable end, 46, (Fig. 2–18)
    47
Fiberboard, 4, 201
Fiberglass insulation, 5
Fiberglass insulation and
  double-wall, 155–57
Flat plate collector:
  bracing materials, 104
  flashing, 106

heat absorption, 109
  mounting, 105–7
Floor insulation:
  blackboard, 151
  crawl space, 150
  ground treatment, 151
  ledgers, 152
    gauging, 154
  roll-type fiberglass, 151
  Styrofoam, 152
Flow regulator, 99, 200
Fluid media collector, 88,
  93, 201
Foundation bed, 35–36, 40,
  201
Foundation exposure:
  area, 12
  insulating, 12
  minimum, 12
Foyer, 9, 201
Frame wall:
  double wall, 121–32, 200
  exterior 6″ studded, 14
Free heat sources, 201
  sun, 11
  water, 11
  wind, 11
French drain, (Fig. 2–14) 40,
  201
Friction fit insulation, 156,
  200
Frost-line, 54, 201

**Gauge blocks, 139, (Fig.
  4–23) 140**
Glass:
  double-pane, 32
  double-Thermopane, (Fig.
    3–1) 80
  insulating, 7
  single-pane, 80
  tilted, 84
  triple Thermopane, (Fig.
    3–1) 80
  vertical, 84
Glazing, 6, 202
Glazing on slant-faced, 112,
  (Fig. 3–22) 113
Gravel bed, (Fig. 2–14) 40
Greenbelt, 87, 202
Greenbelt, floral, (Fig. 3–9)
  88
Greenhouse collector, 8̣,
  197, 202

Ground cover barrier, 151, 202
Ground water, 24, 39, 202
Gusset, (Fig. 2–29) 65, (Fig. 4–39) 160, 202

Hardwood shade trees, 21, 202
Heat absorption rate, 109
Heater elements, 11, 202
Heat gains:
　earth, water, wind, 11
　reflected, 35
Heating systems, solar, 175
Heating zone map, (Fig. 3–3) 82
Heat pump systems, 188, 202
　air to air, 188
　water to air, 189
　　closed loop, 189
　　open, 189
Heat retention, 12
Heat-rise principle, 83, 91, 202
Heat storage, 88
　bin, 89
　media, 93
　media, retention
　　comparison, 93
Heat tape, 112, 203
Heat transfer, 4, 203
Hermetically sealed, 7, 80, 203
Humidity control, 34

Infiltration, 202
Infiltration, key zones, 6
Infrared rays, 77
Initial cost, 171, 203
Inletted brace, 71, 203
Inletted ribbon, 58, 203
Insulated doors, 8, 203
Insulating glass, 7, 80
Insulation, 3
　ceiling, 157
　floor, 150
　layered, 55
　R-values, 82
Insulation barrier, 38, (Fig. 2–20) 52, (Fig. 2–22) 54, (Fig. 3–8) 87, (Fig. 4–52) 175, 203

Integral collector, 176, 179, 203
Integral reinforcement, 36–37, 204
Inverted knee brace, 63

Joists:
　notched, (Fig. 2–25) 58, 59
　one-piece, 59
Joist and plank roof, 34, (Fig. 2–15) 42

K brace, 133, 204
Knee brace, inverted, 64, 204

Lateral pressure, 36, 64, 70, 204
Lateral span, 36, 69, 204
Ledger strips, 152, (Fig. 4–32) 153

Manifold absorber, 101, (Fig. 3–16) 103
Masonry patio, 86
Masonry storage wall, 90
Mechanical cooling, 31
Mechanical heat, 30
Metal tie, 143
Modular span, 159, 205

Nails:
　plate toenails, 62
　sole, 139–141
　underground fastening, 63
Nosebleed, 38, 205

One-piece joist, 59
Optimum insulation, 205
Overinsulating, 155, 206

Parapet, 27
Partial berm, 53, 206
Partition blocks:
　concrete, 206
　wood, 142
Passive cool air return, 90, 91
Passive solar system, 79
　space heating, 83–87, 175–90
　windows, 79
Payback, 14, 22
Perforated drain pipes, 24

Pitch wedge, 158, (Fig. 4–37) 159
Plenum, 187, 206
Plywood header, 125–28, 134–37
POB (point of beginning), 59, 206
Precut stud, 58–59, 206
Pressure-treated wood, 52, 206

Quonset shape, 44, 207

Raised truss, (Fig. 2–30) 66, (Fig. 4–36) 158, (Fig. 4–37) 159, (Fig. 4–38, 4–39) 160
Rectangular absorber, 100 (Fig. 3–15) 102
Reflected heat gains, 85
Reflected heat gains, shutter reflector, 86
R-factor, 5, 82, 207
Reinforcing mesh, 175, 207
Reinforcing rods, 39, 207
Resale feasibility, 43
Retrofit, 92, 147, (Fig. 4–38) 149, 207
Reverse-flow valve, 68, 207
Revetment window, 39, 208
Roll-batt, 5, 55
Roll type fiberglass, 5, 55
Roof overhang, 21
Roof ventilators, 166
Rough window will, 125, 208
R-rating, 5, 82
R-values, 5, (Fig. 3–3) 82
R-values, recommended (Fig. 3–3) 82

Safety valve, 208
Seasonal lag, 19, 208
Secondary entrance, 10
Sediment accumulation, 98, (Fig. 3–13) 99
Serpentine, pattern, (Fig. 3–15) 102
Shadow height, 81, 178
Shadow height and eave overhang, 81
Site factors, 23
Skylight, 33, 208
Sod homes, 3, 208

Soil composition, 23
Solar collectors, 77
  angle, 177
  built-in, 176
  integral:
    constructing, 181
    sizing, 179
  orienting, 176
Solar coordinates, 20, 208
Solar heat, 32
Solar storage, 88
  heat sump, sink, 89
  masonry wall, 90–91, 209
  masonry wall, color of, 92
Solar systems, 195
  active, 78
  passive, 79
Solar water heater, 114,
    (Fig. 3–23) 115
Solar water heating, 110,
    209
Solar wick, 87, 209
Sound deadener, 21, 211
Spillway, 24, (Fig. 2–3) 25
Storm door, 80, (Fig. 3–4)
    83, 209
Stud:
  bowed, 144, 209
  crooked, 144, (Fig. 4–28)
    145
  twisted, 146
Styrofoam, 4, 209
Styrofoam, protecting, 13
Subfloor drainage, 67
Suns angle, 80, 209
Superinsulated house, 14
Super insulation, 5, 14
Surface drainage, 41–42,
    (Fig. 2–21) 54
Swedish drain, (Fig. 2–2) 24,
    40, 209

Tanks, 109
  arrangement, 112, (Fig.
    3–23) 115
  bread box, 110

Temperature:
  constant, 20
  differential, 20, 210
Temperature vent, (Fig. 4–
    54) 180, (Fig. 4–58)
    185
Thermal barrier, 39, (Fig.
    3–8) 87
Thermal breaks, (Fig. 2–13)
    38, 210
  nosebleed, 38
  wick effect, 39
Thermal bridge, 5, 210
Thermal conserving, 210
Thermal construction:
  buyer inspection, 173
    basement, 174
    crawl space, 174
    slab floor, 174
  consistency, 172
  cost effective, 171
  long-range planning,
    172
Thermal cripple stud, 157–
    58
Thermal gifts, 11, 210
Thermal insulation, 4, 210
Thermal roof designs, 156
Thermal truss, (Fig. 4–36)
    157–63, 210
Thermal ventilation, 163
Thermal wick, 39, 210
Thermal windows, (Fig. 3–1)
    80, 210
Thermopane, 7
  double, 80
  triple, 80
Thermostat, (Fig. 4–56) 184,
    210
Timer, 95–96, 210
Topography, 23, 211
Traffic pattern, 10, 48–49,
    211
Transom, 29, 211
Treated lumber, 71, 211
Trombe wall, 92, 211

Truss:
  extended span, 159
    web location, 162
  pitch wedge, 158
  raised, 66
  thermal, 157

Underground, 211
Underground fastening,
    appropriate nails, 65
Unstable bed, 24, 36, 211

Ventilation, 32, 163, 211
  air exchange, 165
  full air exchange, 168
  thermal structure, 163
  vapor blocking, 165
Ventilators:
  roof, 166
  shaft, 33

**Wagonwheel traffic, 48,
    211**
Warped, salvaging studs,
    144, (Fig. 4–28) 145
Water heaters:
  electric, 95
  solar:
    coiled pipe, 100
    flat plate, 100, (Fig. 3–
    14) 101
    rectangular absorber,
    100
Waterproofing:
  AWWF, (Fig. 2–24), 57
  earth shelter, 39–41
Water table, 24, 211
Weatherstripping, (Fig. 3–4)
    83
Wedge, 158, (Fig. 4–37) 159,
    (Figs. 4–38, 4–39)
    160, 161
Window types, 6
  thermal, 7
  Thermopane, 7, 80
Window of vulnerability,
    12–13, 156, 212